CRE▲TIVE
HOMEOWNER®
ULTIMATE GUIDE TO

Trim
Carpentry

CREATIVE HOMEOWNER®

ULTIMATE GUIDE TO

Trim
Carpentry

PLAN · DESIGN · INSTALL

Neal Barrett

CREATIVE HOMEOWNER®, Upper Saddle River, New Jersey

TRIM CARPENTRY

MANAGING EDITOR: Fran J. Donegan
ASSISTANT EDITOR: Evan Lambert
PHOTO RESEARCHER: Robyn Poplasky
INDEXER: Schroeder Indexing Services
LAYOUT AND DESIGN: David Geer
ILLUSTRATIONS: Robert LaPointe, Mario Ferro
  (pgs. 68–69)
PRINCIPAL PHOTOGRAPHER: Neal Barrett
FRONT COVER PHOTOGRAPHY: Gary David Gold/CH
  (Insets, Neal Barrett)

CREATIVE HOMEOWNER

VP/PUBLISHER: Brian Toolan
VP/EDITORIAL DIRECTOR: Timothy O. Bakke
PRODUCTION MANAGER: Kimberly H. Vivas
MANAGING EDITOR: Fran J. Donegan
ART DIRECTOR: David Geer

Printed in China

Current Printing (last digit)
10 9 8 7 6 5 4 3 2 1

Ultimate Guide to Trim Carpentry, First Edition
Library of Congress Control Number: 2005928046
ISBN-10: 1-58011-279-X
ISBN-13: 978-1-58011-279-6

CREATIVE HOMEOWNER®
A Division of Federal Marketing Corp.
24 Park Way, Upper Saddle River, NJ 07458
www.creativehomeowner.com

Metric Equivalents

Length

1 inch	25.4 mm
1 foot	0.3048 m
1 yard	0.9144 m
1 mile	1.61 km

Area

1 square inch	645 mm²
1 square foot	0.0929 m²
1 square yard	0.8361 m²
1 acre	4046.86 m²
1 square mile	2.59 km²

Volume

1 cubic inch	16.3870 cm³
1 cubic foot	0.03 m³
1 cubic yard	0.77 m³

Common Lumber Equivalents

Sizes: Metric cross sections are so close to their U.S. sizes, as noted below, that for most purposes they may be considered equivalents.

Dimensional lumber	1 × 2	19 × 38 mm
	1 × 4	19 × 89 mm
	2 × 2	38 × 38 mm
	2 × 4	38 × 89 mm
	2 × 6	38 × 140 mm
	2 × 8	38 × 184 mm
	2 × 10	38 × 235 mm
	2 × 12	38 × 286 mm
Sheet sizes	4 × 8 ft.	1200 × 2400 mm
	4 × 10 ft.	1200 × 3000 mm
Sheet thicknesses	¼ in.	6 mm
	⅜ in.	9 mm
	½ in.	12 mm
	¾ in.	19 mm
Stud/joist spacing	16 in. o.c.	400 mm o.c.
	24 in. o.c.	600 mm o.c.

Capacity

1 fluid ounce	29.57 mL
1 pint	473.18 mL
1 quart	0.95 L
1 gallon	3.79 L

Weight

1 ounce	28.35g
1 pound	0.45kg

Temperature

Fahrenheit = Celsius × 1.8 + 32
Celsius = Fahrenheit − 32 × ⁵⁄₉

Nail Size & Length

Penny Size	Nail Length
2d	1"
3d	1¼"
4d	1½"
5d	1¾"
6d	2"
7d	2¼"
8d	2½"
9d	2¾"
10d	3"
12d	3¼"
16d	3½"

SAFETY

Although the methods in this book have been reviewed for safety, it is not possible to overstate the importance of using the safest methods you can. What follows are reminders—some do's and don'ts of work safety—to use along with your common sense.

- *Always* use caution, care, and good judgment when following the procedures described in this book.

- *Always* be sure that the electrical setup is safe, that no circuit is overloaded, and that all power tools and outlets are properly grounded. Do not use power tools in wet locations.

- *Always* read container labels on paints, solvents, and other products; provide ventilation; and observe all other warnings.

- *Always* read the manufacturer's instructions for using a tool, especially the warnings.

- Use hold-downs and push sticks whenever possible when working on a table saw. Avoid working short pieces if you can.

- *Always* remove the key from any drill chuck (portable or press) before starting the drill.

- *Always* pay deliberate attention to how a tool works so that you can avoid being injured.

- *Always* know the limitations of your tools. Do not try to force them to do what they were not designed to do.

- *Always* make sure that any adjustment is locked before proceeding. For example, always check the rip fence on a table saw or the bevel adjustment on a portable saw before starting to work.

- *Always* clamp small pieces to a bench or other work surface when using a power tool.

- *Always* wear the appropriate rubber gloves or work gloves when handling chemicals, moving or stacking lumber, working with concrete, or doing heavy construction.

- *Always* wear a disposable face mask when you create dust by sawing or sanding. Use a special filtering respirator when working with toxic substances and solvents.

- *Always* wear eye protection, especially when using power tools or striking metal on metal or concrete; a chip can fly off, for example, when chiseling concrete.

- *Never* work while wearing loose clothing, hanging hair, open cuffs, or jewelry.

- *Always* be aware that there is seldom enough time for your body's reflexes to save you from injury from a power tool in a dangerous situation; everything happens too fast. Be alert!

- *Always* keep your hands away from the business ends of blades, cutters, and bits.

- *Always* hold a circular saw firmly, usually with both hands.

- *Always* use a drill with an auxiliary handle to control the torque when using large-size bits.

- *Always* check your local building codes when planning new construction. The codes are intended to protect public safety and should be observed to the letter.

- *Never* work with power tools when you are tired or under the influence of alcohol or drugs.

- *Never* cut tiny pieces of wood or pipe using a power saw. When you need a small piece, saw it from a securely clamped longer piece.

- *Never* change a saw blade or a drill or router bit unless the power cord is unplugged. Do not depend on the switch being off. You might accidentally hit it.

- *Never* work in insufficient lighting.

- *Never* work with dull tools. Have them sharpened, or learn how to sharpen them yourself.

- *Never* use a power tool on a workpiece—large or small—that is not firmly supported.

- *Never* saw a workpiece that spans a large distance between horses without close support on each side of the cut; the piece can bend, closing on and jamming the blade, causing saw kickback.

- When sawing, *never* support a workpiece from underneath with your leg or other part of your body.

- *Never* carry sharp or pointed tools, such as utility knives, awls, or chisels, in your pocket. If you want to carry these tools, use a special-purpose tool belt that has leather pockets and holders.

CONTENTS

8   **Introduction**

CHAPTER 1

10   **TRIMWORK & DESIGN**

12   **Trim Elements**
Types of Trim

16   **Modern and Traditional Elements**
Learning from the Past • Modern Designs
• Colonial • Georgian • Federal • Greek
Revival • Victorian • Arts and Crafts
• Your Style

CHAPTER 2

30   **TOOLS & TECHNIQUES**

32   **Measuring and Layout Tools**
Measuring Tapes • Folding Stick Rules • Steel
Rulers • Squares • Angle Guides • Chalk Line
• Levels • Stud Finder

36   **Cutting Tools**
Miter Saws • Power Cutting Tools • Power
Miter Saws

40   **Shaping and Finishing Tools**
Sanders • Plate Joiner • Routers

44   **Files and Rasps**

45   **Work-Holding Tools**

46   **Installation Tools**
Power Nailers

49   **Stationary or Bench-Top Tools**
Table Saw • Jointer • Planer

50   **Basic Trim Techniques**
Cutting Stock • Plate Joinery • Scarf Joints
• Coped Joints • Mitered Returns

CHAPTER 3

60   **TRIMWORK MATERIALS**

62   **Lumber for Trimwork**
Pine • Poplar • Red Oak • Selecting Wood
Moldings

72   **Characteristics of Lumber**
Defects in Lumber

76   **Other Trim Materials**

78   **Materials for Wainscoting**
Panel Materials • Panel Faces

82   **Fasteners**

84   **Glue and Construction Adhesive**
Sandpaper • Caulk

CHAPTER 4

86   **DOOR & WINDOW CASING**

88   **Prehung Doors**
Installing Prehung Doors

90   **Casing a Drywall Opening**

92   **Door Casings**
Evaluate the Condition of the Door

93   **Simple Colonial Casing**

94   **Built-Up Colonial Casing**

98   **Traditional-Style Casing**

100   **Neo-Classical Casing**
Building the Head Casing

104   **Victorian Casing**

105   **Arts and Crafts Casing**

106   **Window Trim**
Extension Jambs

108   **Stool and Apron**

112   **Troubleshooting Casing Problems**
Bulging Drywall • Protruding Jambs

114   **Design Ideas: Casing**

CHAPTER 5

116 TRIMWORK FOR WALLS

118   **Baseboard**
One-Piece Baseboard • Built-Up Baseboard
• Evaluate Room Conditions • Baseboard
Installation • Inside Corner Joints • Outside
Corner Joints • Dealing with Out-of-Level
Floors • Three-Piece Base Trim • Working
Around Electrical Receptacles • Working
Around Wall Registers • Base Trim and Stair
Stringers

132   **Picture Rail, Chair Rail, and Plate Rail**
Picture Rail • Chair Rail • Plate Rail

136   **Wall Frames and Wainscoting**
Wall Frames • Tongue-and-Groove Bead-
Board Wainscoting • Flat-Panel Wainscoting
• Modular Construction of Wainscoting
Panels

154   **Design Ideas: Wall Treatments**

CHAPTER 6

156 CROWN MOLDING & CEILING TREATMENTS

158   **Cornices and Crown Molding**
Cornice Materials • Installing Crown Molding
• Installing Built-Up or Compound Cornice Trim

173   **Beamed and Coffered Ceilings**
Installing a Beamed Ceiling • Coffered Ceiling
Construction

178   **Design Ideas: Cornice and Ceiling Treatments**

CHAPTER 7

180 COLUMNS & PILASTERS

182   **Columns**
Building a Square Column

188   **Pilasters**

CHAPTER 8

190 TRIMWORK FINISHES

192   **Painted Finishes**
Removing Hammer Marks

195   **Clear or Stained Finishes**

196   **Resource Guide**

198   **Glossary**

202   **Index**

207   **Photo Credits**

INTRODUCTION

In many ways, our homes tell the story of who we are and the things we cherish. We fill the rooms with objects that comfort us, promote our sense of well-being, and sometimes stimulate our intellect. The colors and furnishings of a home are a large part of that story. But the blank canvas for these trimmings is the building itself. The layout of the rooms, the number and size of windows and doors, and the height of the ceiling form the foundation for all that we bring to the task of transforming a house into a home.

Beyond the basic structure, a prime contributor to the style of any home is the architectural trim or woodwork: the casing, baseboard, paneling, and assorted moldings that mark the transitions between surfaces and define room openings. Some of these elements serve practical functions—such as covering the spaces between wallboard and floor or ensuring that doors operate properly—and some are purely decorative. But each of these trim components contributes to the architectural spirit of a home. The shape of each profile and its relation to the adjoining surfaces and the room as a whole make a statement about style. The nature of trim invites our eyes to move in deliberate ways. It uses the traditional architectural devices of dimension, line, proportion, and shadow to create a particular mood.

Although trim is definitely part of the structure of a home, it is by no means sacred. In a bow to cost sav-

ings, many newer homes are constructed with the simplest possible molding profiles and without any embellishments beyond the basic functional necessities—baseboard and casing. While there is certainly nothing wrong with this approach, more-elaborate treatments can dramatically change the feel of one room or an entire home. In these pages you will find a step-by-step guide to many design options and techniques for replacing existing trim or tackling new trim in a remodeling project or addition. With relatively modest tools and a bit of patience, you can transform your home, and add value—and experience the satisfaction of knowing that you did it yourself.

CEILING BEAMS, opposite bottom, add a distinctive touch to this traditional home.

ARTS AND CRAFTS THEMES, opposite top, contribute to the design of this wall treatment.

ELABORATE COR-NICES, left, were once standard in many American homes.

WINDOW AND DOOR CASINGS, above, should reflect the style of the house.

CHAPTER 1

TRIMWORK & DESIGN

In general, people don't think much about architectural trim. That's not surprising given the type of trim that can be found in most homes built since the middle of the 20th century. Even though trim has the potential to create a sense of style and even drama in a home, the trend among builders, except for those who build exclusive custom homes, has been more toward simplicity and economy in the woodwork they include in their projects. It would be foolish to argue that millwork isn't an expensive component in building a house. But if you are willing to learn to do the work yourself, you can transform your home by adding additional features or changing existing trim to reflect a particular style you admire—and do it for just the cost of the materials.

Trim Elements

The basic types of trim and molding found in the average home are fairly simple, but there is an almost endless variety of molding profiles from which to choose. The trick is to understand what is available and what looks best in your home. Once you understand the elements of interior woodwork, you can decide to follow a traditional design theme or create a more individual look by mixing features of separate styles.

Types of Trim

Beginning at the junction of the floor and wall, base trim is used to cover the gap between the discrete materials used for each surface. Modern homes typically use a one-piece *baseboard* that is 3 to 4½ inches high. A small *shoe molding* is often nailed to the baseboard to cover any gap between the baseboard and the floor. Earlier, traditional styles featured taller and more elaborate treatments. These often combined three or four separate molding profiles to create a stronger visual line at the bottom of the walls.

Casing. The sides and tops of window and door openings are lined with wooden members called *jambs,* and the gaps between the jambs and the wall treatment are covered by trimwork or molding called *casing.* In applications where moving parts are involved, the casing acts to lock the jambs in place, maintaining an even gap around the

THE ARCHED ENTRY shown above is trimmed with bright-white casing that frames the colorful room setting as well as the artwork hanging on the far wall.

HOMES BUILT IN THE FIRST HALF of the century, right, tend to have distinctive trimwork, especially around mantels, windows, and cornices.

window or door, and ensuring reliable operation.

In some homes, windows are trimmed with casing on sides, top, and bottom in what is called a picture-frame style. But in a more traditional treatment, the bottom of a window is provided with a *stool*, a shelf-like horizontal piece that extends across the opening. Under the stool, another piece of molding, called an *apron*, covers the gap between the stool and wall surface. In many cases, the apron is cut from the same molding profile used for the window casing.

Cornice Molding. *Crown* or *cornice molding* is applied at the joint between the walls and ceiling. These treatments can be simple one-piece moldings or elaborate constructions with layers of different profiles. Often a cornice will sit atop a *frieze*, or horizontal band, located near the top of the wall surface.

THE MOLDING PROFILE of the casing shown left works well with the bright color scheme of the room.

CHOOSE CORNICE AND CASING profiles, top, that complement one another.

DISTINCTIVE MOLDINGS, below, add texture and visual interest to a monochromatic color scheme.

1

TRIMWORK & DESIGN

Wall Treatments. Originally conceived to protect wall surfaces from damage by chair backs, a *chair rail* can be a single or compound molding. Although there are some profiles that are sold specifically as chair rail molding, other shapes are often used alone or in combination for this purpose. When *wainscoting,* or wall paneling, is applied to the lower portion of a wall, the molding that acts as a cap can sometimes be considered a chair rail. If the wainscot cap is designed as a narrow shelf with grooved top surface, it is called a plate rail and can be used to display decorative china or artwork. Sometimes a plate rail is used alone, without a wainscot being applied.

A *picture rail* is another horizontal molding band. These are normally mounted high on the wall and include a rounded, projecting profile, which can accept hooks for hanging pictures.

Sometimes moldings are applied directly to a wall surface in square, rectangular, or even parallelogram shapes. These are called *wall frames.* They can be fashioned from either specifically named panel molding or other profiles. Wall frames are strictly ornamental elements, and they are most dramatic when combined with decorative painting techniques or wallpaper treatments.

Ceiling Treatments. Ceilings can be adorned with beams or coffers. In a *beamed ceiling,* either solid structural timbers are left exposed or built-up beams are mounted to the ceiling in a parallel row. Often the beams are trimmed with decorative molding. If the beams run in two directions and form recessed panels, these panels are called *coffers.* Although coffers were originally a detail cast in plaster, it is also possible to use plain or figured wooden surfaces for these panels. Most often, coffered ceilings include some type of molding at the junction of the beam and coffer surfaces.

Columns and Pilasters. Transitions between rooms are frequently a focal point for decorative trim. Round or square *columns* can be mounted on decorative bases or platforms in an archway. *Pilasters* are rectangular, projecting moldings mounted vertically to the wall. These are treated in the same way as a column, with trimmed base and capital, and can be used to bracket room openings or architectural features like a niche, fireplace, or built-in shelving unit.

CHAIR RAIL AND WALL FRAMES, opposite, set a traditional tone for this room.

AN UNUSUAL CEILING, right, calls for an imaginative ceiling trim design.

INTERIOR COLUMNS, below left, may not be structural, but they should appear to be.

PILASTERS, below right, add a classical touch to the design.

Modern and Traditional Treatments

Before you can decide how to proceed with your trim projects, you need to know a bit about your options. While you don't have to feel locked into following any particular style or design tradition, it is helpful to have an understanding of the historical trends and elements that define some of the predominant design trends. Then you can create the trim details to suit your taste using features that resonate with your own aesthetic sensibility. If you are thinking about mixing specific trim details from different periods or disciplines, you might consider borrowing a technique from professional interior designers. Try creating a small sample board for your project, with all of the decorative elements for a room displayed together. Then you can better see how the moldings, colors, and materials affect one another and avoid a costly design mistake.

Learning from the Past

Architectural embellishments have a long and rich history. Carvings and sculptural details were used from ancient times, with the most opulent examples used for public buildings, religious centers, and the homes of the wealthy and powerful. Many of these features were carved in stone and have survived to this day, still valued as artifacts of a treasured artistic heritage. If you look to ancient Greece as one example, you'll find that structural members of public buildings were treated as decorative elements. Columns ad-

hered to strict principles of design; most were fluted and were adorned with carved bases and capitals. Friezes on buildings featured figurative details, often based around the exploits of heroic or mythic characters, and these could be capped by a molded cornice. Many of these elements have been borrowed, in greatly modified form, as inspiration for some of the predominant architectural styles still visible in many public and residential buildings in our country.

Of course, most of the residential detailing in the United States has been fashioned from wood and not stone. And our homes are usually quite a bit more modest than the ancient Greek temples. But the desire to establish a style and make a personal statement about our environment is linked to those ancient roots. Design inspiration can come from many places, and historical precedent is a reasonable place to start.

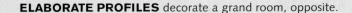

Modern Designs

By the middle of the twentieth century, housing demand in the United States was growing at an unprecedented rate. As soldiers returned from World War II and the country returned to a peacetime economy, financial optimism was growing. Almost overnight, the dream of home ownership became a real possibility for a generation of people. Government subsidized mortgages for veterans and a growing economy provided fuel for the housing boom. And to fill the need for housing stock, builders around the country sprang into action turning old farmland and vacant properties into residential tracts.

ELABORATE PROFILES decorate a grand room, opposite.

SIMPLE DESIGNS fit the contemporary space above.

PAINTED MOLDING, top, complements the decor.

PANELED PILLARS, right, flank a decorative railing.

Changes in Housing. For many of these developments, the operating principles were to build houses as fast and as inexpensively as possible. A new vocabulary for home design evolved, and ranch, raised ranch, split-level, Cape Cod, and Colonial-style homes became the new universe from which home designs were chosen. Any number of traditional features and embellishments were set aside in the pursuit of efficient construction. Sometimes concrete slabs replaced full foundations and basements, porches were jettisoned in favor of small entry platforms, and interior woodwork was limited to either "ranch-" style or "colonial-" style casing and baseboard.

Of course, those who purchased these houses were thrilled to be homeowners and were more than content with the simplified approach to interior millwork that was part of the package. These stripped-down interiors became emblematic of a modern sensibility regarding housing design, and a new standard was born. Those who have grown up with this pared-down approach may, in fact, find that it suits them perfectly. It has the advantage of providing a blank canvas on which to build your environment, and it stands in stark contrast to the heavier and more complex treatments of earlier days. But for those who gravitate toward a more layered view of interior de-

sign, a brief survey of the predominant styles of American housing stock can offer a rich source of inspiration from which to choose.

Trend Development. In some ways, trends in architecture and interior design are analogous to those in clothing design. Styles and original concepts are developed by professionals for a select group of elite customers. When these are executed and viewed by the public, they are often the source of a derivative movement, inspired by the original design. Thanks to the efficiencies of mass production, these styles can be made available to the general public in a simplified form with lower cost. Of course, changes in ar-

chitecture and interior design are less impulsive than those in the fashion industry, and the analogy breaks down quickly. But the popularization of a particular style in building can follow a similar trajectory from original design to mass marketing. Keep in mind that the application of any of the housing styles that follow can be less than strict. But by employing some of the most characteristic features of a particular genre, you can create an environment that you enjoy. The sense of an interior space is conditioned not only by the elements of a specific trim style but by the interplay of those elements with your choice of paint, floor covering, lighting, and furnishings.

1

TRIMWORK & DESIGN

CHAIR RAIL, opposite top left, serves to divide the wall into two decorating areas.

CLASSIC PILLARS, opposite bottom left, define an intimate space within the larger room.

UNIQUE CASING TREATMENT, opposite right, helps the window stand out in this contemporary room.

A COFFERED CEILING, left, adds a look of distinction to this traditional-style room.

Colonial

Early settlers in our country brought with them established tastes and preferences in architectural styles. As the colonies developed, it is not surprising that many of the earliest cultural influences came from throughout Europe. The *American Colonial* style was the first manifestation of a particularly American aesthetic by the new settlers of our land, although it drew freely on a variety of established styles, predominantly *Georgian*. (See page 22.)

In the earliest period of settlement, colonial homes were largely frontier structures. Simple log structures or half-timbered huts were the first individual dwellings. As regions started to become more developed, larger, more elaborate homes appeared and attention was directed to-

ward a more refined interior. In the more public areas of a home, plaster walls were common, and whitewashed finishes were popular. Often, on upper floors, the structural framing was left exposed. Baseboards and cornices, as well as plaster ceilings, started to be used by the early 1700s, and decorative wainscoting was common in the formal rooms of a home.

Fireplaces were a focal point of any home, particularly in the parlor or dining room. Sometimes the walls around the fireplace were paneled, first with plain wooden boards and later with more ornate treatments. Decoration around a fireplace could be as simple as a molded lintel across the top of the opening or complex, featuring pilasters and carvings of classical designs. Floors were often wide pine boards.

Modern Interpretation. As Colonial style is interpreted in modern homes, it is most often the less ornamental elements that have survived, such as an open fireplace with simple millwork, built-in china cabinets or hutches, and simple trim details. Baseboards and casings tend to be flat boards with the addition of a simple backband or shoe molding. Ceilings can be accented with cove molding and rustic beams. Wainscoting is frequently used, but it tends to be constructed with beaded tongue-and-groove boards rather than more formal panels. Sometimes, Colonial style is blended with a farm-style Country aesthetic. Furnishings might include floral-, fruit-, or check-patterned curtains, handmade quilts, simple rustic furniture, or braided rugs.

EXPOSED BEAMS, opposite, are a favorite Colonial detail.

OPEN FIREPLACES, right, add visual interest.

DISTINCTIVE MOLDING, below, enhances a hearth.

ROUGH TIMBERS, below right, add character.

Georgian

Georgian style developed in England in the early eighteenth century, and it relied heavily on elements from classical Greek and Roman architecture: symmetry, regularly spaced windows, and elaborate molding details. Columns and pilasters were used as decorative elements, and definite rules of proportion were strictly obeyed.

Early Georgian interiors may have featured full-height wooden paneling with a painted finish, but later plaster or stucco walls were often covered by paper or fabric with applied molding such as *wall frames*. Both wood and plaster ceiling moldings were used, and the cornice treatments were often quite elaborate. As trade and immigration increased between England and the American colonies, Georgian style made the cross-Atlantic voyage, and many pattern books and architectural manuals were printed as reference for carpenters. Furniture of this style is best represented by the designers Chippendale, Sheraton, and Hepplewhite.

Georgian Today. Today, Georgian-style interiors are characteristically elegant but uncluttered. Walls in formal rooms are often divided into three sections, with a decorative frieze and cornice at the top, a center field with paint or wallpaper finish, and a paneled wainscot with chair rail at the bottom. Classical motifs such as urns or acanthus leaves occasionally appear as decorative elements. Wall frames are sometimes used instead of paneling or wainscoting, or in addition to these elements. These lend themselves to a variety of paint and wallpaper treatments that can impart a more or less formal feel to a space.

GEORGIAN-STYLE INTERIORS, right, grew out of designs developed in early eighteenth century England.

WALL FRAMES, opposite top left, are often found in Georgian interiors.

INTEGRATED TRIMWORK, opposite top right, ties the elements of this Georgian-style room together.

AN ELABORATE CORNICE, opposite bottom, complements the mantel moldings.

Federal

The *Federal* style became popular in the years following the American Revolution. This style was initially based on the work of the Adam brothers from Scotland, but builders in the newly formed United States soon put their own mark on the genre. Details from Greek and Roman buildings were freely borrowed as ornamentation, and features such as curves, ellipses, and elongated windows were used to modify rectangular Georgian homes. Many Federal-style homes have an arched Palladian window above the front entry.

CURVES FIGURE PROMINENTLY in Federal-style designs, as shown in the curved room at right.

GREEK AND ROMAN THEMES, below, play a large part in the molding and trimwork selected for Federal-style rooms.

Greek Revival

After the War of 1812, affection for British influence in design started to fade. American designers, most notably Thomas Jefferson, became influential, and an offshoot known as *Greek Revival* started to spread. Contributing to the popularity of Greek Revival design was the fact that it referred back to the ancient democracy as the roots for the new democratic nation. In fact, this style resonated so successfully with the American spirit that it became known as the "National Style." These buildings feature elaborate cornice trim with wide friezes, columned porches, and gabled or hipped roofs. Interiors tend to be less ornate than in either Federal or Georgian styles.

GREEK INFLUENCES are obvious in the bathroom shown at right. Note the elaborate cornice treatment.

UNDERSTATED DETAILS, below, became a hallmark of a style that came to be known as the "National Style."

Victorian

Victorian style takes its name from the reign of Queen Victoria of England, who ruled from 1837 to 1901. This genre covers a variety of individual movements, including *Gothic Revival, Italianate, Queen Anne, Stick, Eastlake,* and *Shingle* styles. Each of these fashions has its particular characteristics, but all are marked by an extremely ornate sensibility. Spires, towers, spindled porches, decorative brackets, and patterned shingles were commonly used elements, and as a result, the tendency toward overwrought excess has become synonymous with Victorian sensibility.

Victorian Trim. Interior millwork featured moldings layered upon one another in elaborate combinations. Images could be carved into the surface or applied to almost any millwork item or combination of items. Often these decorative elements did not even mirror or respond to similar moldings elsewhere in the room but instead provided a general sense of complexity and ornamentation. Doors and windows were trimmed with pilaster casings that included plinth and corner blocks. Elaborate apron panels under windows and architraves over doors added other decorative elements.

STONE AND METALWORK, above, were often combined with elaborate moldings.

MIXING DESIGN DETAILS, right, is common in Victorian-inspired designs.

PATTERNED WALLPAPER, bottom, supports the elaborate mantel trim.

ELABORATE CASINGS, opposite, convey the Victorian design sense.

Arts and Crafts

If the Victorian style was a celebration of the fruits of the Industrial Revolution, with its mass-produced ornament and overwrought excess, the *Arts and Crafts* style developed as a rejection of those same values and tastes. In England, William Morris and John Ruskin set the tone for this movement, promoting an ethic of simplicity in design and rejection of the industrially produced aesthetic. Their philosophy incorporated more than purely visual ideals. They spoke broadly of the effects of the home environment on quality of life, and they related design principles to hygiene, sanitation, and a general sense of right living. Before long, American designers picked up this theme, and Arts and Crafts design flourished in a variety of separate styles like *Mission* and *Craftsman*. Despite its elaborate appearance, much Victorian furniture and ornament were not particularly well made. And in their effort to develop a new design philosophy, the Arts and Crafts designers placed great emphasis on the quality of construction.

Trimwork Evolution. Trim systems in the Arts and Crafts style are typically rectilinear and angular. The decorative motifs that appear most often are derived from medieval, Japanese, and Islamic influence. Wide, flat casing, baseboard, and friezes are often used, as particular value is given to the decorative grain of the wood. The millwork is generally finished to allow the wood grain to be seen, with warm reddish-brown or dark-brown stains most common.

Your Style

Of course, the design of interior trim does not always adhere to any of these particular design disciplines, and the above list is not intended to be a comprehensive catalogue of historical trends. But by examining these concepts of style, you can get a sense of how trim details evolved. You can also see how each of these approaches relates to one another. Sometimes one style grows organically from a prior fashion; at other times, a new form is the result of a strong reaction against a popular trend.

BUILT-INS, opposite, are favorite design elements.

BEAMED CEILINGS, above, decorate public rooms.

FLAT CASINGS, right, provide strong visual lines.

NATURAL WOOD, below, is a common design theme.

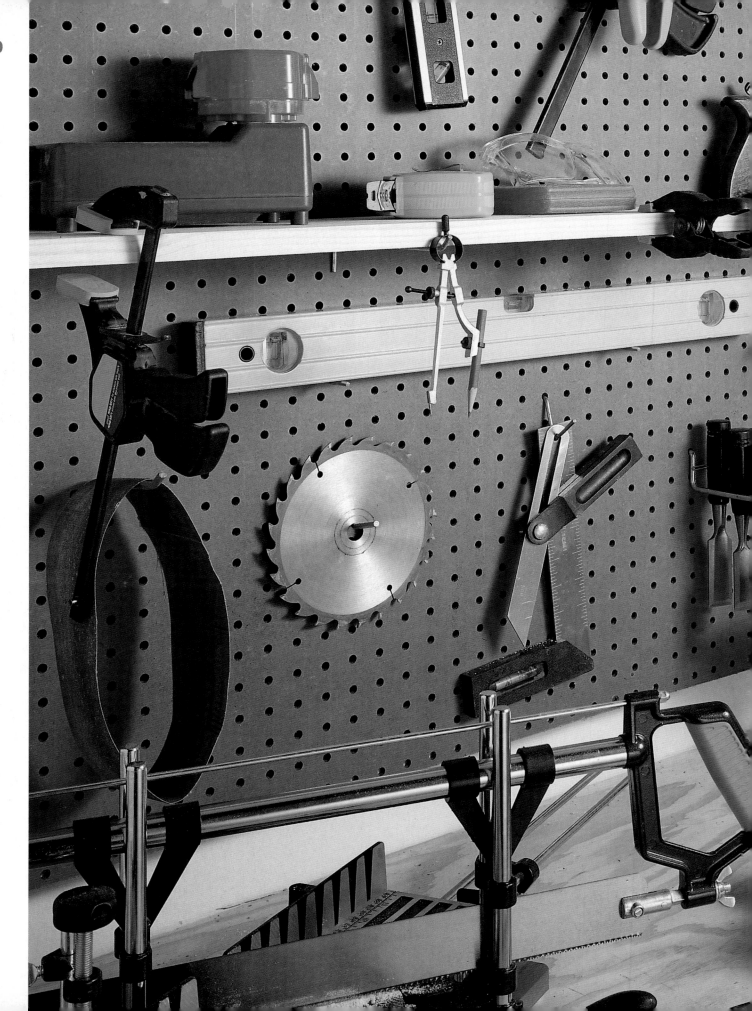

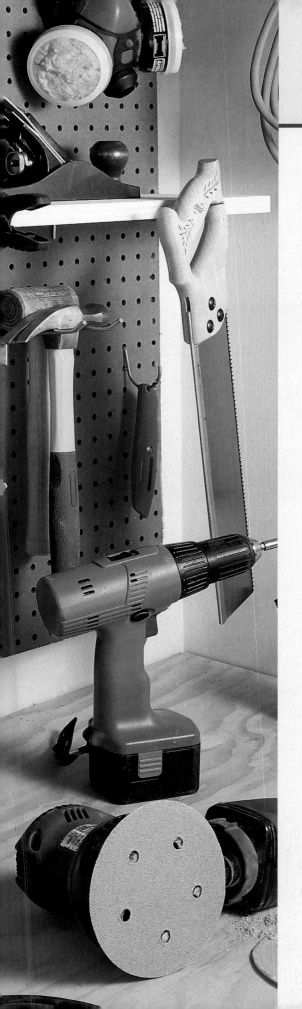

CHAPTER 2

TOOLS & TECHNIQUES

Tools for trimwork range from the most rudimentary implements to some pretty obscure and specialized machines. And, despite the tendency of some to accumulate every tool possible, you don't need them all. For the neophyte, the best approach is to start with a few basic items and learn to use them safely and confidently before branching out to the more advanced and specialized tools. Purchase tools as the need arises, rather than to stock your workshop. In that way, you will be motivated to use and master each item instead of allowing it to sit gathering dust for years before its initial use.

Measuring and Layout Tools

Your choice of measuring tools for any task depends, at least partially, on the scale of the job and tolerances you must keep. The secondary factor has to do with personal preference, for often there is a choice of appropriate tools. As you work with a variety of tools, you will naturally gravitate toward some over others. Just make sure that your preference for comfort or convenience does not result in a sacrifice of accuracy.

When it comes to marking stock to be cut to size, or laying out more complex joints, the accuracy of your marks is critical. Although the tool most associated with carpentry layout is the flat carpenter's pencil, this tool is really not very useful for trimwork. The thick, soft lead of the pencil and its fat body make it awkward to use and prone to rapid dulling; the result is a wide, vague mark. For trimwork the better choice is a hard pencil—#3 is perfect—that can be sharpened to a very fine point. If you keep a fine point on the tool, it will provide you with an extremely precise mark.

For the finest work, even a sharpened pencil mark can be too vague. In those situations where you want the highest degree of accuracy, a knife mark is the best choice. The type of knife you use is not important—an inexpensive utility knife will work as well as a fancy rosewood-handled layout knife—but the edge and tip should be razor sharp.

Measuring Tapes

A *measuring tape* is a great device for estimating materials and laying out a job. The most common sizes of steel retractable tape are ¾ inch wide by 12- or 16-feet long and 1 inch wide by 25 feet long, although reel-style tapes are available to 100-foot lengths. For room measurements and all-around general use, the 1-inch by 25-foot model is your best bet. The wide blade will support itself over a long span and most rooms are less than 25 feet in length. Most have a locking lever that keeps the blade from retracting. Tapes usually have each "foot" mark clearly delineated as well as arrows or other indications for 16-inch spacing—this is especially handy for stud locations. You will typically find graduations down to ⅟₁₆ inch, with some models having ⅟₃₂-inch graduations for the first foot of the tape.

Folding Stick Rules

The *folding stick rule* is one of carpentry's oldest measuring devices and still very useful. These come in 6- and 8-foot lengths that fold into a compact 8-inch-long package. A stick rule is great for those situations where you need to

measure something that is just out of reach, and you need to suspend the ruler over an unsupported space. It is also handy to gauge the extent of an overhanging detail or to measure the inside dimension of an opening. Most models have a sliding extension at one end for easy inside measuring. For easy folding, periodically apply a tiny drop of oil to each folding joint.

Steel Rulers

Steel rulers usually come in sizes from 6 inches to 24 inches, although a yardstick could easily be included in this category. For the most accurate measurements, it's hard to beat a steel ruler because the graduations are scribed or etched

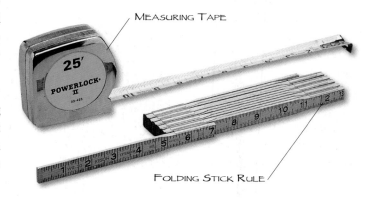

MEASURING TAPE

FOLDING STICK RULE

into the surface, and they are, typically, finer lines than those painted on a wooden ruler or tape. In addition, it's easy to find rulers that have graduations as fine as 1/64 inch.

Squares

A *square* is the primary tool for testing that two edges are perpendicular, but it is also important for layout. Squares are available in different sizes and configurations for various uses.

Framing Square. This tool is made of steel or aluminum and has legs of 16 and 24 inches. In addition to inch measurements along each blade, you will find a chart for determining the angles for rafters of various slope roofs. A framing square is handy for laying out stud walls, but it is also useful in trimwork to check that larger panels are square or for testing door and window openings. The long blade of the square is also valuable as a straight edge.

Sliding Combination Square. In addition to being a precision square, this tool has a milled edge on the body that sits at 45 degrees to the blade for testing miter cuts. The body can slide along the graduated blade and lock in place at different settings so that you can use it as a depth or marking gauge. Most models also include a steel scriber and a small level vial on the body.

Try Square. This tool has a 6- or 8-inch blade with a fixed body. These are convenient for testing the accuracy of cuts on small parts. For the highest degree of accuracy, you can purchase an *engineer's precision square*. These steel squares are available in blade sizes from 6 to 12 inches and are guaranteed to conform to extremely fine tolerances (typically .016mm).

Speed Square. Although designed as a rafter layout tool, a *speed square* is valuable in trim work. You can use the speed square as a crosscutting guide for the circular saw to help in making square cuts on narrow lumber.

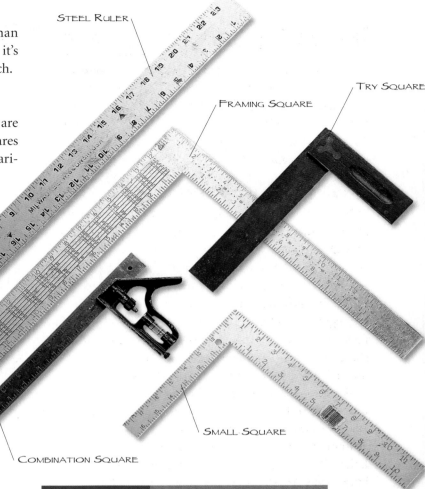

STEEL RULER

FRAMING SQUARE

TRY SQUARE

COMBINATION SQUARE

SMALL SQUARE

SPEED SQUARE

Trim Tip PARALLEL LINES

If you need to mark a line parallel to a straight edge, reach for your sliding combination square. Slide the body along the blade until you reach the distance your line needs to be from the edge. Hold the body along the edge and your sharpened pencil against the end of the blade. Slide both square and pencil down the edge to scribe your line.

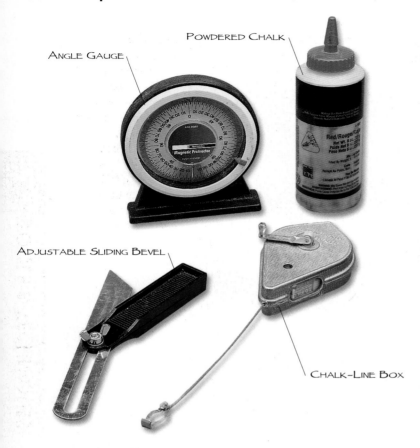

ANGLE GAUGE

POWDERED CHALK

ADJUSTABLE SLIDING BEVEL

CHALK-LINE BOX

Trim Tip GOOD MARKS

When marking a board to be cut to length or determining a guideline on a wall, place a "V" at the desired mark rather than a vague line. Use the point of the "V" to indicate the exact point of measurement; then use a square, protractor, or straightedge to lay out the cut or layout line.

Angle Guides

Things would be much simpler in trim work if all angles were either 90 or 45 degrees, but life is just not like that. So, in order to be able to work with various angles you will need a *protractor* or *angle gauge*. The particular configuration of your tool is not critical, but it's worth investing in a steel tool rather than a plastic model.

Adjustable Sliding Bevel. An *adjustable sliding bevel* has no graduations to indicate particular angle measurement, but it is a great device for copying any angle. Simply loosen the nut; hold the body against one side of the angle; and slide the blade until it rests against the opposite side of the angle. Tighten the blade to retain the setting. You can then use the gauge to trace the angle onto another surface for direct cutting or bisecting with a protractor.

Chalk Line

A *chalk-line box* is a simple, but very valuable, tool for marking a long straight line between distant points on a wall, floor, or ceiling. It consists of a metal or plastic enclosure with a reel that holds a cotton string; the string has a metal hook on its free end. Pour powdered chalk into the box, and extend the string between the points you wish to connect. Hold the string taut and gently lift and release it so that it snaps once against the surface to mark the straight line.

Levels

The concepts of plumb and level are primary to good trim carpentry work. In carpentry terms, something is level when it is perfectly parallel to the ground, with no slope. Something is plumb when it is perfectly vertical. Plumb and level lines are always perpendicular to one another.

Spirit Level. The most common tool used to test these qualities is the *spirit level*. A spirit level has two or three fluid-filled arched vials, each with a small air bubble inside. Hold the level against a horizontal or vertical surface to check if it is plumb or level; the bubble should be exactly between the gauge marks.

Water Level. A *water level* can be used to set a level mark at two distant points. It consists of a hose, filled almost completely with water, with transparent ends. If you hold both ends up, the waterline at one end will always be level to the waterline at the opposite end.

Laser Level. A *laser level* projects a horizontal or vertical beam of light. Some models are self-leveling, but on others you need to adjust the unit first with a vial gauge. Rotary models can project the beam on all four walls of a room at the same time. Once you have your level or plumb line established, you can place marks appropriately to guide your measurement or installation.

Plumb Bob. One of the oldest methods of gauging if something is plumb, or of striking a plumb line, is to use a *plumb bob*. This tool is simply a string with a pointed weight attached to one of its ends. Most bobs are fashioned of brass, and some of the old models can be quite decorative. If you suspend the bob from any point you can always be sure that the string will describe a perfectly plumb line.

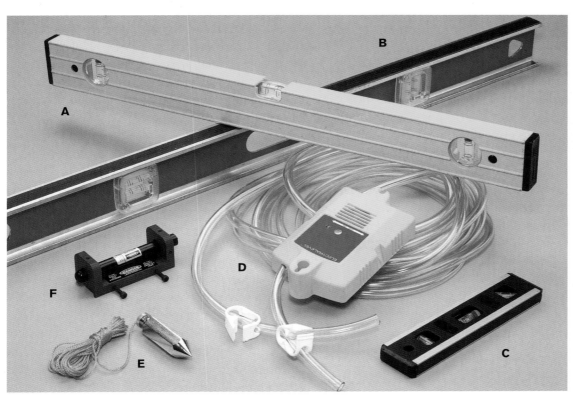

LEVELS:
A—2-ft. spirit level, **B**—4-ft. spirit level, **C**—6-in. spirit level, **D**—water level with electronic level sensor, **E**—plumb bob and string, **F**—laser level, which can be attached to a standard level

Stud Finder

Most trim carpentry involves attaching pieces of wood to a wall or ceiling surface. Since most rooms are finished with drywall or plaster, it is important to fasten parts to the underlying framing members whenever possible. While you can always poke holes to locate studs or joists, a much neater and quicker technique is to use a *stud finder*. Older models relied on magnets to sense nails or screws driven into the framing. Most electronic models have sensors that detect difference in capacitance to locate the studs. The most recent developments use a type of radar technology to sense the framing inside the wall. Electronic stud finders use a series of sounds or lights to indicate when the tool is directly over a stud.

STUD FINDERS help locate framing within a wall without damaging the surface of the wall. Most newer models use lights and sounds to indicate the location of the stud.

Trim Tip   MAKE A MEASURING JIG

Taking an accurate inside measurement—such as an exact window or door opening—is one of the challenges of trim work. To obtain exact measurements, take two sticks, each somewhat longer than one-half the overall dimension. Hold the sticks together and slide them apart until the ends touch the walls of the opening. Use clamps to lock the dimension; you can then use the guide to transfer the measurement to your trim piece.

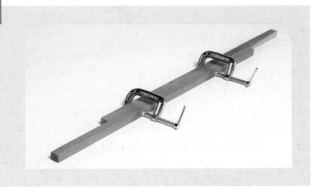

Cutting Tools

For many specific jobs, as well as those times when an extension cord is not handy, a hand saw is the tool of choice. The saws most associated with the carpenter's trade are the traditional *crosscut* and *rip saws.* Each of these saws has a blade approximately 22 to 26 inches long that tapers from the handle toward the tip. A crosscut saw typically has 8 to 10 teeth per inch and a rip saw 4 to 5 teeth per inch. When using either of these saws, you should position yourself so that you can take long, straight strokes, with your arm and shoulder in line with the blade. If the saw is properly sharpened, you should not need to force the saw, but simply guide it back and forth, allowing the weight of the blade to determine the rate of cut.

A handy alternative to western-style hand saws is the Japanese *Ryoba.* This dual-purpose saw has fine crosscutting teeth on one edge and coarse ripping teeth on the opposite edge. All Japanese saws cut on the pull stroke, rather than the push stroke like western saws. This allows the saw blade to be thinner and therefore yields a smaller *kerf,* or width of cut. Using a Japanese style saw takes some practice, but once you master the technique, you will find it a very valuable addition to your toolbox.

Backsaw. A *backsaw* has a rectangular shaped blade with a steel or brass reinforcement along the top spine. The reinforcing spine allows the saw to have a thin blade that still stays straight. This type of saw comes in many sizes and tooth configurations, each with a particular use in mind. The smallest backsaws are called "dovetail" saws since they are designed to cut fine furniture joints called dovetails. Larger saws are handy for use in a miter box to cut molding to precise angles.

Coping Saw. A *coping saw* consists of a handle attached to a C-shaped frame. A thin blade is stretched between the ends of the frame. This configuration enables the user to make sharp turns with the saw to follow complex molding shapes. This tool is primarily used in the cutting of "coped" (or fitted) joints. Most carpenters install the blade so that the saw cuts on the "pull" stroke.

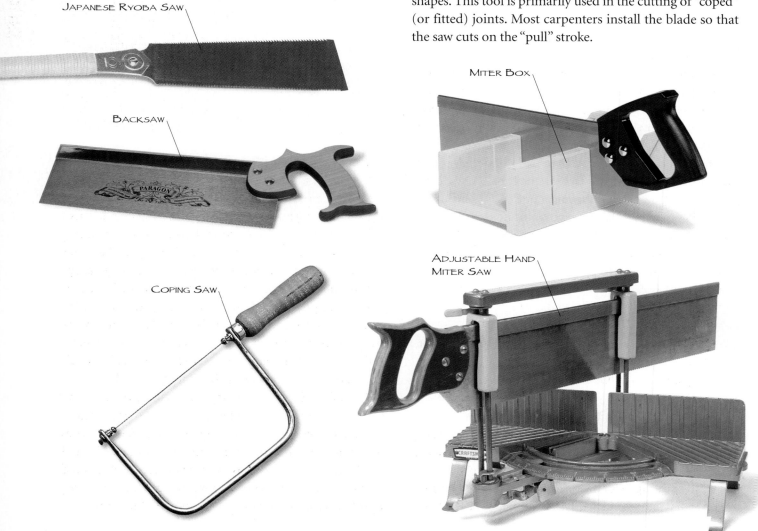

JAPANESE RYOBA SAW

BACKSAW

COPING SAW

MITER BOX

ADJUSTABLE HAND MITER SAW

Trim Tip   HAND CHISELS

A basic set of butt chisels, ranging in width from ¼ to 1½ inches, is a worthwhile investment for trimwork. You'll find them handy for fine paring of joints and cutting mortises for door hardware. In order to keep them sharp, purchase a good quality sharpening stone and honing guide—and use them often.

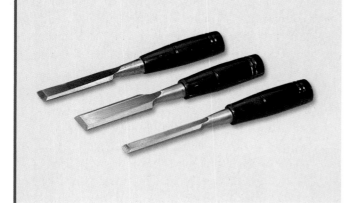

Circular Saw

Saber Saw

Miter Saws

If you only have a few miter joints to cut, it's hardly worth investing in a power miter saw. Fortunately, there are less expensive, and low-tech, alternatives—the wood or plastic miter box, and metal hand miter saw. The simplest tool for cutting simple miters is the *miter box*. A miter box has a U-shaped cross-section with saw kerfs cut at 45 and 90 degrees through the guide rails. These are meant to be used with a backsaw which has a reinforcing spine along the top edge of the saw blade. You can find an inexpensive miter box, complete with back saw, at most home centers. Unfortunately, the miter box has the limitation of not allowing any adjustment in the angle of cut.

For more flexibility, you can turn to the *hand miter saw.* Some miter saws use a backsaw and some are designed to hold a saw that resembles a hacksaw. In either case, the saw is supported in a guide, and you have the ability to adjust the angle of cut from 45 degrees left to 45 degrees right, providing more flexibility than the miter box.

Power Cutting Tools

When you need a power saw for crosscutting or ripping solid lumber and sizing plywood panels, the *circular saw* is usually the first choice. Tool selection is based on the diameter of the cutting blade, and there are a number of sizes available. But for general use, pick a saw with a blade that is

7¼ inches in diameter as this size should handle most cutting jobs. These models are adjustable for depth and angle of cut, and most will cut stock up to 2¼ inches thick at 90 degrees. Expect your saw to have a fixed upper blade guard and a lower retractable guard that operates by spring tension. Some saws offer an electronic blade brake that stops the blade when you release the trigger, and this is a great option for increased safety. If it does not come with the saw, you should purchase an accessory rip guide for cutting strips of uniform width from wide stock. There are a number of different types of blades available for circular saws. Initially, you should purchase a combination blade for all-around use and a crosscutting blade for fine work.

Saber Saw. Sometimes called a *portable jig saw,* this is an extremely versatile tool that is great for cutting curved or intricate shapes. These tools accept a wide variety of blades for rough and finish cutting of wood, as well as plastics and metal. Most saws have an adjustable base for bevel cuts and a switch to allow the blade to move in either an orbital (for wood) or reciprocating (for plastic or metal) motion.

MAKING A MITER-SAW STAND

A miter saw is a great tool for cutting both flat stock and molding, but when the material is long, safety and accuracy concerns mandate that you provide more support than the saw table alone can offer. There are plenty of commercial miter-saw stands available for purchase; most have locking casters and folding outboard stock rests. However, it's easy for you to construct your own stand from a piece of plywood, some 2x4 stock, a piece of one-by pine, and a pair of sawhorses. Fashion a support platform in the shape of a ladder by nailing or screwing together some 2x4 stock. Cut a piece of ¾-inch plywood to fit over the top of the frame. Apply some construction adhesive to the top edges of the frame, and screw the plywood to the base. Mark the location of saw mounting holes on the plywood surface, and drill pilot holes for mounting bolts. Fasten the saw base to the platform, and then add a support block at either end of the platform, making sure that the top edge of each block is level with the saw table. Clamp the saw platform to a pair of sawhorses to ensure stability of the work table.

Difficulty Level: **Easy**

TOOLS
Power drill with screwdriver bit • caulking gun • pencil • socket wrench • clamps

MATERIALS
2x4s • ¾-inch plywood • construction adhesive • lag screws and washers • utility screws

BUILD A FRAME for the table using 2x4s set on edge. Use wood screws to assemble the frame.

CUT THE TOP using ¾-in. plywood. Set it in the adhesive and fasten with screws.

DRILL THROUGH THE PLYWOOD and secure the saw using lag bolts or lag screws.

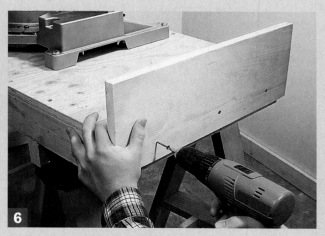

ATTACH A MOLDING SUPPORT to each end of the platform so that the top is level with the saw table.

INCREASE STABILITY of the assembly by running a bead of construction adhesive on the 2x4s.

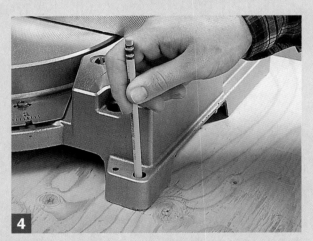

PLACE THE SAW in the middle of the platform, and mark the bolt-down locations.

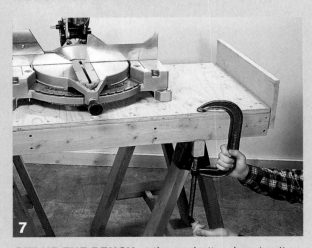

SET UP THE BENCH at the work site, clamping it firmly to stable sawhorses.

Power Miter Saws

When your trim projects become more extensive, a *power miter saw* will undoubtedly become one of the primary tools on the job. These are essentially a circular saw mounted on a pivoting stand. The motor and blade can swivel from side to side over the table to cut the desired angle. Most saws have preset detents at 90, 45, and 22.5 degrees.

Compound Miter Saws. These tools have the added capability for the blade to tip to one side to cut a bevel angle, in addition to the miter. A *sliding compound miter saw* adds one more feature to the mix by providing guide rails that allow the blade to be pulled through the cut, toward the operator. With sliding capability, these saws allow you to cut wide stock, cut joints on crown molding with the material held flat on the saw table, and cut grooves or tenon joints by limiting the depth of cut with a stop. Saws are available in a variety of sizes which are determined by blade diameter—most fall in the range of 8½- to 12-inch sizes. When selecting a saw, pay particular attention to the capacity ratings of each particular model—both the thickness and width of stock it will cut. While sliding compound saws are the most versatile of all miter saws, they are quite expensive; some models can exceed $600.

POWER SAWS increase your versatility. Shown left and below are a standard miter saw and a sliding compound miter saw.

2

TOOLS & TECHNIQUES

Shaping and Finishing Tools

Planes are one of the tools most often associated with carpentry. The image of the carpenter, with shavings flying, is almost an icon in woodworking. Aside from the image, however, the plane is a necessary part of your tool collection. While there are planes designed for many specific tasks, for a beginner approaching trimwork, a *block plane* will serve most purposes quite well. Block planes are about 6 inches long with a cutting iron approximately 1½ inches wide. The cutting iron is mounted, with the bevel facing up, at a low angle—this makes the tool especially well suited to trimming the end grain of a board, but it will also do a fine job planing the edge or face of a board.

You will find a block plane very handy for final fitting of a trim board to an uneven surface, or fine-tuning a miter joint. For best results, always keep the cutting iron razor sharp.

BLOCK PLANE

Sanders

For most people who work with wood, sanding is the least appealing part of any project—it is dusty and can be tedious—and it can seem hard to justify the effort. However, much of the final impression of a job lies in the quality of the finished surface, and sanding prepares the way for a first-class finish.

Belt Sanders. For the coarsest jobs, you can't beat a *belt sander* for fast stock removal. These tools usually accept 3- or 4-inch-wide belts in a variety of grits from very coarse (40 grit) to very fine (220 grit). A belt sander can be your best friend on a job, but it can also get out of control easily and do some damage. Make sure that you orient the sander so that the belt moves parallel to the grain, and always keep the machine moving down the length of the workpiece when the belt is running or you may gouge the surface.

Random Orbital Sander. A *random orbital sander* is a finishing sander that has a disc-shaped pad. The sanding pad turns on an eccentric spindle so that it creates tiny swirl marks on the wood surface. This type of tool has the ability to remove stock quickly, but it also can leave a fine finish on the surface. Look for a model with a 5-inch-diameter pad because that size sanding disc is the most widely available.

Belt Sander

Random-Orbital Sanders

Orbital Sheet Sanders

Orbital Sheet Sanders. These tools have been the standard finishing sanders for many years. They are offered in ¼- and ½-sheet sizes and are generally the least expensive machine option for finish work. These sanders provide the best choice if you need to sand vertical surfaces.

Hand Sanding. Power sanders are great tools, but there are times when you just have to do the job by hand. For small flat surfaces, you can use a block of wood as a sanding block. Or you can go the commercial route and purchase a rubber or cork block. For sanding molded profiles, use a bit of creativity to fashion a sanding block or pad that matches the profile. You could use a pencil or dowel as a backer to sand flutes in a pilaster, or a small can, jar, or the cardboard core from a roll of paper towels as a backer to sand a cove molding.

Plate Joiner

You could easily spend years mastering the art of cutting various joints in wood—and many people have done just that. To do trimwork, you really do not have to master those skills. However, there are situations when you will need to join materials without screws or nails, and a simple, flexible approach can be found in plate joinery. Joining plates are football-shaped wafers of compressed wood, about ⅛ inch thick, that come in a variety of sizes. (See "Joining Plate Sizes," right.) To use the plates, cut a semi-circular slot in each half of the joint with a *plate joiner*. The tool has a spinning blade that you advance into the wood to a preset depth. Location and alignment of the slot is controlled by two fences on the joiner, and there are adjustments that allow angle settings as well.

Once your joint is cut, spread a bit of glue into each slot and also on the surface of a joining plate. Push the plate into one of the matching slots, and assemble the joint. Use a clamp to hold the parts together while the glue sets. The glue causes the compressed wood of the plate to expand.

Joining plates have been dubbed "flat dowels" by some woodworkers, since they have largely replaced dowels as a means of joinery. Cutting a plate joint is much quicker than drilling matching dowel holes and has the added advantage of having some "play" in the joint. The slots are slightly longer than the plates, providing room to adjust a joint.

Plate Joiner

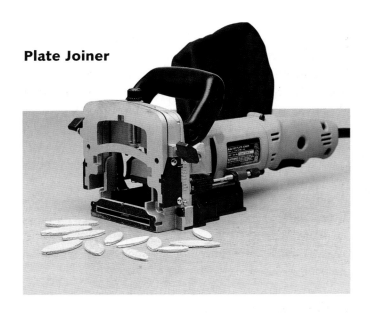

JOINING PLATE SIZES

#0: About ⅝ inch wide by 1¾ inches long (47 x 15 mm)

#10: About ¾ inch wide by 2⅛ inches long (53 x 19 mm)

#20: 1 inch wide by 2½ inches long (56 x 23 mm)

Trim Tip ROUTER TABLES

A router is a versatile tool, and you will inevitably want to explore its full capability. (See "Routers," page 42.) By mounting the router upside down in a *router table,* you can shape pieces that are too narrow or too short to be cut with the tool held by hand. Commercial router tables are available in many configurations, some for table-top use and others that are freestanding. Most tables will accept any model router, although some may require that you drill new holes for mounting the machine to the table.

When you use a router table, the cutting bit is exposed, so you need to take extra precautions for safety. Always firmly clamp a fence to the table so that no more than one half of the bit is exposed. And, whenever possible, use hold-down fixtures and guards to keep the work from kicking back and to keep your hands away from the cutting edge. When cutting small parts, push sticks are a necessity.

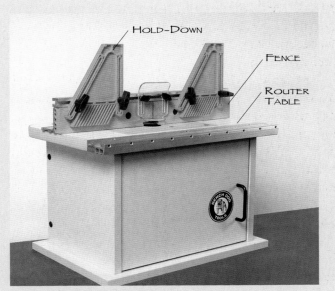

SINCE THE ROUTER BIT is inverted in a table, the direction of rotation is reversed. Therefore, when facing the table, you will need to feed the material from right to left.

Routers

A portable *router* gives you the ability to cut a wide range of molding profiles, as well as cutting grooves and trimming edges. Cutting bits are available in a dazzling array of profiles. Routers are rated by motor size and also by the size of the shank the collet (tool holder) will accept. For a first purchase, look for a model with a rating of 1½ to 1¾ horsepower with a ¼-inch collet. This is adequate for just about any task that you encounter and is a reasonable investment.

A basic router has a *fixed base* that requires you to set the depth of cut by turning a locking adjusting ring on the base; the depth must be set before turning on the tool. You will also see models that feature a *plunge base* that allows you to

Router, Guide, and Bits

SETTING UP A ROUTER

Professional cabinetry shops create molding profiles using large cutters mounted in powerful shaping machines. The home workshop equivalent is a router. Thanks to a wide variety of bits, you can use the tool to shape your own custom profiles. When using a router, unplug the tool before changing bits, and always wear safety glasses.

Difficulty Level: **Easy**

TOOLS
Router • bits • locking wrench • safety glasses

MATERIALS
1-by stock

ADJUST THE DEPTH OF CUT by turning the depth ring or the depth knob.

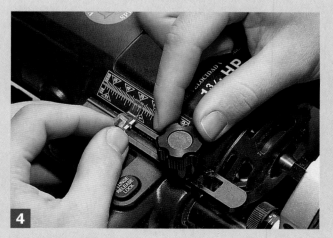

CUTTING BITS have a mounting shank. Place the shank in a sleeve, called a collet, located under the motor.

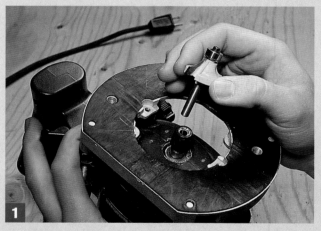

PLUNGE ROUTERS have a mechanism for adjusting the depth of cut.

lower a spinning bit into the work surface. While a plunge-base router is the more flexible tool, it is a bit less stable than a comparable fixed-base tool. For molding edges, either type of base is fine, but for stopped internal flutes or grooves, you will need a plunge-base machine.

When using a router, always move the tool against the direction of rotation of the bit. As a general rule, this means that if you are facing the edge to be cut, the router should be guided from your left to your right.

If your router does not come with an accessory edge guide, you should certainly consider purchasing one. Many bits feature a ball-bearing pilot to guide the cut, but if you want to use other bits, the guide is almost a necessity.

INSERT THE SHANK, and tighten the bit in place using the wrench that came with the tool.

TEST THE SETUP on scrap lumber before moving on to the molding stock.

BASIC ROUTER BITS

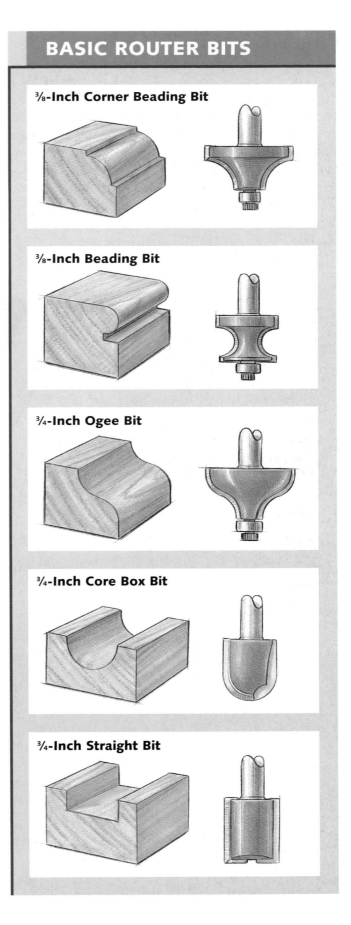

³⁄₈-Inch Corner Beading Bit

³⁄₈-Inch Beading Bit

³⁄₄-Inch Ogee Bit

³⁄₄-Inch Core Box Bit

³⁄₄-Inch Straight Bit

Files and Rasps

Trimwork sometimes involves delicate fitting of two wood parts together, or one piece of wood against another surface such as plaster, drywall, brick, or stone. In those cases, the only true rule is to use the tool that works best—sometimes it could be a saw, others a knife, and still other times a file or rasp could be just right. *Files* and *rasps* come in a wide variety of shapes that make them perfect for the final fitting of coped joints, especially those that involve a complex profile.

One of the frequent challenges that can arise when casing a door or window is that the drywall will bulge out into the room, creating a hump in the wall surface. This situation is a natural by-product of taping a drywall joint, but it is a problem for the person applying the trim. One way to attack the problem is to use a *surform tool* to shave down the built-up drywall compound. The surform has an expanded metal blade that is held in a frame so that it can be used like a rasp or plane.

Although you cannot sharpen files and rasps, you can, and should, keep them clean. The tool for this job is called a *file card*. Use the card like a brush to remove any built-up debris from file and rasp teeth.

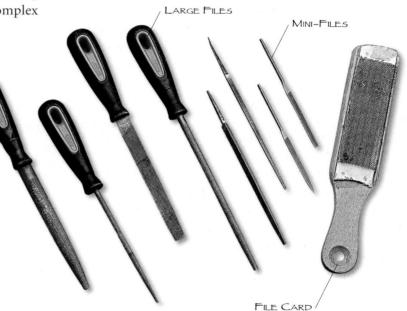

LARGE FILES

MINI-FILES

SURFORM TOOL

FILE CARD

PRY BARS, END NIPPERS, AND LOCKING PLIERS

Trim carpentry is often a game of finesse. Many jobs require careful and patient fitting and re-fitting in order to achieve a tight fit between two parts. In that pursuit, many different tools can be brought into the mix, but some of the most effective, and necessary, are listed below.

When you need to remove an old molding, or coax a new piece into position, a *pry bar* is the tool for the job. These come in a wide variety of configurations, but the most useful for trim are the versions with flat ends, appropriately called flat bars. You will find some bars as short as 4 inches and some longer than 24 inches. If you select two different styles, usually those on the smaller side, you will be set for most jobs. In addition, it's useful to have a few different *putty knives* handy for scraping, gentle prying, and filling nailholes.

If your project includes removal of existing molding, you will need a way to remove the old nails from that stock. Two great tools for the job are *end nippers* and *locking pliers*. If you were to hammer the nails back through the face side, there is a great risk of chipping the material. With either of these tools, you can grab the protruding end of the nail and pull it through the back side of the board. This technique maintains the face side of the molding, allowing you the option of reusing it.

LOCKING PLIERS

END NIPPERS

Work-Holding Tools

When you get involved in almost any wood cutting or shaping process, the issue of how to hold the workpiece will arise. You simply cannot do most woodworking operations, safely and accurately, if you are crouched on the living room floor. Of course, you can always hijack the kitchen or dining room table, but that's not always a popular, or practical, approach. The alternative solutions you can devise are endless, but some basic options will cover most situations.

Saw Horses. *Saw horses* are a simple and flexible support system for all types of work. You will find commercial models in steel and plastic, and you can always make your own from wood. Just about any horses that you buy will fold up for compact storage, and that can be a compelling reason to go the commercial route. Look for models that are sturdy and that will hold your work and tools at a comfortable height.

Clamping Worktables. Several manufacturers offer a folding worktable with moveable top panels that function as a vise for work holding. These tables provide an ample top surface that can hold a miter saw firmly between its clamping dogs and can also provide work-holding power for planing, sawing, routing, or chiseling. Their portability lets you take the worktable to the work site.

Clamps. The variety in styles and sizes of *clamps* is vast. And it is a traditional woodworker's refrain that "you can never have enough clamps." Clamps are used to hold a joint together while glue sets or while you drive a mechanical fastener. But they are also handy, when you do not have access to a workbench and vise, for stabilizing a board for sawing or planing. Small clamps are great for temporarily holding a molding in place or positioning a stop for repeat cuts on the miter saw. For a beginning tool kit, start with two or three of each of these types: spring clamps, C-clamps, lightweight bar clamps, and quick-release clamps. You will soon

ADJUSTABLE CLAMPING WORKTABLE   CLAMPING DOG

HOLDING TOOLS are like having an extra set of hands. The clamping worktable, above, and a vise, left, can help make a number of jobs go easier.

learn which type is most useful for your style of work.

Vise. If you have the luxury of having a dedicated workbench, one of the nicest modifications you can make is to add a *vise*. Vises for woodworking are available in many sizes, configurations, and prices. For most trim jobs, a lightweight vise that clamps to the top of a worktable will be sufficient. Whatever type you select, make sure that it has a provision for lining the jaws with wood so that you do not mar your workpieces when holding them.

C-CLAMP

SPRING CLAMP

LIGHTWEIGHT BAR CLAMP

QUICK-RELEASE CLAMP

Installation Tools

The *hammer* is the most basic of hand tools—and probably the oldest. Primitive humans used some sort of hammering device at the dawn of civilization, but it is still a valued tool in the carpenter's tool kit. Although the popular image of hammer use in our culture is a rather crude one, in experienced hands a hammer can be a precise and subtle tool. For trimwork, look for a 16-ounce claw hammer. You will find models with curved and straight claws. Some "experts" will suggest that the curved claw model is preferred for trim; in fact, either style will be fine. Materials for the shaft include wood, fiberglass, and steel and, once again, personal preference rules. Of course, each manufacturer will offer their version of the "best" hammer, but you should choose one that feels comfortable and seems well balanced. If at all possible, test the hammer by driving some nails before purchasing it.

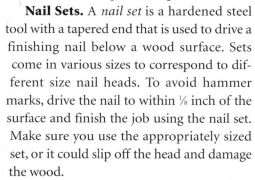

Curved Claw

Straight Claw

Nail Sets. A *nail set* is a hardened steel tool with a tapered end that is used to drive a finishing nail below a wood surface. Sets come in various sizes to correspond to different size nail heads. To avoid hammer marks, drive the nail to within ⅛ inch of the surface and finish the job using the nail set. Make sure you use the appropriately sized set, or it could slip off the head and damage the wood.

Power Drills and Screwdrivers. These are tools that you will reach for frequently on most trim projects. You will use these to drill pilot holes for nails and screws, to drive screws for installing hardware or drywall, and to assemble jamb sets. This is a case where cordless models are certainly a worthwhile investment. Most tool companies offer combination drill/drivers with adjustable clutch settings. These can operate at high or low speeds, and you can set the torque for any job requirement—high for drilling in wood or low for driving small screws. You will find models rated from 7.2 to 24 volts, but as a nonprofessional, if you select a 12- or 14.4-volt unit, you will have plenty of drilling power. An additional attraction of the cordless models is that they all come with keyless chucks, so you don't have to worry about keeping track of the chuck key.

Cordless Drill and Charger

FINISH NAILER

BRAD NAILER

NAIL CLIPS

Compressor

In addition to having a power driver, you'll want to have an assortment of hand drivers, since there will always be those jobs where a power tool is too large or awkward. Try to include at least two sizes of driver in each common screw category: flat blade, Phillips and Robertson (square drive).

Power Nailers

If your plans include extensive trimwork, the advantages of a *pneumatic nail gun* are obvious—increased speed and no hammer marks. But, even for a small job, there are reasons to consider a nail gun. First, the nails used in a finishing nail gun are thinner than those you drive by hand, so there is less chance of splitting the wood when nailing near an edge.

You can adjust the pneumatic pressure that drives the gun, so with a simple pull of the trigger, you can drive and set the nail below the wood surface. When working with hardwood molding, you need to drill pilot holes for nails that will be driven by hand, but a pneumatic gun will shoot them home in one step.

Compressors. To drive a pneumatic nail gun, you will need a *compressor*. Look for an electric model in the range of 1.5-2.5 horsepower. These are available in designs that are either oil-lubricated or oil-less, and for occasional use in applying trim, either style will be fine. Make sure that you get an air hose that is at least 25 feet long, or you will find yourself moving the compressor every few minutes.

2

TOOLS & TECHNIQUES

USING A NAIL GUN

The ability to drive and set a nail in one step can save much time and effort even when applying trim to a small room. Look for a gun that will accept nails up to 2½ inches long. For fine work, a brad gun will shoot shorter and thinner fasteners. These tools are widely available from rental agencies, so you do not need to purchase one for a small job.

Difficulty Level: **Easy**

TOOLS
Air-powered nailer • compressor

MATERIALS
Nail clip

PNEUMATIC NAILERS use long clips of glued-together nails for easy loading.

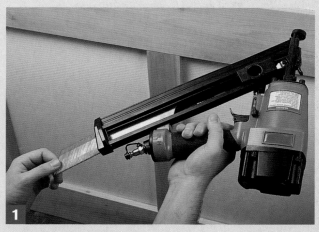

FOR BEST RESULTS, make sure the firing head is perpendicular to the work surface.

FOR SAFETY, most pneumatic nailers won't fire unless the tip is pressed firmly against the work.

Trim Tip   USING SAFETY EQUIPMENT

Trim is not very dangerous work, but there are two areas where it pays to be cautious. The first is with power tools, particularly saws. You should check the manufacturer's operating instructions and follow the rules for safe operation. The second is with wood chips and sawdust. Guard against injury by wearing safety glasses or goggles and, in some situations, by wearing a dust mask or respirator. Also, you will find gloves handy for sanding and finishing work, and you will come to appreciate kneepads when installing baseboard or wainscoting.

SAFETY EQUIPMENT: A—rubber gloves, **B**—work gloves, **C**—knee pads, **D**—safety glasses, **E**—safety goggles, **F**—particle mask, **G**—respirator, **H**—ear protectors

DOWELING AND POCKET SCREW JIGS

In commercial furniture and cabinet construction, dowels are still used as one of the primary systems to join lumber and plywood together. Those commercial systems rely on large machines with multiple drilling heads to bore the required holes in exact alignment. While the ease of plate joinery has made the use of dowels less popular for trimwork, a plate joiner is still a pretty expensive tool. If you only have a few joints to fashion, dowels are still a viable option, and a doweling jig is considerably less expensive. If you leaf through any tool catalogue or visit a home center, you will see any number of doweling jigs for sale. Just about any jig design will work well if you take care to accurately lay out the loca-

tion of your holes. Follow the manufacturer's recommendations for operation of the jig, and use a sharp drill bit when boring the holes.

Pocket screws are another handy option for joining two pieces of lumber for a frame, extension jamb, or simple cabinet box. The system relies on a special jig that positions a drill bit to bore a shallow, angled pilot hole for specifically designed screws. These joints are quite strong and are easy to machine, but the screw holes are visible on the back side of the joint. Although there are proprietary plugs you can purchase for the screw holes, this system is best used where one side of the material will not be exposed—a wainscoting frame is a perfect use.

DOWELING JIG

BIT GUIDES

DOWELING JIGS provide an easy way to use dowels to join two pieces of wood together.

CLAMPING PLIERS

TAPERED BIT

POCKET SCREW JIGS position drill bits to bore angled pilot holes for special screws.

Stationary or Bench-Top Tools

For all trim projects, accuracy is important, and when you are not a professional, it is hard to dedicate enough time to become proficient in every task. Even for the full-time carpenter, there are just some jobs that are easier and faster to achieve with a stationary tool than with a hand-held one. Straightening the edges of boards and ripping them to width are two such tasks. These jobs, among others, are easier and faster when you can use a tool that is specifically designed for the job, instead of adapting a hand tool. So, if your project budget permits, consider these as possible additions to your arsenal.

Table Saw

A small bench-top table saw can be extremely helpful on a trim job. If you need to rip strips for extension jambs or trim moldings to width, a table saw is the best tool for the job. Over the last few years, lightweight 8- and 10-inch saws have become very popular as alternatives to freestanding contractor-model saws. These saws offer a small miter gauge for square and angled crosscuts, a fence for ripping stock to width, and a tilting arbor for bevel cuts. These saws are not the equivalent of floor model saws when it comes to power and accuracy, but for light-duty use they can do a great job.

Since a bench-top saw is intentionally lightweight, it is important that you clamp or bolt it to a heavy worktable before making any cuts. A stable base is important for safe and efficient operation. Also, make it a habit to check the rip fence setting at both the front and back of the blade because these accessories are notorious for not automatically locking parallel to the blade.

Jointer

A small table-top *jointer* with a 4- or 6-inch-wide head can be very useful for straightening the edge of a bowed board or removing saw marks from ripped stock. These tools are scaled-down models of a cabinet-shop staple that is used in preparing lumber from rough stock. The jointer has two separate tables that surround the spinning cutterhead. To make a cut, hold a board against the vertical fence and push it across the infeed table, past the cutterhead and over the outfeed table. The depth of your cut is determined by the height of the infeed table—most bench-top tools use a hand wheel or lever to control table

Table Saw

Jointer

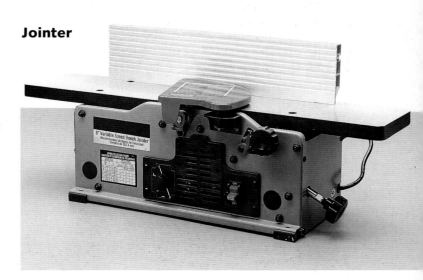

height. **Safety note:** The cutter heads are extremely sharp on this tool. Never joint material shorter than 12 inches long, and always use pushing paddles for stock that is less than 2 inches thick.

Planer

As your trim projects get more ambitious, you might run into situations where the thickness of stock materials does not suit your requirements. When that happens, you could bring your lumber to a custom woodworking shop or mill to have it planed, but you could also obtain a *bench-top planer* and do the job yourself. Many manufacturers now offer lightweight 12-inch-wide models, and most models do a very nice job. The best procedure with these tools is to always take a light cut, and work down toward your desired thickness with multiple passes.

Basic Trim Techniques

Trim carpentry covers a pretty wide range of tasks and skills, and each particular discipline has an appropriate level of allowable deviation. At one end of the spectrum, a carpenter who is framing a house might work to a tolerance of $\frac{1}{8}$ inch; anything more exacting could be construed as wasting time. However, a cabinetmaker could easily be concerned with measurements as fine as $\frac{1}{64}$ inch or smaller, as gaps in a joint or irregularities in spaces around a door are readily visible and are signs of shoddy workmanship.

Applying interior trim falls closer to cabinetmaking than framing in the demand for accuracy. However, much depends on the type of trim that you are installing and the type of finish that will be applied. It's always nice to aim for perfection, and there is great satisfaction in putting together a tight miter joint or fitting a door with uniform margins all around. In practice, though, you will need to acquire your own sense for the appropriate level of accuracy on your jobs. It's rare for two carpenters to have the same approach to their work, and most have developed an intuitive judgment that operates in the background of each task.

In practical terms, you should not be able to see a space in a joint or a difference in the amount of overhang on opposite sides of a piece of trim. If your job is to receive a clear or stained finish, the demands are pretty high because any filler you use in a gap can easily be seen. When a painted finish is planned, you have a bit more leeway because fillers and caulk can correct many small problems. Keep in mind, however, that wide spaces in joints can telegraph through paint surfaces, and caulk does not cure all careless mistakes. In addition, if a joint depends on glue to keep it together, a tight fit is doubly important, as glue offers little strength when it must bridge a gap. It is much better to strive to develop good technique for measurement and fitting than to routinely rely on gap-filling measures.

Cutting Stock

Circular Saws. It's exciting to look over a neatly stacked pile of lumber, waiting to be installed on the job. But, before picking up a hammer, you will need to cut each piece to size, and you want to do it safely and accurately. To break down long pieces of stock into manageable length, as well as to make accurate finish cuts, a circular saw is likely to be one of your most useful tools. For all-around use, equip your saw with a combination blade; a 24-tooth, thin-kerf carbide tipped blade is a good choice. Carbide blades are more expensive than plain steel, but they maintain a sharp edge far longer. If you don't abuse the blade, or use it to cut through nails, it should last you for years. After prolonged use a carbide blade will start to dull, but it is easy to find a shop to sharpen a blade at a fraction of the cost of a new one.

To make fine finish cuts in solid stock, purchase a finish, or crosscutting, blade that has a 40-tooth configuration. Cutting plywood and other panel stock requires an even finer tooth blade. The thin veneer of a manufactured panel is very susceptible to chipping out where the blade exits the cut, and a finer blade minimizes this tendency. So, if you

24-TOOTH COMBINATION

140-TOOTH PLYWOOD

40-TOOTH FINISHING

INSTALL A RIP GUIDE on the circular saw to rip strips of uniform width from a wide piece of stock.

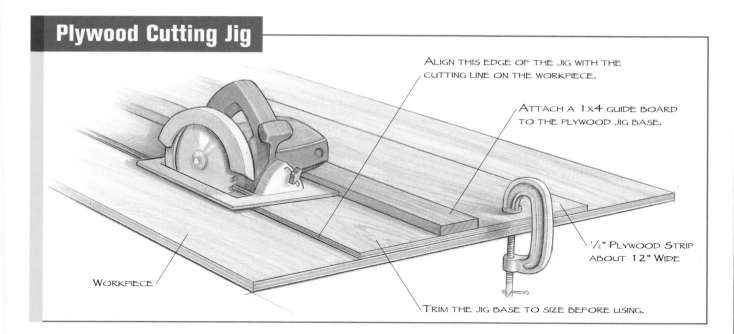

Plywood Cutting Jig

ALIGN THIS EDGE OF THE JIG WITH THE CUTTING LINE ON THE WORKPIECE.

ATTACH A 1x4 GUIDE BOARD TO THE PLYWOOD JIG BASE.

1/2" PLYWOOD STRIP ABOUT 12" WIDE

WORKPIECE

TRIM THE JIG BASE TO SIZE BEFORE USING.

have expensive panel stock to cut, consider a dedicated plywood blade with around 140 teeth. These are available in plain steel, so the expense is comparable to an all-purpose carbide blade.

Whenever you pick up a circular saw, be sure that you are prepared to give it your full attention. These are powerful tools, and careless or inattentive use can result in wasted materials or, worse, an injured operator. Begin by making sure that your work is properly supported. Place adequate support blocks under the piece being cut, so that the weight of the wood does not cause the blade to bind. Check periodically to see that the blade guard operates properly—un

plug the saw and clean any built-up sawdust from around the guard so that it does not stick. Set the depth of cut to be about ⅛ to ⅜ inch more than the thickness of your stock. Glance at the power cord to the saw, and make sure that it is not tangled, liable to catch on an obstruction, or lying in the path of the blade. Pull the saw trigger and let the blade come up to speed before starting your cut; then push it slowly and steadily, in a straight line, through the cut.

Saw Guides. It takes some practice to make an acceptable freehand cut with a circular saw, but, fortunately, you don't have to wait that long to begin work. For rip cuts, all circular saws are designed to accept an accessory rip guide.

TO USE A SAW GUIDE first measure the distance from the blade to the edge of the saw shoe.

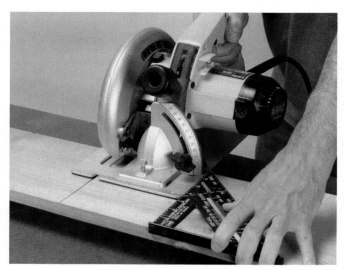

A SPEED SQUARE is a handy guide for making crosscuts using a circular saw.

Some models come with a guide and for others you need to purchase it separately. To use the guide, simply set the desired width of cut—measuring from the guide to the outside edge of the blade—then run it along the edge of the stock while cutting.

For short crosscutting jobs, you can use a square as a saw guide. First, mark your desired cut-line across the workpiece. Measure the distance between the edge of the saw blade and the outside of the saw shoe, or foot. Place another mark that same distance away from your cut-line and align a square with that mark. Hold the outside edge of the saw shoe against the square while you make the cut. The same principle can be used for cutting panel stock. Instead of a square, simply clamp a long straightedge across the panel and use it as a guide for the saw. (See "Plywood Cutting Jig," page 51.)

Miter Saws. Most processes in trimwork involve making joints in wood. Sometimes a joint could be as simple as butting two pieces of wood together, end to end or end to edge. At times, a joint will involve an angled cut. Miter cuts entail cutting an angle across the face of a board or piece of molding. Bevel cuts are angle cuts that run through the thickness of a piece of stock. Some joints require a cut that includes both a miter and bevel angle—these are commonly called compound miters.

Power Miter Saw Setup

Difficulty Level: **Easy**

TOOLS
Power miter saw • secure saw mount to bench • adjustable sliding bevel

MATERIALS
1-by stock

RELEASE THE LOCKING BUTTON in order to free the saw arm. On most saws the button is spring loaded.

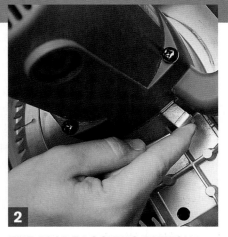

THE BLADE LOCKING BUTTON is located near the blade guard. It locks the blade in place so that you can change or tighten it.

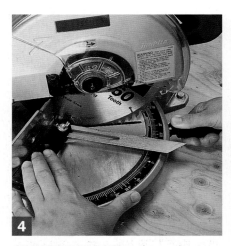

ADJUST THE SAW to the angle at which you want to cut. Release the handle to swing the saw left or right along the miter scale.

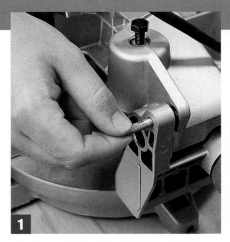

SET THE DEGREE SETTING using the handle on the scale. On most saws, the handle simply screws into position.

THE LOCKOUT BUTTON is a safety measure found on saws. You must depress the button before you can squeeze the trigger.

In general, the angle that you cut on each half of a joint is equal to one-half of the total angle of the joint. For instance, for two pieces that will be joined at 90 degrees, each part needs to be cut at a 45-degree angle. Regardless of the specifics of the joint, in most cases the best tool for the job is a miter saw. Whether you use a simple hand miter saw or a sliding compound saw, the basic principles remain the same. Adjust the saw to the desired angle of cut; hold the piece of molding against the saw fence; and align the cutline with the edge of the saw blade. Then slowly make your cut, keeping the molding steady so that the blade can move cleanly through the material.

Power Miter Saws. If your plans include a good-sized trim job, the investment in a power miter saw is well worth considering. These saws provide the ability to make quick and accurate cuts, as well as the ability to trim existing cuts for small adjustments—something that a hand miter saw cannot do. Miter saws generally have preset detents at common cutting angles: 15, 22.5, 30, 45, and 90 degrees.

Bevel and miter cuts can be described as either open or closed. If you look at the finished surface of a piece of molding, an open cut would expose the interior thickness of the material. Conversely, a closed cut would hide the interior thickness of the stock.

TO CHANGE BLADES, mount a new blade on the arbor; then tighten it with the wrench that came with the saw.

Using a Hand Miter Box

Difficulty Level: **Easy**

TOOLS
Hand miter box • secure saw mount to bench

MATERIALS
1-by stock

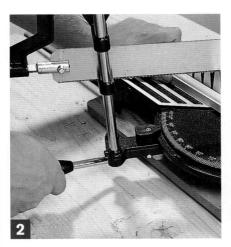

SECURE THE STOCK before cutting. Many hand miter boxes have a built-in clamp for holding thin stock in place.

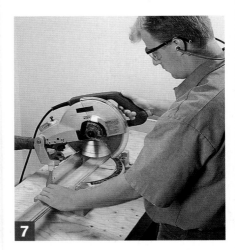

ADD POWER through a properly grounded electrical receptacle, and go to work. Wear safety glasses or goggles when using a power saw.

MOVE THE SAW into the correct position by using the handle on the front of the miter scale. Move it left or right of the 0-deg. central setting.

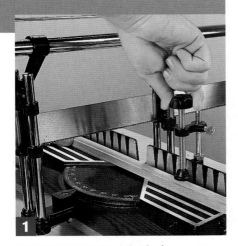

ON MOST SAWS, such as this thin, fine-toothed blade built into this saw, the blade travels back and forth on a pair of guides.

Plate Joinery

The plate joiner is a versatile tool that is extremely valuable for trim applications. You can adjust the blade to cut various sized slots in the mating surfaces of two pieces of stock. Then you apply a small bit of glue to each slot and the compressed, football-shaped joining plate. Slide the plate into one half of the joint, and assemble the parts.

Plate joints can be useful in a number of situations, including joining wide pieces of casing and wainscoting frame stock. All plate joiners have adjustable fences that can be moved to locate the slot at the desired height in the stock. You also have the option of using the flat bottom surface of the machine as a registration surface. Hold both the stock and the joiner tight to a flat tabletop while you cut.

Using a Plate Joiner

Difficulty Level: **Easy**

TOOLS
Plate joiner • clamps • smooth, flat work surface • masking tape • pencil

MATERIALS
Joining plates • 1-by stock • wood glue • glue brush

1

PLACE A MARK to indicate the center of the joining plate slot on the surface of the board. If you want to avoid marking up your stock, use a piece of masking tape. Clamp the board to the worktable and use both hands to control the plate joiner when cutting.

2

FOR SLOTS IN THE EDGE of a board, lay out the center point of each slot; then clamp the board to the table. A flat work surface can function as a reliable registration surface for cutting the slots if both workpiece and plate joiner are held firmly to the surface.

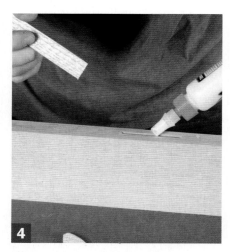

4

USE A THIN WOODEN SHIM to spread a small amount of glue on the inside of each joining plate slot. The moisture in the glue will cause the plate to swell, further strengthening the joint.

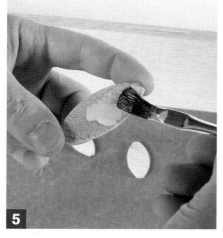

5

SPREAD GLUE on both sides of each joining plate before inserting it into its slot. A small disposable brush is the perfect tool for this job.

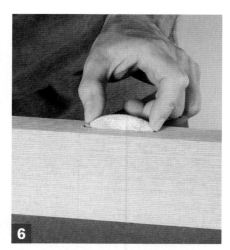

6

INSERT THE JOINING PLATE into its slot. The slots are intentionally sized a bit longer than the plates to allow for a small amount of lateral adjustment.

Scarf Joints

Molding is usually available in lengths up to 14 or 16 feet, depending on your supplier and species of lumber. In larger rooms, or if your stock is of short length, you may need to splice together two or more pieces to cover a long wall. If you were to simply butt the square ends together, even the smallest bit of shrinkage would result in a visible gap between the parts, so the solution is to join the pieces with a scarf joint. In a scarf joint, the two parts are cut at an angle of 45 degrees, with one of the parts overlapping the other. The joint is typically glued and nailed together, forming an almost invisible joint. If there is any shrinkage over time, instead of an open gap, only more wood is exposed.

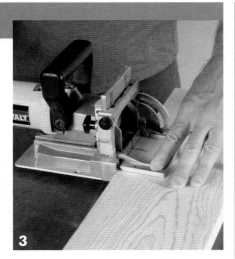

3

ALL PLATE JOINERS have registration fences that you can use to locate the vertical position of a slot in the edge or end of a board. Flip the fence into position, and hold it firmly on the surface of the board while making the cut.

Making Scarf Joints

Difficulty Level: **Easy**

TOOLS
Power miter saw or hand miter box • power drill and bits • hammer and nail set • sanding block

MATERIALS
Baseboard molding • finishing nails

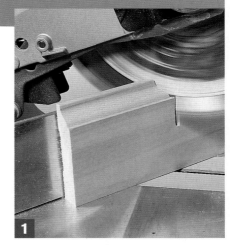

1

PLAN THE CUT by locating the scarf joint over a wall stud. Using a miter saw, cut matching 45-deg. cuts on each piece that will form the scarf joint.

7

ASSEMBLE THE JOINT; adjust the position; and pull the joint tight. Clamp the joint for at least one hour to allow the glue to develop a strong initial bond. Do not stress the joint for at least 12 hours.

4

ATTACH THE MOLDING on the wall, overlapping the miter cuts. Strengthen the joint by first applying carpenter's glue to both sides of the joint. Drive finishing nails through the joint. Sink the nail heads below the wood's surface.

5

FILL THE NAILHOLES with wood filler. Sand the area smooth and finish as desired. To further disguise a scarf joint in baseboard, add a shoe molding or a base cap. Offset scarf joints in built-up assemblies.

Coping Chair Rail Molding

Difficulty Level: **Challenging**

TOOLS
Clamps • measuring tape
• utility knife • coping saw
• flat and round rasps
• sandpaper

MATERIALS
Chair rail molding

1

MAKE THE MITER CUT, and measure the molding. Leave an extra inch or two to make adjustments.

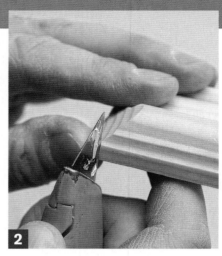

2

USE A UTILITY KNIFE to trim off the feathered edge of the miter cut, which is easily broken.

Coped Joints

When two pieces of square, flat stock meet at an inside corner joint, the parts can simply butt together and the joint will stay tight. But, when you need to make an inside corner joint with profiled stock, the situation is very different. In these cases, whether baseboard, chair rail, or cornice molding, the pieces should be joined in a coped joint. In a coped joint, the profile of one piece of molding is trimmed to fit over the matching profile of a second section of molding when the two meet in an inside corner. Baseboards, chair rails, and cornice molding can all benefit from coped joints.

The reasons for using a coped joint instead of an inside miter joint are twofold. First, not all corners are square, and a coped joint is forgiving of variations in angle. Second, even if an inside miter joint appeared tight at first fitting, the process of nailing it in place would tend to drive the joint apart, leaving you no way to remedy the situation except to fill the joint with caulk.

Cutting Coped Joints. To make a coped joint, install the first piece of molding square into the corner, and nail it in place. Cut a piece of stock to rough length (about 2 inches longer than finished dimension) for the next piece of molding. Use a miter saw to cut an open 45-degree bevel cut on the end that will receive the coped joint. An open bevel has its long point on the back surface of the stock, and it exposes the profile of the molded surface.

Use a coping saw to cut along the exposed profile, keeping the saw blade angled to provide a back-cut or clearance angle that is slightly greater than 90 degrees. The back-cut will allow you to easily adjust the coped profile without re-

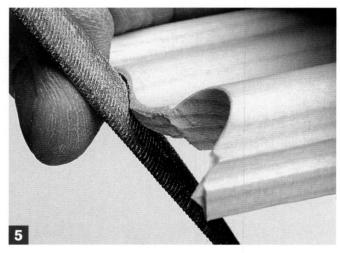

5

AFTER THE INITIAL CUTS it is time to make the final passes with a file or rasp. A tapered half-round rasp works well to clean up the edges of rounded areas.

moving too much stock and ensures a tighter joint. For wide or thick molding, many pros use a combination of jig saw for straight cuts and coping saw for tightly curved cuts. (In many cases, it simply takes practice to trim the waste with a jig saw.) Feel free to switch back and forth between these tools to create the most efficient work flow.

Cutting Technique. When cutting a coped joint, it is a good practice to keep the saw blade about $\frac{1}{16}$ inch to the waste side of the profile line. Many people find it easier to stay to the waste side of the profile line by outlining the profile with a pencil to help it stand out. Once you made the necessary cuts with the saw, it is then a simple matter to use

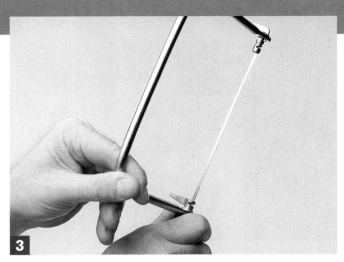

TURN THE BLADE of the coping saw so that the teeth are facing at a right angle to the bow of the saw.

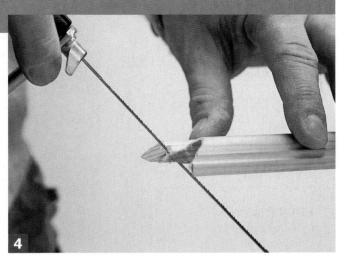

BACK-CUT THE MOLDING along the edge line of the miter. It is best to keep the blade of the saw about ¹⁄₁₆ in. to the waste side of the cut line.

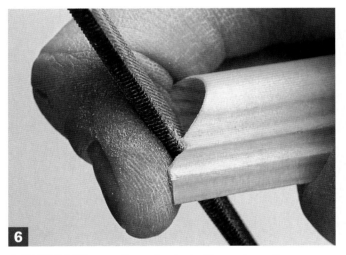

A FLAT RASP as well as a laminate file works well on square edges where the molding will fit into place against the adjoining section of molding.

TEST YOUR WORK by placing the coped edge against the molding it will adjoin. In most cases, the piece with the straight-cut edge will already be in place.

a rasp or file to refine the cut to the line. Use a tapered half-round rasp to work the edges of rounded surfaces. Use a flat rasp on square edges.

This technique can be a true time saving measure, as it is easy to slip with the coping saw on an intricate profile and ruin a joint—something you are less likely to do when finishing the cuts with a rasp.

Test your work. When you're satisfied that the joint is snug, cut the other end of the molding to length. Expect your first few attempts at coping to be a bit frustrating, but with practice, the process becomes easier and should not take more than a few minutes per joint.

Trim Tip   HELPFUL TOOLS

A good coping saw may be your best friend when cutting coped joints, but don't forget the more common tools that can help you achieve success. A dark pencil to outline the profile can help keep your cuts on track, and a good set of files and rasps will go a long way for making the final adjustments to the cuts. And, of course, it is best to be prepared to attempt to make the joint fit snugly more than one time.

Making Mitered Returns

Difficulty Level: Moderate

TOOLS
Hammer • nail set • measuring tape • pencil • power miter saw or hand miter box • power drill and bits • small glue brush

MATERIALS
Chair rail molding • wood glue • finishing nails

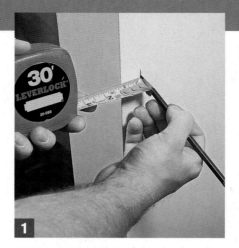

1

MARK THE EDGE of the dead-end piece about 1 in. back from the edge of the wall. In most cases, this is all the space you will need to expose the mitered return.

2

CUT THE MOLDING to length, allowing for a 45-deg. miter cut that will face the wall. If both ends of the molding will have a mitered return, plan accordingly.

3

INSTALL THE MOLDING to a guide line for chair rails such as this. Attach the section by drilling pilot holes and using finishing nails to avoid splits. Sink nailheads with a nail set.

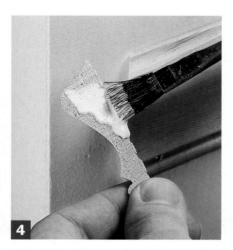

4

CUT THE RETURN from a piece of molding large enough to hold safely and securely against the saw fence. Apply glue to both surfaces.

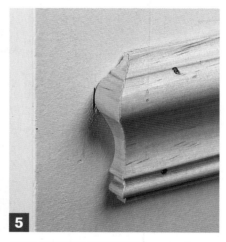

5

ATTACH THE RETURN by pressing into place. You can set a small finishing nail in the return, or simply clamp the return piece until the glue sets.

Mitered Returns

As you move through the different tasks in trimming a room, you will usually encounter a situation where the end of a piece of molding will be exposed. This is a common condition at the ends of window stools, casing caps, aprons, or chair rail, but it also occurs with baseboard and cornice molding. Of course, the simplest solution would be to cut a square end on the stock, sand it smooth, and paint it. But this treatment has an unfinished look and indicates a lack of care in the job. Another approach would be to cut an open 45- or 30-degree angle on the end of the molding. This is an accepted detail on shoe molding, when it must end at door openings, but otherwise, it too looks incomplete. The preferred method is to fashion a mitered return on the end of the molding, creating a finished and intentional transition between the molding and the wall surface.

To create a mitered return, you will need to cut a small section of the molding profile and to attach it to the end of the molding run. This will give the appearance of the shape of the molding wrapping around the edge of the molding.

MAKING A SIMPLE CUTOFF JIG

Every tool has its limitations. And even though a sliding compound miter saw can do many things, cutting a short piece of stock for a mitered return is not one of its best uses. In designing for flexibility, the fence on this type of saw is necessarily open around the cut, and does not provide good support for short cutoffs. A simple alternative for this particular job is to build a simple crosscutting jig that you can use with a back saw. Screw two pieces of scrap 1x4 stock to the edges of a piece of 1x6. The entire assembly needs to be only about 18 inches long. Use a reliable square to mark across the top edges of the 1x4, and carry the guide marks down the outside faces. Use a backsaw to carefully cut down along your marks, stopping when the blade rests against the top of the 1x6.

To use the jig, simply place your molding in the box, resting against the back inside edge. Align your desired cut line with the kerf in the jig and slide the saw back and forth in the kerf to make the cut. You can use the jig for both large and small moldings—anything up to 5½ inches wide.

Difficulty Level: **Easy**

TOOLS
Power drill with screwdriver bit • combination square • pencil • backsaw

MATERIALS
1-by stock • utility screws

DRILL AND COUNTERSINK pilot holes; then screw a piece of 1x4 stock to either edge of a length of 1x6.

USE A SQUARE to mark cut lines across the top edges of the 1x4's and down the outside faces.

USE A BACK SAW to carefully cut down along your layout marks until the saw teeth just graze the top of the 1x6.

TO TRIM THE MOLDING, align the cut mark on your molding with the kerf on the jig.

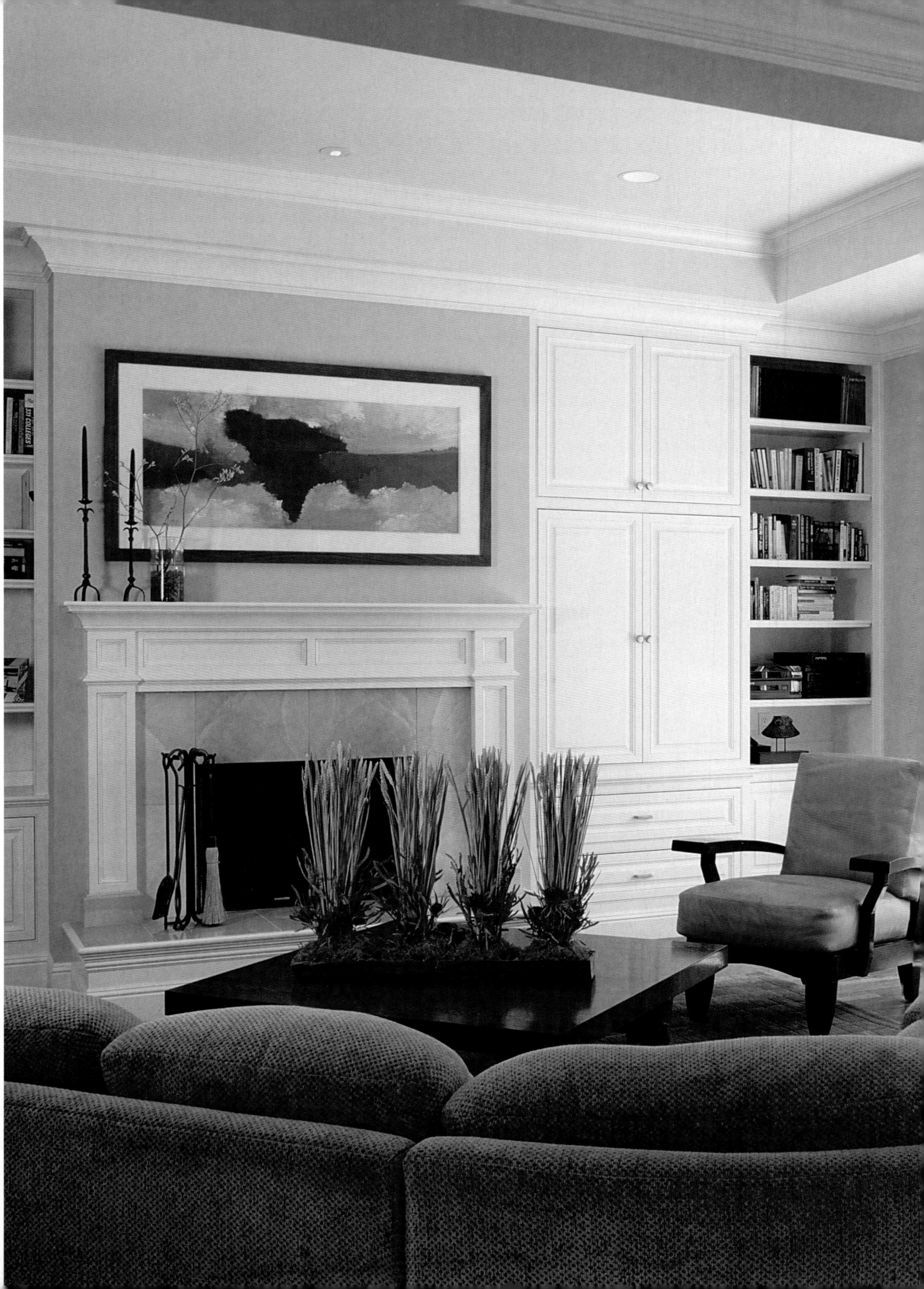
331 COLLEGES

TRIMWORK MATERIALS

The choice of materials for any trim project will depend on a number of factors. Of course, budget is always a concern, for no matter how extravagant your project, cost is an issue in determining how a job will be approached. But hand-in-hand with financial considerations go those of design and appearance because, after all, that is what trim is all about. Fortunately, the library of stock molding profiles is quite substantial, and the choices are great. If you cannot find a particular profile at your local home center, there are specialty millwork suppliers that usually offer a large selection of moldings.

Deciding on a molding profile is only part of the process. Your choice of lumber species and finish are equal partners, and they affect one another in noticeable and subtle ways. Balancing material and finish choices can be complicated, but the combination provides you with the ability to customize even the simplest trim application.

Lumber for Trimwork

If you stroll down the lumber aisles at the local home center, you will see racks of interior moldings and boards in pine, red oak, and poplar. These species are the most common choices for interior millwork, and most stock molding profiles are available in these woods. *Millwork* is the term used to describe lumber that has been machined into particular profiles. This can include flat stock for door jambs, as well as intricate molding.

Pine

Pine has long been the default choice for interior millwork for a number of reasons. Because pine trees grow faster than many other species, manufacturers have a source of lumber that can be renewed, keeping the cost of materials more manageable. Door and window manufacturers have used pine because of its high resin content, which makes it more resistant to rot than some other species. Builders like pine because it is relatively lightweight, it is easy to install, and it takes a nice finish.

Lumber Grades. Most interior trim jobs use a combination of molded stock and flat lumber. When you shop for pine lumber, you will find that it is available in either *clear* or *common* grades. While the details of lumber grading can get somewhat technical, a functional approach is simple. Clear, or select, grades have relatively few defects such as knots or pitch pockets, while common-grade lumber can include more of these defects. The difference in price in these material grades can be substantial, but for most trim work you should choose clear, or select, stock. The reasons for using clear grades have more to do with just the appearance of the job. The additional labor involved in cutting around defects, and the inevitable waste, makes the efficient use of lesser grades questionable, even for a painted finish. And knots that are left in

FINGER JOINT

SELECT PINE   COMMON-GRADE PINE

CLEAR, OR SELECT, PINE, left, has few defects; common-grade pine, right, contains more knots and pitch pockets.

place will usually become visible after a time, even through a first-quality paint job.

Molding Types. When it comes to choosing molding, the choices are slightly different. It is difficult, if not impossible, to find molding profiles cut from common-grade lumber. Clear-grade lumber is used for most profiles because knots and sap pockets would create inevitable holes in the molding and can dull expensive cutters. Clear-grade material is suitable for both stain-grade and painted finishes.

Finger-Jointed Molding. If you are looking to save some money, and your job is definitely to be painted, you can consider *finger-jointed* molding. This term describes molding stock that has been built up of short lengths of lumber. The ends of each short piece are machined in an interlocking finger profile and glued together. The built-up lumber is then run through a molder, just like clear stock, and the profile is cut.

The use of short pieces of lumber saves money. In this process, no effort is made to match the color or grain of the lumber, but knots and other defects are excluded. As a result, you can use this stock for paint-grade work and save quite a bit on the cost of material; however, finger-jointed stock is usually only offered in the most common molding profiles. Many suppliers now apply a primer coat to their finger-jointed stock, so you can save both money and labor by using this material.

MATERIAL AND FINISH go hand-in-hand when designing a trim package. In the room opposite, white-painted wainscoting complements the wall color.

STOCK MOLDING PROFILES

Most lumberyards and home centers provide a display with a sample of available molding profiles. Each retailer has a selection of moldings that they carry as stock items, and while most are similar, you may find more profiles at one dealer over another. Moldings that are manufactured by one of the large millwork suppliers will be identical from one source to another, but those that are turned out by a local millwork house might not exactly match those of another manufacturer. In other words, a colonial casing from your local home center may not match the one from Johnny's Lumber Barn, despite having the same descriptive name. Because of this possible discrepancy, it is best to purchase all of each molding profile from one supplier.

3 ½" CLEAR PINE COLONIAL CASING

2 ½" CLEAR PINE COLONIAL CASING

2 ¼" FINGER-JOINTED, PRIMED CLAMSHELL CASING

TYPICAL MOLDING PROFILES available from most home centers include the casings shown above.

Trim Tip IF YOU DON'T SEE IT, ASK

If you do not see a molding profile on display that fits your needs, it is still possible that your retailer can obtain what you want. Most dealers have access to a more extensive selection of profiles than they choose to stock, so it's worth asking if they have a catalog of available moldings. Of course, expect to pay a premium for special orders, but in most cases, it will be less expensive than commissioning a custom molding.

Poplar

Although pine is the primary softwood that is used for interior trim, poplar is a hardwood species that shares many of the qualities of pine, and it can be used in similar situations. Poplar is soft enough so that you can nail it without drilling pilot holes, and its closed-grain structure finishes well. The natural appearance of poplar can range from a warm cream color to a quite distinct green or purple, and it has a rather bland grain pattern, so it is most often painted. But if the material is carefully selected, you could use it with a stained finish. Poplar is frequently used by millwork houses for their custom paint-grade molding. It is a fast-growing species, and it is one of the least expensive hardwoods.

Red Oak

When home builders decide to provide an upgraded trim package, red oak is often their first choice of materials. Its open-grain structure can create bold contrast, especially when the wood is stained. But red oak also has a pleasant reddish-brown natural color, leaving open the option of treating it with a clear finish and no stain. Depending on the way the lumber is cut from the log, it can display a grain that is linear, with long parallel grain lines, or graphic, with peaked cathedral shapes that run the length of a board.

Because it is used extensively for interior trim, many of the stock profiles that are available in pine are also available in red oak.

THE BACK SIDE OF MOLDING

When you examine most commercial molding, especially those pieces wider than 2 inches, you will notice that the back side has been slightly hollowed out. This relief cut serves two purposes. First, by reducing the thickness, it helps to lessen the tendency of the stock to cup. And, second, it allows the molding to bridge any irregularities in the wall surface and stay tight at the outside edges—where it counts.

WIDE MOLDINGS often have relief cuts on the back. The hollowed-out sections help reduce cupping.

RELIEF CUTS

HARDWOOD VERSUS SOFTWOOD

In a home center, poplar and other hardwood boards are often sold according to the same system that is used for softwood lumber. In this convention, boards are given a nominal size description, 1x2, 1x4, etc., that corresponds to the size of the board that is rough-sawn at the mill before it is planed smooth. The actual size board that you purchase is always less than the nominal size. For instance, the 1x2 and 1x4 boards are actually ¾ x 1½ inches and ¾ x 3½ inches. These boards are sold in even foot lengths from 6 to 16 feet.

If you shop for material at a hardwood lumberyard, however, you will find another classification system. Hardwood lumber is also classified according to the thickness of the material before it is planed smooth, but the descriptive categories are different. Trees are sawn at the mill into boards of varying thickness measured in quarters of an inch. For example, a board that is 1 inch thick would be called 4/4 stock and one 2 inches thick would be 8/4 stock. These rough-sawn boards are then dried and sold to a wholesaler or end user who planes them to a finished thickness. In addition, hardwood lum-

ber is normally sold in boards of random width and length. So specifying the amount of material needed for a particular job requires a bit more effort and results in a greater amount of waste.

ROUGH-CUT RED OAK

S4S 1x6 PINE

HARDWOOD AND SOFTWOOD have different classification systems that denote stock size.

PAINTED FINISHES, opposite, are usually applied to molding made from softwood.

STAINS AND CLEAR FINISHES, right, are usually reserved for hardwoods.

HARDWOOD LUMBER THICKNESS CHART

SIZE NAME	ROUGH THICKNESS	PLANED THICKNESS
4/4	1"	13/16"
5/4	1¼"	1 1/16"
6/4	1½"	1 5/16"
8/4	2"	1¾"
10/4	2½"	2 5/16"
12/4	3"	2¾"

Selecting Wood Moldings

Keep in mind that although each molding profile usually has a particular use associated with it, you are not bound to use it in any specific way. For example, it is not unusual to find a baseboard profile used as a frieze board in a cornice. Or a panel molding can be added to a casing or chair rail to help create a distinctive look.

In addition, you can cut a stock molding apart and use just part of the profile, either alone or in combination with other pieces. This technique may require additional modification, such as planing the back flat, but it provides another tool for expanding your design options.

Built-Up Designs. Another option is to create designs using two, three, or even four common profiles in one assembly. Some examples are shown on the opposite page, but you can easily create your own designs with a little experimentation. By varying the use of moldings and combining them in layered assemblies, you can achieve a wide variety of effects that create extravagant architectural details or may go well beyond the obvious applications.

Custom Profiles. If you find that you cannot achieve the look you desire with stock molding, even by combining profiles, you can turn to a custom molding supplier. Most areas of the country have custom millwork shops that offer

Common Molding Profiles

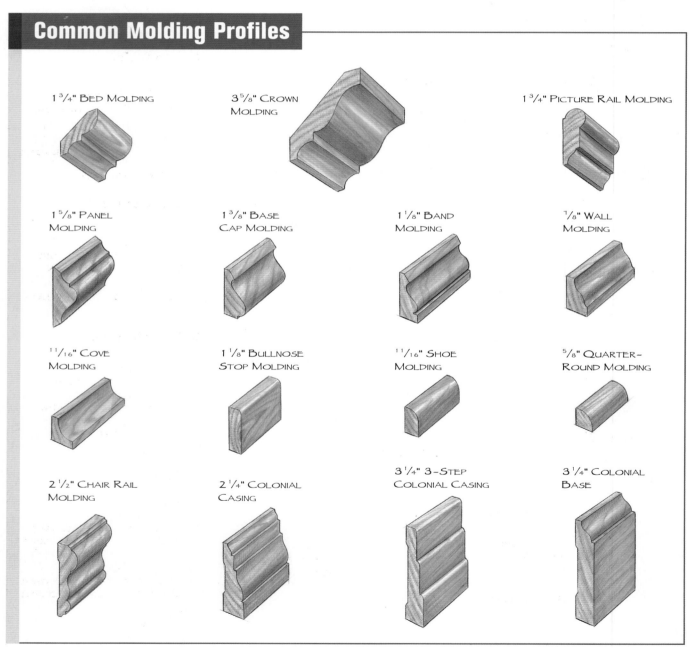

1 3/4" BED MOLDING

3 5/8" CROWN MOLDING

1 3/4" PICTURE RAIL MOLDING

1 5/8" PANEL MOLDING

1 3/8" BASE CAP MOLDING

1 1/8" BAND MOLDING

7/8" WALL MOLDING

11/16" COVE MOLDING

1 1/8" BULLNOSE STOP MOLDING

11/16" SHOE MOLDING

5/8" QUARTER-ROUND MOLDING

2 1/2" CHAIR RAIL MOLDING

2 1/4" COLONIAL CASING

3 1/4" 3-STEP COLONIAL CASING

3 1/4" COLONIAL BASE

a wide selection of profiles, as well as the capability to match an existing molding or a drawing that you provide. And if you can't find a local supplier, there are plenty of shops that will ship anywhere in the country. Most have Web sites, so you can see molding samples and profile drawings to help you select your profiles.

As you might expect, having custom moldings made can be expensive—especially if a new cutter must be ground for the job. The cost for these services is based on a combination of material and labor costs to install the knives and run the molder—knife grinding is additional and is based on the size of the knife and depth of profile. Most of these shops have an extensive collection of molding cutters from past jobs that they can use. You would be well advised to examine their list of available profiles, to see if one can fit your job, before spending the additional dollars to have a new knife ground.

Once you enter the realm of custom molding, you open the door to a large world of material choices. Of course, for paint-grade work, poplar would be the first choice. But if you are attracted to a natural finish, you can consider any of the native or imported hardwoods that are becoming more popular due to their own distinct character, color, and grain. (See pages 68–69 for sample custom profiles.)

Built-Up Molding Profiles

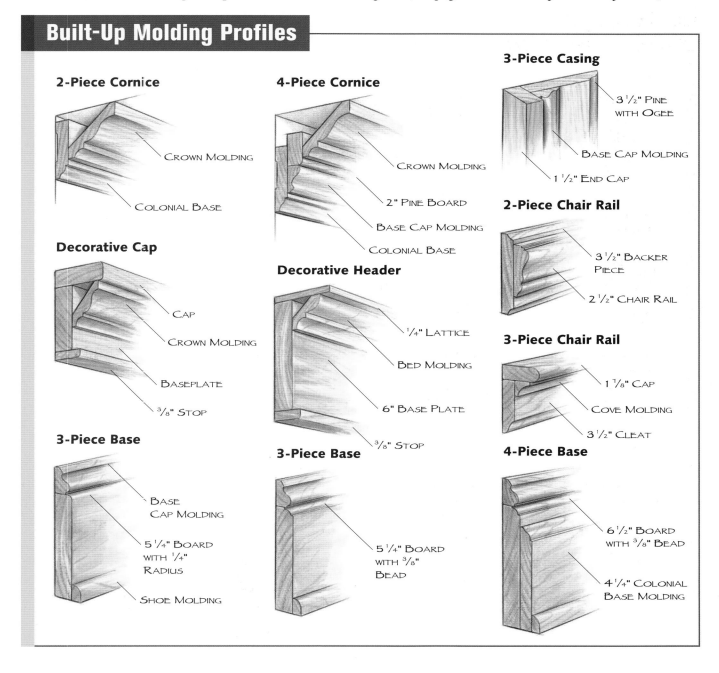

2-Piece Cornice
- Crown Molding
- Colonial Base

Decorative Cap
- Cap
- Crown Molding
- Baseplate
- 3/8" Stop

3-Piece Base
- Base Cap Molding
- 5 1/4" Board with 1/4" Radius
- Shoe Molding

4-Piece Cornice
- Crown Molding
- 2" Pine Board
- Base Cap Molding
- Colonial Base

Decorative Header
- 1/4" Lattice
- Bed Molding
- 6" Base Plate
- 3/8" Stop

3-Piece Base
- 5 1/4" Board with 3/8" Bead

3-Piece Casing
- 3 1/2" Pine with Ogee
- Base Cap Molding
- 1 1/2" End Cap

2-Piece Chair Rail
- 3 1/2" Backer Piece
- 2 1/2" Chair Rail

3-Piece Chair Rail
- 1 1/8" Cap
- Cove Molding
- 3 1/2" Cleat

4-Piece Base
- 6 1/2" Board with 3/8" Bead
- 4 1/4" Colonial Base Molding

3

TRIMWORK MATERIALS

Custom Molding Profiles

Cornice

$^{11}/_{16}$" × 3 $^{1}/_{4}$"

$^{13}/_{16}$" × 3 $^{1}/_{2}$"

$^{15}/_{16}$" × 3 $^{7}/_{8}$"

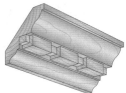
$^{3}/_{4}$" × 3 $^{7}/_{16}$"

$^{13}/_{16}$" × 3 $^{11}/_{32}$"

1" × 3 $^{7}/_{8}$"

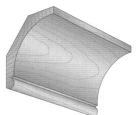
1 $^{1}/_{16}$" × 4 $^{1}/_{2}$"

$^{9}/_{16}$" × 3 $^{15}/_{32}$"

$^{13}/_{16}$" × 3 $^{1}/_{2}$"

$^{3}/_{4}$" × 3 $^{1}/_{2}$"

$^{13}/_{16}$" × 3 $^{1}/_{4}$"

$^{3}/_{4}$" × 3 $^{1}/_{8}$"

Chair Rail

$^{13}/_{16}$" × 2 $^{1}/_{4}$"

$^{11}/_{16}$" × 2 $^{1}/_{2}$"

1 $^{1}/_{2}$" × 2 "

$^{3}/_{4}$" × 2 $^{1}/_{4}$"

$^{11}/_{16}$" × 2 $^{1}/_{2}$"

$^{11}/_{16}$" × 2 $^{1}/_{2}$"

$^{13}/_{16}$" × 2 $^{5}/_{8}$"

$^{13}/_{16}$" × 2 $^{1}/_{2}$"

$^{11}/_{16}$" × 3 "

$^{3}/_{4}$" × 2 $^{7}/_{8}$"

$^{13}/_{16}$" × 3 $^{3}/_{8}$"

$^{3}/_{4}$" × 2 $^{7}/_{8}$"

Casing

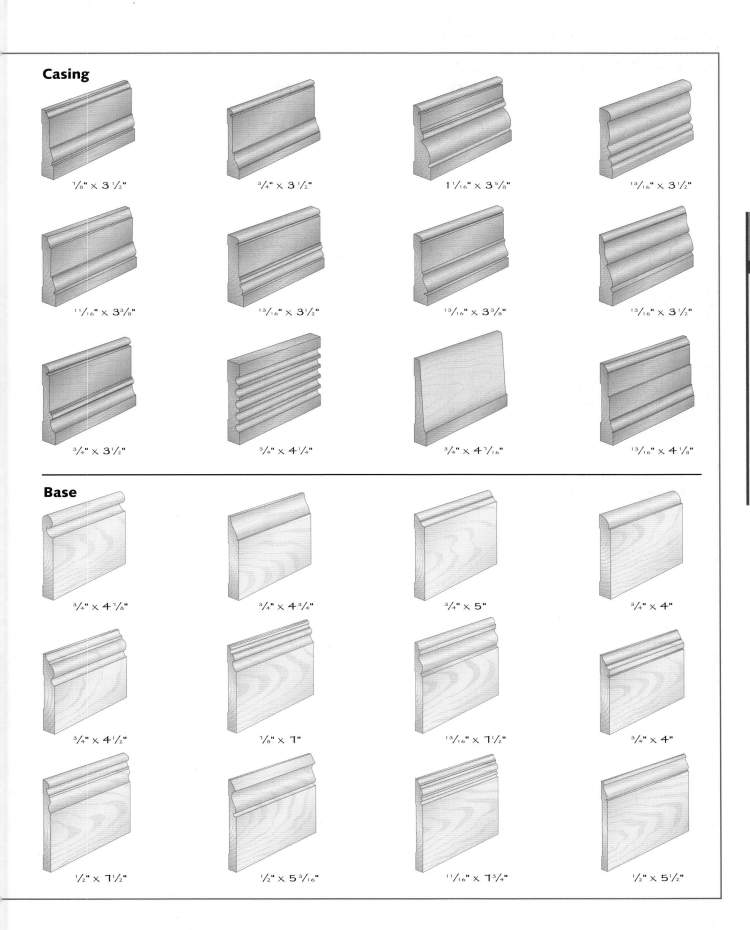

$\frac{7}{8}$" × 3$\frac{1}{2}$"

$\frac{3}{4}$" × 3$\frac{1}{2}$"

1$\frac{1}{16}$" × 3$\frac{5}{8}$"

$\frac{13}{16}$" × 3$\frac{1}{2}$"

$\frac{11}{16}$" × 3$\frac{3}{8}$"

$\frac{13}{16}$" × 3$\frac{1}{2}$"

$\frac{13}{16}$" × 3$\frac{3}{8}$"

$\frac{13}{16}$" × 3$\frac{1}{2}$"

$\frac{3}{4}$" × 3$\frac{1}{2}$"

$\frac{3}{4}$" × 4$\frac{1}{4}$"

$\frac{3}{4}$" × 4$\frac{1}{16}$"

$\frac{13}{16}$" × 4$\frac{1}{8}$"

Base

$\frac{3}{4}$" × 4$\frac{1}{8}$"

$\frac{3}{4}$" × 4$\frac{3}{4}$"

$\frac{3}{4}$" × 5"

$\frac{3}{4}$" × 4"

$\frac{3}{4}$" × 4$\frac{1}{2}$"

$\frac{7}{8}$" × 7"

$\frac{13}{16}$" × 7$\frac{1}{2}$"

$\frac{3}{4}$" × 4"

$\frac{1}{2}$" × 7$\frac{1}{2}$"

$\frac{1}{2}$" × 5$\frac{3}{16}$"

$\frac{11}{16}$" × 7$\frac{3}{4}$"

$\frac{1}{2}$" × 5$\frac{1}{2}$"

Matching Lumber. If you select a custom hardwood molding, you may need some matching lumber as well. In most cases, your local home center won't be much help in this regard. Sometimes a custom millwork house will supply lumber in a matching species, but some are not equipped to provide sales of plain lumber. The alternative source is a dedicated hardwood supplier. These dealers are often a bit more difficult to locate, since most of their customers are cabinet and furniture shops, but many are willing to sell to retail clients. And if you only need a small amount of lumber, you can always approach local woodworkers—more often than not they are happy to help out

an enthusiastic do-it-yourselfer. When all else fails, there are many lumber dealers who will ship material anywhere in the country. Just remember to factor in the cost of shipping when you put together your budget.

FINDING MATCHING LUMBER, below, is required on some trim projects.

PAINTED FINISHES, opposite, work well on both softwood and hardwood.

OPEN- AND CLOSED-GRAIN HARDWOODS

In broad terms, hardwoods are divided into those with an open grain and those with a closed-grain structure. Woods with open grain include ash, red and white oak, walnut, butternut, elm, and mahogany. Some of these species feature a distinct difference in the density of the early and late seasonal growth that makes up each annual ring. As a result, when the wood is sliced, it displays a characteristic coarse appearance with alternating dense and porous grain. When these woods are stained, the open grain readily absorbs the color, while the dense areas are more resistant. This can create a striking effect, but for some situations it may appear too busy. Other open-grained woods have a more uniform grain, but one which is nonetheless porous, causing uneven absorption of the finish. When preparing an open-grained wood for a smooth finish, you should apply paste grain filler to fill the more porous areas of the wood surface.

OPEN-GRAIN WOOD absorbs stains more readily than closed grain. Red oak is open grain; poplar is closed grain.

This technique prevents the finish material from being absorbed into the grain, which would otherwise leave a textured coating on the surface.

Closed-grain woods include birch, cherry, hard and soft maple, poplar, gum, and sycamore. These are woods of more uniform density and, except for figured varieties, generally present a quieter and more reserved appearance than the open-grained woods.

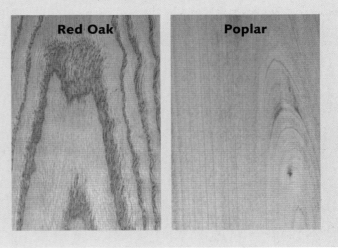

Red Oak | Poplar

Characteristics of Lumber

Whether you are dealing with molding or flat lumber, wood is a dynamic material. Although it is solid and hard, it is not a static substance, and it responds to fluctuations in temperature and humidity by expanding, contracting, cupping, and warping. The degree to which any piece of wood reacts to changing conditions is dependent on a number of factors, and the study of this subject has filled many volumes. But for the purpose of trim installation, some basic knowledge can be useful.

QUARTER-SAWN WHITE OAK

FLAT-SAWN WHITE MAPLE

NOTE THE GRAIN PATTERN of the samples of quarter-sawn and flat-sawn lumber shown above.

Quarter-Sawn Lumber. When boards are cut from a log, the orientation of the grain in the boards is determined by the way that the growth rings intersect the board surface. At one extreme is a *quarter-sawn* board in which the rings are perpendicular to the surface; this is also called vertical grain. To manufacture quarter-sawn lumber, the boards are sawn perpendicular to the exterior of the log. In this process, the yield from the log is reduced and the boards are relatively narrow. The stock displays straight, parallel grain lines on a board surface and, in some species like oak, characteristic rays become visible. These boards resist cupping and warping, and they are less likely to swell and contract than flat-sawn stock. Because there is more waste and also higher labor costs involved in cutting quarter-sawn lumber, it commands a premium price.

Flat-Sawn Lumber. In *flat-sawn* lumber, the boards are cut parallel to one side of a log, and the growth rings intersect the surface at a more acute angle. This technique provides the best yield from a log, but the lumber is less stable than quarter-sawn, and the grain patterns are more variable. In practice, much lumber falls somewhere between true vertical grain and flat-sawn patterns. If you have the luxury of examining a pile of lumber to make your selection, you can often select boards with similar grain for a particular project.

COMPLEMENTARY TRIM is used to highlight the newel posts at left.

Trim Tip   BACK PRIMING

Wood expands and contracts as moisture is absorbed or lost from its cell structure. And when you use any wood in a project, anything you can do to minimize that movement will result in a better result—less splitting of the stock and tighter joints. One simple technique you can use is to make sure that all surfaces of your trim are sealed. For paint-grade work, simply apply a coat of paint or primer to the back side of the stock before installing it. For parts that will receive a stained or clear finish, apply a coat of varnish or polyurethane—stain alone is not a good sealer. This technique is especially important in areas that are subject to high humidity, such as kitchens, bathrooms, and utility rooms.

BACK PRIMED TRIM is destined for high-humidity areas, above.

MOLDING DETAILS enliven simple square columns, below.

Expansion and Contraction. Movement due to expansion or contraction occurs almost exclusively across the grain of a board, and not along its length. For practical purposes, the majority of trim applications will not be greatly affected by this movement, as most details are constructed of narrow pieces where the movement is negligible. However, you will notice that wooden doors and windows tend to swell in the hot and humid summer months and then contract in the winter. Another case where wood movement must be taken into account is when you install a shoe molding around a hardwood floor. In this situation, it is important that you nail the molding to the baseboard instead of the floor boards so that the boards can expand and contract independent of the molding. And if wide, solid wood panels are used in a wainscot application, it is also important to design the installation so that the panels can expand and contract without cracking or showing gaps.

Defects in Lumber

When you shop for lumber, it is important that you pay careful attention to the quality of the stock. As a natural material, wood is subject to a number of defects, and these can present problems in a job where straight edges, flat surfaces, and tight joints are important. Defects in lumber can be due to natural causes that arise during the growth of a tree, or due to the way it is cut, dried, and handled.

For most small trim projects, you will probably be able to select the material you will be using by going through the bin at the home center or the local lumberyard. If you order through a reputable millwork shop, you should receive good-quality stock.

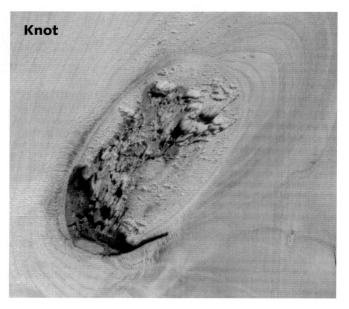

Knot

Knots. *Knots* in a board are an indication of where a branch grew off the trunk of the tree. Small, solid knots are usually not a problem for trimwork, and they are allowable defects in even select stock. Large knots, however, are not features that you generally want to include in your work, so think carefully about the yield you will get after cutting around them. Keep in mind that stock with knots should be primed with a good-quality primer before painting. Unprimed knots will eventually bleed through any paint job.

Bark Inclusions. Sometimes trauma to a tree during its growth cycle can cause *bark inclusions* in the interior portion of the tree. These areas are too soft and unstable to be used as finish lumber and should always be discarded. *Pitch pockets* and *worm holes* are also seen in some lumber species. If these are small and infrequent, you can generally work around them, but if too prevalent, you could end up with a large pile of firewood. Keep in mind that particular defects are more common in some types of lumber than in others. Pitch pockets are quite common in cherry lumber, and walnut boards often show more knots than other species.

Checking and Spalting. *Checking, splitting, honeycombing,* and severe *warping* are symptoms of improper drying. Checks, splits, and honeycombing occur because of different rates of shrinkage between the surface and core of a board.

Warping can occur because of improper stacking of lumber in a kiln or because of naturally occurring stress in the wood.

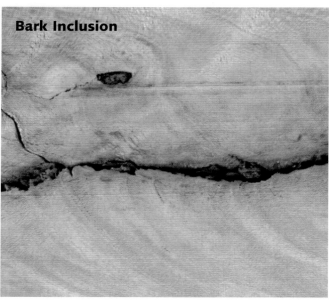

Bark Inclusion

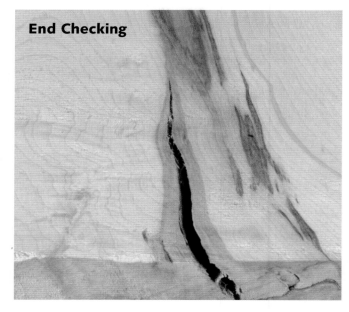

End Checking

Trim Tip | DEALING WITH PLANER AND MOLDER MARKS

When lumber is first cut from a log, it is rough-sawn into boards and then dried. In most cases, before it reaches the retail outlet, it is put through a surface planer which uses a spinning cutterhead to yield an even face and uniform thickness. The same general process applies to molding stock, which is shaped by a series of profile knives. Both processes leave a pretty smooth surface on the wood, but if you look carefully, you will usually be able to see a faint series of parallel knife marks down the length of a board or molding. Sometimes these marks are not visible until you apply the first coat of finish to the wood—and then it's a bit late.

When boards are ripped to width or crosscut to length, either at the lumberyard or in your home shop, the saw blade inevitably leaves a trail of marks on the cut surface. Once again, if you do not smooth these sur-

faces, the marks will be visible once the finish is applied and are the sure sign of shoddy workmanship.

The remedy for these conditions is simple, but labor intensive. Expect to sand all wood surfaces in preparation for finishing, even if they feel smooth to the touch. Also make it a practice to lightly ease all sharp edges with a sanding block so that every surface has a finished look and feel.

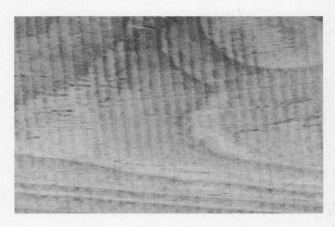

SURFACE PLANERS leave their mark on finished boards. Sanding is the only remedy.

Sometimes, especially in lighter materials like maple and ash, stains will appear cross the wood surface. These can be caused either by a fungus or by the use of wet *stickers*, which are the strips used between adjacent boards as the lumber dries.

Spalting is caused by a fungus that affects maple, causing a dark stain. Spalting is technically a decayed state, and material affected with this condition is not generally used for trim. However, spalted maple is highly valued by bowl turners for its spectacular visual effects.

Interior Checking

Worm Holes and Spalting

Other Trim Materials

Although most people think of wood when the subject of trim arises, these days there are other options. When a job is destined to be painted, you can consider molding made of composite wood materials or even plastics.

Medium Density Fiberboard. *Medium density fiberboard,* or MDF, is a product that is made from ground wood fibers bound with adhesive under pressure. The resulting material is uniformly dense and very stable. Manufacturers can mill the raw material, much like wood, into various profiles, and the resulting moldings have an exceptionally smooth surface. Most of these moldings are primed at the factory, providing an excellent base for a painted finish. The extreme density of MDF makes it quite a bit heavier than a comparable piece of wooden molding; and it must be treated much like hardwood, in that you need to drill pilot holes before nailing. Because it has no grain structure, the edges of cuts tend to be pretty delicate, and the material can chip easily when fitting an intricate joint; use extra care in those situations.

Resin Moldings. *Polyurethane* and *polystyrene* moldings provide another option for paint-grade jobs. These products are especially attractive for ceiling moldings because they are extremely lightweight and install very easily.

Plastic moldings can be cast in a wide variety of shapes, and extremely large and elaborate profiles are easy to achieve. For the installer, you eliminate the need for cutting coped joints at inside corners, as the plastic resin cannot be worked like wood. Instead, these intersections are treated with miter joints and any gaps must be filled with joint compound or caulk.

Some resin moldings are designed for use in curved applications. They are flexible enough so that you can bend them to fit a concave or convex wall surface. There are also manufacturers that will cast these moldings to fit an arched or elliptical opening. For these situations, you would need to specify the dimensions of the opening, or send a template, to have the pieces made. Most of these systems use a combination of adhesives and nails to hold them in place, and they generally come primed to accept either a painted or opaque stain finish.

If you are looking for columns or ornamental pedestals to bring classical style to a room, you might look at some in fiberglass instead of wood. In most cases, a polymer column is less expensive than one of wood, and it typically requires less maintenance—especially if you are considering a damp location such as the kitchen or bath. These products are offered in both stock and custom sizes so that almost any situation can be accommodated.

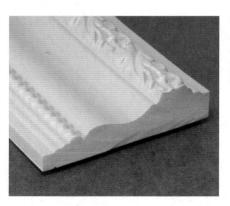

RESIN MOLDING can be installed with nails and glue like traditional wood molding.

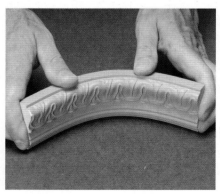

FLEXIBLE RESIN MOLDING can be bent to match most curved walls— either concave or convex surfaces.

RESIN MOLDINGS come in hundreds of profiles and designs. This room contains resin crown, casing, and panels.

MAKING YOUR OWN MOLDING

Commercial molding manufacturers use heavy duty molders and shapers to produce the different profiles they offer. Working at home, you cannot expect to duplicate that capability. However, with a router and small table saw, you can produce a modest selection of moldings to function as elements of window and door trim, chair rail, baseboard, or wainscoting.

For a few small pieces of molding, use a hand-held router to cut the profile. Clamp a board to the worktable to keep the stock secure while routing. You may need to place spacer blocks beneath the board to provide clearance for the ball bearing pilot. Allow the router to get up to full speed before starting the cut. Then advance the tool along the edge to cut the molded shape.

Router Tables. If you need a lot of molding, the easier method is to mount the router in a router table. Commercial router tables are available in a variety of prices and configurations, some for tabletop use and others that are freestanding. Whatever type of table you use, make sure that it is either clamped firmly to a worktable or screwed to the floor to keep it from moving around while you work.

If you examine a catalog of router bits, you might be surprised at the number of different profiling bits that are available. Some of the larger bits are only available with a ½-inch-diameter shank, and require a heavy duty router for safe use, but many are suitable for smaller routers that accept bits with a ¼-inch-diameter shank.

Mount your chosen bit in the router, and install the router in the table. Adjust the height of the tool, and then set the fence to expose the desired profile. Even though many bits have a ball-bearing pilot guide, it is safest to use a fence on the router table—the face of the fence should align exactly with the bearing. Adjust the guard on the table to cover the spinning bit and install finger-board hold-downs to keep the stock pushed tight to the table surface.

For the safest procedure, do not attempt to cut a molding profile on a narrow board. Instead, cut the molding on the edge of a wide board, and then use the table saw to rip the profile off the edge. Then, repeat the procedure for each piece you need. When the board gets too narrow, put it aside for another use.

Difficulty Level: Moderate

TOOLS
Router and bit • clamps • table saw • push stick

MATERIALS
1-by stock

1 **TO MAKE A NARROW MOLDING,** first rout the desired profile on the edge of a wide board. Use a bit with a ball-bearing guide or install an accessory edge guide to determine the position of the bit. Make a test cut on some scrap stock to be sure that adjustments are correct; then cut the profile on the edge of the stock.

2 **USE THE TABLE SAW** to rip the narrow molding from the edge of the wide board. If possible, use a finger-board hold-down jig to exert even pressure on the board and prevent kickbacks. The hold-down jig also eliminates any need to position your fingers near the blade. Always use a push stick as you reach the end of the cut.

3

TRIMWORK MATERIALS

Materials for Wainscoting

Wainscoting is the term used to describe a solid wood or paneled treatment of the lower part of a wall. This treatment can cover a wide range of styles and materials, from simple painted boards to intricately molded hardwood panels. While the installation and design options for your wainscoting will be treated elsewhere, the materials you require are related to those for the rest of your trim projects – and the suppliers are generally the same.

Bead Board. The simplest wainscoting, and one of the most popular, is an application of narrow tongue-and-groove boards with a beaded profile to the lower section of a wall. The material for this treatment is often made of fir lumber and sold either under the name of "bead-board wainscoting" or "beaded porch ceiling boards," after one of the more popular uses for the stock. You can usually find this material in bundled packages at home centers or in random lengths at a traditional lumberyard. Similar profiles are also available in a wide range of hardwood species from specialty suppliers.

BEAD-BOARD
WAINSCOTING

Plywood Panels. To achieve the same general look, but with less labor, some people use plywood panels with a grooved design cut into the surface instead of individual boards. Although there is some sacrifice in detail, these panels have the advantage of eliminating potential gaps at the board seams as boards dry out. As with most plywood panels, these are manufactured in 4 × 8-foot sheets, but some home centers offer smaller, precut panels.

CONSTRUCTION-GRADE VERSUS HARDWOOD PLYWOOD

For interior trim, it is usually best to avoid construction-grade plywood. This material is made from layers of softwood veneers and typically has defects and voids in the core. The veneers used for the core are quite thick and the number of laminations is relatively few, resulting in an inherently unstable panel. Even though it is offered in A and B grades with smooth faces, it is just not made to standards comparable to that of hardwood panels, and can yield a poor surface, even for paint-grade work. Save this material for exterior jobs or utility applications.

Hardwood plywood generally features many thin laminations and a void-free core. Although this material also can exhibit a tendency to warp, especially when cut, the surface quality of the face veneer and ability to hold fasteners is far superior to construction-grade stock.

9-Ply Hardwood Plywood

5-Ply Construction-Grade Plywood

Classic Wainscoting. More-formal wainscot systems involve a combination of wood frames and either solid wood or plywood panels. Frame stock is typically the same type of material that you would purchase for other trim applications, such as pine, poplar, or oak boards. If you want to embellish the panels with molding, and to cap the top of the installation, there are many profiles that can be used to add depth and character.

Flat panels are usually formed from manufactured panel stock. The advantages of this material over solid wood are considerable. First, plywood panels are almost always less expensive than an equivalent amount of solid wood, especially when you factor in labor and waste. Second, manufactured panels are much more stable than solid wood; they usually stay flat and do not expand and contract with seasonal changes in humidity. These materials have a smooth, sanded face that requires minimal preparation for finishing, and if you want a clear finish, the grain of the face veneer is more consistent from panel to panel than solid wood.

WAINSCOTING, opposite, can be created from a number of materials, including solid wood and plywood.

BEAD-BOARD WAINSCOTING, right, fits in with a number of traditional design schemes.

Panel Materials

Panel stock is most often carried in thicknesses of ¼-, ½-, and ¾-inch although it is manufactured in sheets as thin as ⅛ inch and as thick as 1½ inches. When you shop for this material, you will find that a variety of core options are available. Traditional plywood has a *veneer core*—formed from thin layers of wood pressed together—with a decorative veneer on each face. The grain of each layer is arranged at 90 degrees to that of the adjacent layer, so the panel is dimensionally stable. One drawback to traditional plywood is that these panels often do not stay flat, especially after they are cut. In a wainscot application where the material will be fastened to a wall, this is usually not a problem, but for other jobs this can be troublesome.

MDF Panels. Some panels are made with a *medium-density fiberboard* (MDF) *core.* A mixture of wood fibers and glue that is pressed together and heated, MDF is extremely smooth and uniformly dense. An MDF panel without a face veneer is considerably cheaper than a sheet of plywood and provides an excellent surface for a painted finish. The price of an MDF panel with a face veneer is usually close to that of a plywood panel, but it is more likely to remain flat when cut into workable parts. If you are buying MDF panels for a job, you should plan to have a helper to handle the material, as it is extremely heavy. Also, the nature of the core is such that machining it yields a lot of very fine dust. So be prepared with dust masks, eye protection, and a good shop vacuum.

Manufactured Panel Core Materials

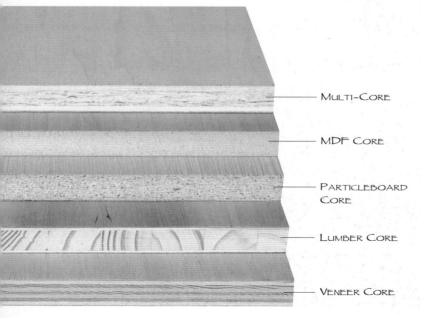

MULTI-CORE

MDF CORE

PARTICLEBOARD CORE

LUMBER CORE

VENEER CORE

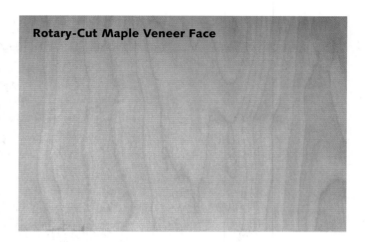

Rotary-Cut Maple Veneer Face

Trim Tip — PANEL DIMENSIONS

Standard dimensions for a plywood panel are 48 x 96 inches, but those with a particleboard and MDF core are slightly larger, 49 x 97 inches. Most home centers sell panels that have been cut to smaller dimensions, and if you purchase your material at a lumberyard, they will usually cut panels into manageable sizes for you, but expect to pay a cutting charge.

Particleboard Cores. Panels with a *particleboard core* are another option. The construction of these panels is similar to that of MDF-core stock, except that the core consists of flakes of softwood lumber and glue. These panels are also formed under heat and pressure, and while quite stable, they do not feature a particularly uniform core. As with MDF panels, these are sold with and without a face veneer, but the raw panels are not as well suited to paint-grade use. In general, these are a less desirable choice for a wainscoting application.

Lumber-Core Panels. *Lumber-core* panels are the elite class of manufactured panel stock. Strips of solid lumber are glued together and covered with a thick layer of veneer called cross-banding. The face veneer is then applied to each side of this sandwich to yield the finished product. Since this is a premium product, and is most often used in furniture manufacture, you would need to obtain this type of panel by special order—and expect to pay a premium price. It is not unusual for a lumbercore panel to cost twice the price of a comparable plywood panel.

Advances in technology have yielded a number of composite *multi-core* panels, which mix different materials in the core in an effort to reduce weight and cost while

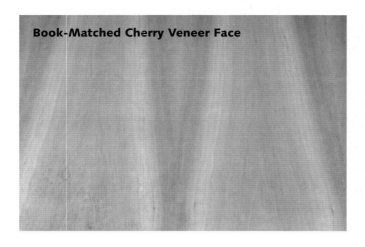

Book-Matched Cherry Veneer Face

Quartersawn White Oak Veneer Face

maintaining a stable product. One of these products uses the idea of traditional plywood, but alternates layers of wood and MDF. Another panel features a core of particleboard covered by thick cross-bands under the face veneer.

Panel Faces

The veneers that are applied to panel faces can display various patterns, depending on the way that they were cut from the log and joined together. Some veneers are peeled from a log that is mounted on a huge lathe. These are called *rotary-*

cut veneers, and they show a characteristic grain pattern that is rather wild. In some species, a rotary-cut veneer can feature grain that moves in a zig-zag pattern down the sheet. Rotary veneers can be very large, and often one sheet can cover an entire panel.

Some veneers are sliced or sawn into sheets that are parallel to one side of a tree; these are called plain-sliced veneers, and they usually show cathedral shaped grain patterns. Plain-sliced veneers are often *book-matched,* or joined together, so that symmetrical patterns appear across the panel. *Quartersawn* veneer is cut parallel to the radius of the log. These veneers show straight grain, and in some oak species, characteristic ray flake.

When shopping for panel stock, pay close attention to the veneer on the face. If you need more than one panel, try to select them so that the veneers are close in color and grain pattern. Whatever type of panel you select, inspect the face for any defects such as torn out veneer, wood-filler patches, and deep scratches. For use in wainscoting, you only need material with one good face, so if available, purchase stock with a back veneer of inferior grade to save some money.

MATERIALS AND FINISH selection contribute to the distinctive look of this staircase.

Fasteners

Fasteners are an essential part of trim work. Almost every process demands that you use some type of mechanical fastener to hold a molding to a surface or join two pieces of wood. The primary fastener for trim is the *finishing nail.* These nails feature a relatively narrow shaft with a slightly larger head. Typically, the head has a small dimple in the top surface to engage the tip of a nail set. Select an appropriately sized nail for each task—for example, for fastening trim boards to framing members, the nail should enter the framing member at least 1 inch. Remember to take the thickness of the drywall or plaster surface into account.

For fastening small pieces of molding, wire nails, or *brads,* are often used. These are essentially very fine finishing nails available in sizes between ⅝ and 1½ inches long.

The nails that are used in nail guns are classified in the same manner as traditional finishing nails, but they are slightly different in configuration. With normal nails, as the length of a fastener increases, the diameter also gets larger. But the nails for a nail gun are of one constant diameter, regardless of the length. Consequently, a nail gun can drive a long nail and still leave a relatively small diameter hole.

Screws. Screws are another important fastener. For many years, brass screws with slotted heads were the norm for woodworking, but the expense and relative soft nature of brass have made these obsolete except for decorative applications. And the popularity of power screw drivers has almost eliminated the slot head, replacing it with the more reliable Phillips and Robertson (square drive) styles.

Screws are available with round, oval, flat, and buglehead styles. If you need your screw to sit flush with the

FINISHING NAILS have a dimple in top to hold a nail set. When installing molding, the nail should penetrate into the underlying framing by at least 1 in.

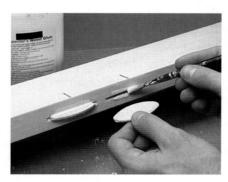

WHEN COVERED WITH GLUE and inserted into the slot cut by a plate joiner, joining plates provide a reliable fastening option.

NAIL SIZES

NAIL SIZE	LENGTH
3d	1¼"
4d	1½"
6d	2"
8d	2½"
10d	3"
12d	3¼"
16d	3½"

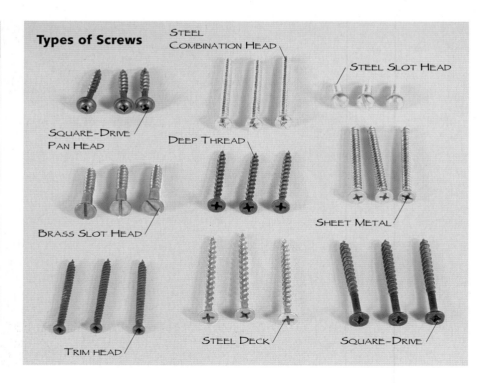

wood surface, or want it completely hidden by a plug or filler, you should choose flat or bugle-head styles. Next, select the screw material. Plain steel screws are the least expensive alternative, but hardened steel offers a tougher screw that is less likely to snap under pressure or strip out if the driver slips. Finally, consider the style of the screw body. Traditional wood screws have a body with threads that only extend about two-thirds of the way up the shank, and the body tapers from the head to the tip. Sheet metal and deep-thread styles have bodies of constant diameter, and the threads extend farther up the screw. Trim-head screws have small diameter heads that can be used like finishing nails.

Dowels. Dowels are wooden cylinders of a specific di-ameter that are coated with glue and inserted in matching holes in the two sides of a joint. For commercial applications, dowels are available in precut lengths with either spiral or longitudinal grooves down the dowel length. These grooves provide a means for excess glue to escape the hole. If you are using plain dowel stock, it is a good practice to carve one or two shallow grooves down the length of each dowel with a knife or chisel.

Joining Plates. These are football-shaped wafers of compressed wood. They are designed to fit into matching semicircular slots that are cut in each side of a joint using a plate joiner. Joining plates come in three standard sizes, and there are also other plates available for specialized uses.

USING HOLLOW-WALL ANCHORS

It's always preferable to fasten trim parts to the framing inside a wall or ceiling, but there are times when there is no stud, plate, or joist where you need one. In those situations you have two options. You can rip into the wall and install some blocking, or you can use one of the various hollow-wall anchors to install your part.

Difficulty Level: **Easy**

TOOLS
Power drill and countersink bit • pencil • screwdriver

MATERIALS
Wall anchors • wood plugs • glue

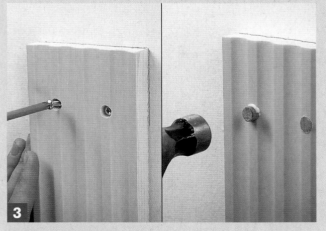

1 **DRILL THROUGH THE PIECE** to be installed using a countersink bit. The bit will mark the drywall for drilling.

2 **REMOVE THE MOLDING**, and drill pilot holes. Insert anchors into the pilot holes.

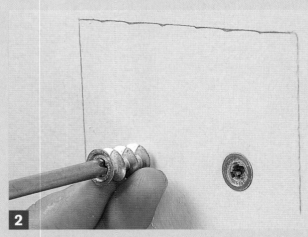

3 **ATTACH MOLDING**, and cover screw heads with dowels. Trim the dowels, and finish the workpiece.

3

TRIMWORK MATERIALS

Glue and Construction Adhesives

In the pursuit of tight, strong joints, woodworking adhesives are an important addition to your arsenal of tools. The standard glues for most joints are *polyvinyl acetate (PVA) adhesives,* known casually as *white* and *yellow* glues. While the white variety can be used for most porous materials, the yellow variety—also called aliphatic resin glue—has been specifically formulated for woodworking applications. Brown-colored versions are available for use with woods of darker tone. For applications that need water resistance, there are formulations of yellow glue that are rated as *waterproof.* These glues are technically known as cross-linking PVA. They are easy to use, nontoxic, and clean up easily with water before curing.

Polyurethane adhesives also offer water resistance and are compatible with a number of different materials. One unique feature of this glue is that it requires moisture to cure, so it is often recommended that you slightly dampen the wood surface before applying the glue. This glue tends to foam up as it cures, and it can be difficult to clean up a joint without leaving a residue. In addition, polyurethane glue will stain your skin, so you need to wear gloves when working with it.

Epoxies are available in a variety of formulas with different strengths and setting times. These adhesives require

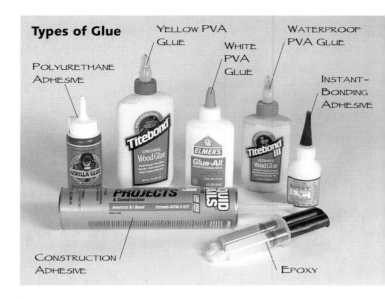

Types of Glue — POLYURETHANE ADHESIVE, YELLOW PVA GLUE, WHITE PVA GLUE, WATERPROOF PVA GLUE, INSTANT-BONDING ADHESIVE, CONSTRUCTION ADHESIVE, EPOXY

that you mix a hardener with a resin to start the chemical reaction that cures the epoxy. Quick-setting versions are sold in convenient double-tube dispensers that provide the proper ratio of hardener to resin. For joints that require the highest bonding strength, especially in varied materials, epoxy is the best choice. But epoxy is also a toxic material, so be sure to wear gloves and a respirator to protect yourself from exposure.

Instant-bonding adhesives, sometimes called "super glue," have limited use in woodworking, but there are times when this can be a life-saver. Technically called cyanoacrylate adhesive, this glue sets in a matter of sec-

FOR TIGHT JOINTS, apply a bead of glue to miter cuts. Complete the job using finishing nails.

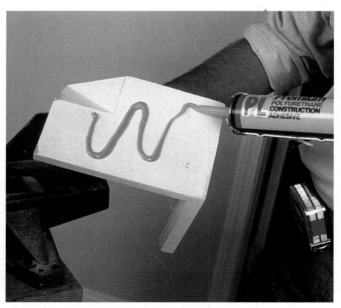

STANDARD CONSTRUCTION ADHESIVE is often all that is required for applying resin-type moldings.

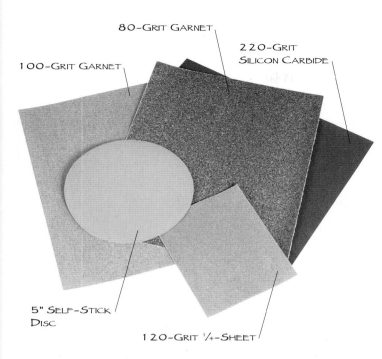

80-GRIT GARNET

220-GRIT SILICON CARBIDE

100-GRIT GARNET

5" SELF-STICK DISC

120-GRIT ¼-SHEET

onds, so clamping is virtually unnecessary. This adhesive can be very useful to repair small chips and torn-out grain in a wood surface.

Construction adhesive is a thick-bodied substance that comes in a tube for use in a caulk gun. There are different formulations of adhesive for specific uses such as bonding paneling or drywall, or resin molding installation.

Sandpaper

It's rare to find someone who truly enjoys sanding, but it is an important part of most woodworking projects, and if approached methodically, it need not be a particularly tedious or difficult task. The first step is to have the right material for the job, and that means sandpaper.

You will see sandpaper that is manufactured with different abrasives, and each has its preferred use. Garnet paper is best for sanding by hand. Machine sanding requires a longer lasting, tougher abrasive, and aluminum oxide is generally considered the best choice. Silicone carbide paper is a good choice for sanding finishes between coats as it holds up well in fine grits.

Sandpaper is rated according to the coarseness of the abrasive particles and type of backer. Lower grit numbers correspond to coarser abrasive. You can find papers rated from 40 to 1500 grit, but for general trim projects, your most frequent selections will fall between 100 and 220 grit. Backers for sandpaper can be either cloth or paper, with paper more common in sheets and discs, and cloth most prevalent in belts. The weight of the backer is classified

from "A" to "X" with "A" being the thinnest and most flexible. For hand sanding, "A" weight is most appropriate, and for orbital machine sanding "C" weight is best.

Sandpaper is sold in full sheets of 9 × 11 inches, as well as in ¼- and ½-sheet sizes for pad sanders. You will also find discs and belts of various sizes to fit different types of power sanders. Most discs come with a backing of Velcro or pressure-sensitive adhesive for mounting to the sanding pad.

Caulk

For jobs that are destined to be painted, caulk can be the trim carpenter's best friend. But it's also important to realize that caulk is not a replacement for doing a careful job of fitting and assembling joints. Although we generally think of walls and ceilings as flat, in most cases you will find dips and humps in these surfaces. And when trim is applied, there is sometimes a small gap between the two materials. These are the places where caulk is an indispensable tool. A judicious application of caulk can blend an applied molding to a wall or ceiling surface, creating a seamless appearance. Small gaps in trim joints, especially at inside corners of baseboards and cornices, can also be filled with caulk.

Acrylic latex caulk is the best all-around choice for interior trim work. This material is easy to apply, and you can shape a caulk joint with a wet finger or putty knife. It cleans up with water while still fresh, and it readily accepts a painted finish after proper curing. Expect latex caulk to shrink a bit as it cures, so for wide joints you might have to reapply the material before painting. For best results, prime the woodwork and wall or ceiling surface before applying the caulk.

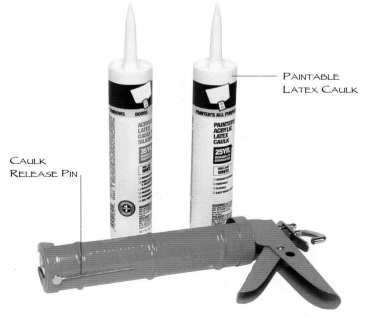

PAINTABLE LATEX CAULK

CAULK RELEASE PIN

CHAPTER 4

DOOR & WINDOW
CASING

Most homes feature some sort of trimwork around windows and doors. Unfortunately, in many cases, it is stock Colonial or clamshell casing that ends up finishing windows and doors. Although inexpensive, these casings provide minimal visual impact and contribute little to the overall design of a room. But other options are readily available. Your local home center or lumberyard may stock dozens of wider casings that have much more interesting profiles. Select one of these moldings, or create a design of your own by installing individual pieces in layers to create a unified design. Augment the molding by using corner and plinth blocks to achieve certain period looks.

Prehung Doors

If you want to add a door to a room, selecting a prehung door can make the installation simple and quick. With a prehung door, you eliminate the need to fit the door to the opening, to cut mortises for the hinges and lockset, and to fit the door stops. All the really fussy and time-consuming work is already done for you, and for the beginner or pro, this can be a real advantage.

Most lumberyards and home centers carry a variety of door styles for prehung applications. In addition, you can often choose between pine jambs that can be painted or stained, or hardwood jambs, with red oak being the most common choice. Interior doors can have a flush design—with a flat veneered or fiberboard surface—solid wood panels, or molded fiberboard panels. Of course, it is also possible to custom order a more unusual combination of door and jamb and have it prehung for you.

When ordering a door, you will not only need to specify the style, material, and size, but also the direction you

Installing a Prehung Door

Difficulty Level: Moderate

TOOLS
Hammer • nail set • spirit level • saw • utility knife

MATERIALS
Shims • finishing nails • prehung door

1 **USE A NAIL SET** or punch to loosen the hinge pins on your prehung door. Lift the pins from the hinges, and gently pull the door free from the jamb assembly.

2 **STAND THE JAMB ASSEMBLY** in the door opening with both side jambs resting on the floor. Use a 24-in. level to check that the head jamb is level in the opening.

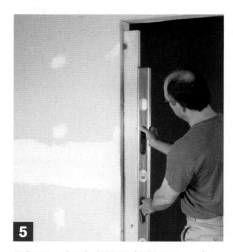

5 **USE A LONG STRAIGHT 2x4** and 4-ft. level to check that the jack stud on the hinge side of the door is plumb—if it is not, you will need to place shims between the jamb and stud.

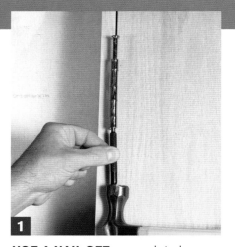

6 **USE 8D OR 10D** finishing nails to fasten the hinge jamb to the jack stud. Place two nails near the top of the jamb; then check that the edge of the jamb is plumb before nailing the rest of the jamb.

7 **USE A FLAT BAR** to pry the jamb out, and slide tapered shims behind the jamb. Be sure to use two shims, one driven from each side, to keep the jamb square. Use shims every 16 in.

wish the door to open. The convention that applies to this issue is as follows: if you open the door toward you and the hinges are on the right side, the door is a right-handed door; if the hinges are on the left when it opens toward you, it is a left-handed door.

The width of a standard prehung door jamb used with typical 2×4 wall framing is 4⅟₁₆ inches, which allows the door jamb to just barely protrude beyond the drywall surface. This compensates for small irregularities in wall thickness.

Installing Prehung Doors

To begin your installation, remove the door from the frame by knocking out the hinge pins. You can use a nail set or punch to drive the pins out. Stand the frame in the opening, and check that the head jamb is level. If one side is higher than the other, block up the low side until it is correct; then note the thickness of the blocking required. Mark the bottom of the high side jamb to remove that same amount, and cut it with a circular saw, jig saw, or handsaw.

Test the Frame. Place the frame in the opening again to make sure that the head is level. Next, check to see if the jack stud on the hinge side of the door is plumb. If it is, use 8d or 10d finishing nails to nail the top of the jamb to the stud; then place the level on the edge of the jamb to make sure that it is plumb in both directions. Adjust the jamb as necessary, and nail the bottom. Position the nails near the top, bottom, and center of the jamb.

Out-of-Plumb Jack Stud. If the jack stud is not plumb, use a flat bar to pry the jamb away from the stud, and slip tapered shims behind the jamb to hold it in position. To keep the jamb straight, place shims, in pairs, about every 16 inches along the length of the jamb. Drive nails just below each pair of shims to keep them in place. Once the hinge jamb is nailed, rehang the door and use it as a guide in positioning the opposite jamb. Place shims between the jamb and opposite jack stud to achieve a uniform gap between the door and jamb. Again, position nails just under the shims.

Test the operation of the door to make sure that it opens and closes properly. Examine the fit of the stop against the closed door. There should be no gaps at the swinging side, and a uniform gap of ⅟₁₆ inch or less on the hinge side, so the door does not bind. Finally, use a sharp utility knife to score the shims flush to the jamb, and snap off the protruding ends.

3 IF NECESSARY, place shims beneath one of the side jambs to bring the head level. Measure the height of the shim; then mark the bottom of the opposite jamb to remove that same amount.

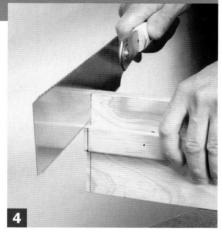

4 CUT THE BOTTOM of the high side jamb along your layout mark. A small Japanese Ryoba saw is an excellent tool for the job, but you can use any saw that is handy.

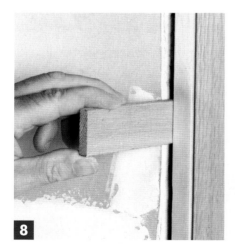

8 RE-HANG THE DOOR, and use it as a guide in adjusting the latch jamb. Place shims between the jamb and jack stud to maintain a uniform gap between the door edge and jamb.

9 USE A SHARP UTILITY KNIFE to score the shims at the point where they protrude beyond the wall surface. After scoring the shim, you should be able to snap it off easily.

Casing a Drywall Opening

Many newer homes feature drywall jambs in passageways between rooms, but it is not difficult to add a wooden jamb and casing to the opening. The first step is to engage in some demolition work. In drywall openings, a metal corner bead is applied to the corners to form a straight, neat edge. As a result, these corners tend to flare out, and they are thicker than the rest of the wall—a potential problem when applying casing.

Expose the Corner Bead. Beginning at the bottom of the wall, use a flat pry bar to expose the corner bead and pry it away from the wall. Most beads are installed with 1¼-inch

drywall nails and will come away easily. Work your way up each corner and across the top of the opening; then pry off the drywall strip that lines the inside of the opening to expose the jack studs and header. If the drywall extends into the opening, use a drywall saw to trim it flush to the inside surfaces of the studs and header.

Custom Jambs. You can certainly purchase standard jambs from a lumberyard, but it is easy to make the jambs for the opening from 1×6 pine stock. For normal wall construction, rip jamb stock to a width of 4⁹⁄₁₆ inches. It's always a good idea to check the thickness of the wall to see if there is variation in the measurement. Adjust your jamb width as required, allowing ¹⁄₁₆ inch more than the overall wall thick-

Asssembling a Jamb

Difficulty Level: **Easy**

TOOLS
Drill • router or circular saw • hammer or nailer • clamps • combination square • chisel

MATERIALS
Wood glue • nails • jamb stock

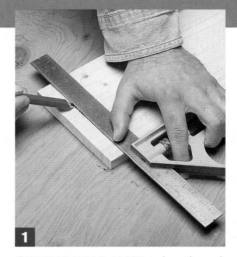

1

CUT THE HEAD JAMB to length, and mark the joint outline with a square for a ¾-in. jamb leg.

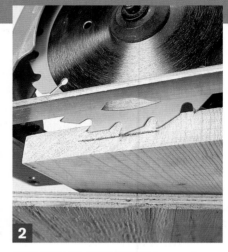

2

SET THE BLADE DEPTH on a circular saw to reach halfway (⅜ in.) through the thickness of the board.

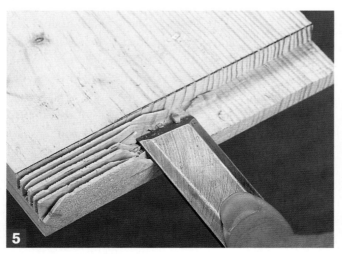

5

YOU CAN USE THE SAW to remove all the wood, or clean up the thin strips between kerfs using a sharp chisel.

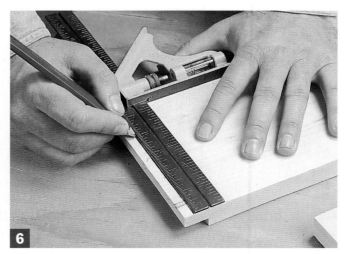

6

WHEN THE RABBET is cleaned up and ready for assembly, mark a nailing line on the outside of the joint.

ness. Next, measure the width of the rough opening in several places along the jack studs. Take the smallest measurement and subtract 1¼ inches to arrive at the length of the head jamb. Cut the side jambs about ¼ inch shorter than the rough opening height.

Use the router and edge guide, or a circular saw, to cut a ⅜-inch-deep by ¾-inch-wide rabbet across the top of each side jamb. Fasten the side jambs to the head jamb with screws or nails and glue. If you use screws, drill and counterbore pilot holes in the side jambs and small pilot holes into the end-grain of the head jamb to avoid splitting the stock. To simplify installation, tack a scrap board across the bottom edges of the side jambs to hold the parts square.

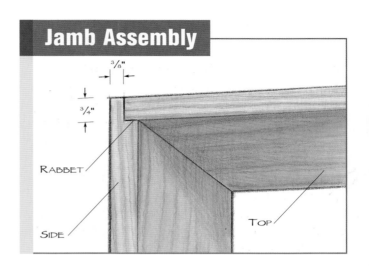

Jamb Assembly

⅜"

¾"

RABBET

SIDE

TOP

3

TO CONTROL THE RABBET CUT, firmly clamp a guide board and the jamb to a stable bench.

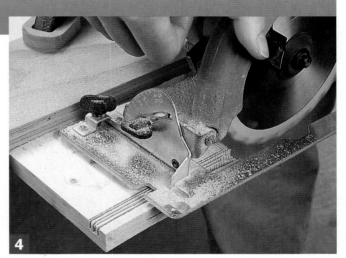

4

MAKE THE INNERMOST CUT with the saw along the guide. Then make multiple passes to kerf the remaining wood.

7

ADD GLUE to the mating surfaces of the jamb parts just prior to assembling them.

8

SQUARE UP the jamb frame before fastening. You may want to set the pieces around a square block for support.

Installing Simple Colonial Casing

Difficulty Level: **Easy**

TOOLS
Hammer • combination square • power miter saw • nail set

MATERIALS
Clamshell or ranch casing • finishing nails • wood glue

1

MARK THE REVEAL by sliding the blade on the combination square. Cut a miter on one end of the casing.

2

ALIGN THE SHORT SIDE of the miter with one reveal mark; transfer the opposite mark to the casing.

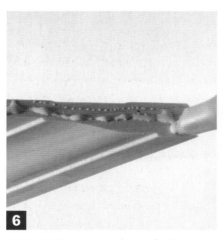

6

APPLY A SMALL BEAD of glue to both miter surfaces. Nail the side casing to the jamb and wall framing.

7

DRIVE A 4D FINISHING NAIL through the edge of the casing to lock the miter joint together.

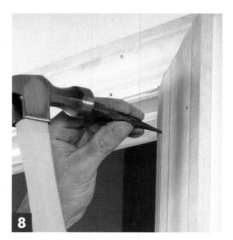

8

USE A NAIL SET to recess the nailheads about ⅛ in. below the wood surface.

Door Casings

Some casing styles feature mitered corners at the joints of the side and head casing; other styles use butt joints; and there are certain treatments that layer a mitered molding over butt-jointed flat stock. All styles, however, have one element in common, and that is called a reveal. Instead of fastening the casing flush with the door side of the jamb, it is traditional to hold it back to allow a small, uniform margin of jamb to be exposed on its edge. The setback is known as the reveal, and this treatment applies to window casing and door casing alike. The actual dimension of the reveal you use is up to you, but ⅛ to 5⁄32 inch is typical. If the reveal is too large, you reduce the amount of jamb available for nail-

ing the casing, and if it is too small, even the smallest discrepancy becomes visible. Whatever measurement you decide to use, it is important that you make it the standard for the entire job so that you maintain a uniform look throughout. Use a combination square as a gauge, and place light pencil marks at the corners, center, and ends of your jambs to indicate the amount of setback.

Evaluate the Condition of the Door

Begin by making sure that the head and side jambs are level and plumb. When you check the side jambs, use a long straightedge with the level to span the entire jamb length. Then use a framing square to check the head and side jambs. If you find that the corners are not square, use a slid-

3

USE 4D FINISHING NAILS to tack the head casing to the head jamb of the door. Leave the nailheads exposed.

4

CUT A MITER on a piece of side casing. Rest the miter on the floor or spacer (for carpet or finished floor).

5

MARK THE LENGTH of the side casing pieces by running a pencil along the top edge of the head casing.

ing bevel gauge to determine the actual angle. Transfer the angle to a piece of scrap lumber or cardboard; then use an angle gauge to measure the angle. Use one-half of that angle for your miter saw setting to cut the corner joint.

Simple Colonial Casing

The one-piece "Colonial" casing is one of the simplest treatments for door and window casing. Along with the "clamshell" or "ranch" molding, it is one of the standard choices for homebuilders throughout the country. The techniques for either type are essentially the same.

In a mitered casing installation, the desired result is a continuous and seamless border of molding around the door opening. Begin by laying out the jamb reveals at the

Trim Tip — MARK ONCE

As a general rule, you are always better off directly marking the size of a trim piece than measuring its length. Whenever you measure and mark a piece for length, there is an inevitable degree of variation in the way the dimension is transferred to the work piece. By marking the size of a piece directly in its ultimate location, you reduce the opportunity for careless errors.

top corners, bottom, and midpoint of the jamb. Next, cut a miter on one end of the head casing stock and hold it in place, aligning the short end of the miter with one of the reveal marks on the side casing. Use a sharp pencil to mark the short point of the opposite miter on the other end of the molding.

Attach the Head Casing. Cut the piece to length, and tack it in place by driving 4d finishing nails driven into the edge of the jamb and 6d or 8d finishing nails into the wall framing—leave the nailheads protruding at this point in case you need to remove the part for adjustment.

Cut the matching miter angles on the side casing pieces, but leave them a few inches long. Instead of measuring the side casing pieces, it is easier, and more accurate, to directly transfer the length onto the stock. Simply invert one of the pieces of side casing so that the long point of the miter rests on the floor and the outside edge of the casing rests against the long point of the head casing. Mark the length of the casing, and make the square cut. If you need to make allowance for carpet or finish flooring, simply place an appropriate spacer under the point of the casing.

Attach Side Casing. Once the casing is cut to length, spread some carpenter's glue on the mating surfaces of the miter joint, and tack the casing in place. Drive 4d finishing nails into the edge of the jamb and 6d or 8d finishing nails to fasten the casing to the framing under the wall surface. Space the pairs of nails about 16 inches apart. Check that the miters are nice and tight; then drive a 4d finishing nail through the edge of the casing to lock the joint together. Set the nailheads below the wood surface.

Installing Built-Up Colonial Casing

Difficulty Level: Moderate

TOOLS
Hammer • nail set • router and bit • plate joiner and wafers (optional) • nail gun and nails (optional) • power miter saw • clamps

MATERIALS
1x2 boards • 1x4 boards • panel or base cap molding • 4d and 6d finishing nails • wood glue

1

A ROUTER with an edge-profiling bit makes quick work of molding the edges of casing stock. Clamp the casing blank to the worktable before beginning the cut. You can also mount the router in a router table.

2

CUT APPROPRIATE MITERS for the corner joints. Mark the center of each joining plate slot on the face of the casing; then clamp a piece to the worktable to cut the slot. Hold the plate jointer and stock tightly on the table.

Built-up Colonial Casing

Factory-made Colonial casing is designed to mimic the more elaborate forms of a traditionally installed, built-up casing. Using readily available stock, you can create a larger and more detailed casing that conveys a more nuanced sense of style than is available with an off-the-shelf profile. The process is not difficult; it uses 1×4 and 1×2 boards, and stock panel or base cap molding. 1×4 boards form the foundation of the casing. While you can certainly leave the edges of the boards square, or ease them gently with sandpaper, the casing will be more interesting if you add a molded profile to the inside edge. In order to do this, install an ogee or cove bit in the router, and use it to cut the profile along one edge of each 1×4 board.

Cut the Head Casing. First, mark the reveals on the jamb edges. Then cut a piece of 1×4 to length for the head casing with an appropriate miter cut on each end. Although it is not technically necessary to create a glue joint between the side and head casings, it is good trim practice when dealing with wide, flat stock.

Tight Connections. Another useful technique is to use a joining plate in the joint between the two casing parts. The joining plate serves two functions. First, it strengthens the joint, and second, it keeps the faces of the adjoining parts perfectly aligned. Mark the location of the center of each slot on the top surface of the head casing and cut the slots. Then tack the head casing in position over the door opening. Trim the side casings to size; cut the matching plate slots; and install those, applying glue to the slots and joining plates before nailing the parts in place.

Installing the Backband. Cut 1×2 stock to wrap around the outside edges of the flat casing—this treatment is known as a *backband*. Notice that the cuts at the corner joints need to be 45-degree bevels, rather than flat miters. Install the backband to the outside edges of the flat casing using 6d finishing nails. Begin with the head casing and then move to the sides. Finally, cut the panel or base cap molding to size so that its outside edge sits tight to the inside face of the backband. Install using 4d finishing nails.

CREATE A CUSTOM DESIGN by adding a simple backband and some panel molding to flat Colonial casing.

3

TACK THE HEAD CASING to the head jamb with 4d finishing nails; then spread glue on the miter surfaces, in both slots, and on the joining plate. Insert the plate in one side of the joint, and assemble the joint.

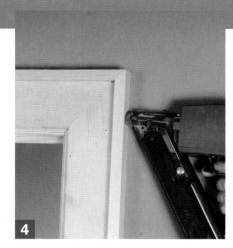

4

CUT BACKBAND STRIPS to size with appropriate bevels for the corner joints. Use 6d finishing nails, or a nail gun, to fasten the strips to the outside edges of the casing.

5

CUT PANEL MOLDING to fit tightly inside the backband border. Nail the molding to the casing with 4d finishing nails.

Trim Tip CLOSING GAPS

When dealing with wide casing, it is pretty common to require a bit of adjustment to get the miters to close tightly. If the doorjamb protrudes beyond the wall surface even $\frac{1}{16}$ in. you may have difficulty closing the miter joint. In this case, you can place shims behind the outer edges of the casing to create a tight joint. Score the shims with a sharp knife, and snap off the protruding portion. The backband will cover the gap between the casing and wall.

USE SHIMS to help the miter joints close tightly. Score and remove the protruding section of the shims.

BUILT-UP MOLDINGS add texture and design interest to the casings around doorways, doors, and windows.

ROUTING A MOLDING PROFILE

The great selection of router bits provides you a means of creating your own molding profiles to personalize a trim installation. Most profile bits feature a ball-bearing pilot at the bottom of the bit, which you can use to guide the cutter along an edge. One of the advantages of cutting your own molding is that you can generate slightly different profiles with the same bit by varying the depth of the cut.

Mount the bit in the router following all manufacturer's recommendations and cautions. Adjust the appropriate depth of cut for the bit and material thickness. Clamp a small piece of scrap lumber to your worktable, and test the cut before moving on to valuable material. When you are satisfied with the profile, clamp your stock to the table and make the cut. Remember to move the router from left to right as you face the edge of the board.

If you need to cut a profile on a lot of material, you should consider using a router table for the job. Once you have set up and adjusted the router in a table, you can push the material past the cutter instead of needing to clamp each board individually. Even though your bit may have a ball-bearing pilot, always install the router table fence and align it with the face of the pilot. By using accessory hold-down jigs on the table, you can eliminate any danger of kickback as well as maintain even pressure on the stock. This will avoid burn marks and irregularities in the profile.

Narrow moldings present a different problem. Because it is difficult to use a router on narrow stock, play it safe and always rout the profile on the edge of a wide board, and then transfer the work to a circular saw or table saw to rip the molded piece off of the wide stock to the desired dimensions.

Difficulty Level: **Easy**

TOOLS
Router and bit • clamps

MATERIALS
1-by lumber

SELECT A PROFILING BIT with a roller guide that rides along the edge of the board.

ADJUST THE DEPTH OF CUT on the router. Some have a collar on the housing; others have a calibrated knob.

TO WORK SAFELY, clamp the board securely to a bench, and be sure the clamps are out of the router's path.

USE HOLD-DOWN ACCESSORIES when routing profiles on a router table.

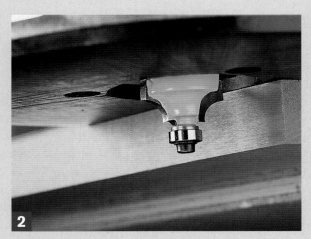

2

SET THE ROUTER on the edge of the board to see the depth of the bit. Make a test cut on scrap.

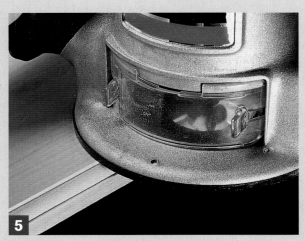

5

ALWAYS MAKE YOUR CUT pushing against the rotation of the bit, and use multiple passes to avoid chatter marks.

THE BEST APPROACH to selecting a casing style, above, is to use the same design throughout the house.

TRADITIONAL-STYLE CASING, below, is a simple but distinctive treatment for doors and windows.

Installing Traditional-Style Casing

Difficulty Level: Moderate

TOOLS
Hammer • nail set • plate joiner and wafers • nail gun and nails (optional) • power miter saw

MATERIALS
1-by casing stock • backband
• 4d and 6d finishing nails
• wood glue

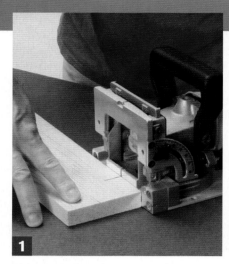

1

MARK THE LOCATIONS of joining plate slots in the bottom edge of the head casing; then use the plate joiner to cut the slots.

2

CUT PLATE SLOTS in the top ends of side casings. To avoid kickback when cutting into end grain, clamp the stock to the table, and use two hands to control the plate joiner.

Traditional-Style Casing

In the period from the 1920's through the 1940's, many homes were built in a style that is often called "traditional." These homes predate the use of the "ranch" and "colonial" casings that are so frequently used today. Door and window openings featured wide flat casings with a simple backband. This treatment creates a nice framework for these room openings and is definitely worth considering. One of the nice features of this trim detail is that the flat casing stock is joined at the head with a simple butt joint. This eliminates the need for fussing with a miter joint on wide stock—a situation that can get tricky if the wall surfaces are not absolutely flat.

Lay Out the Casing. To determine the length of the head casing, measure the distance between the reveal marks on the side casing and add twice the width of a piece of side casing—for 3½-inch-wide stock you would add 7 inches. Lay out and cut the joining plate slots in the bottom edge of the head casing. Cut the side casings to length; cut matching slots in the top end of each piece. Tack the side casings to the door jamb; then apply glue to the joining plate slots and plates. Install the plates to the top of each side casing; slip the head casing into position; and nail it to the head jamb. If necessary, slip tapered shims behind the outer edge of the casing stock to ensure that the joints between side and head casing are flush.

Cut the Backband. Measure and cut the backband stock to length with appropriately beveled ends. There are many situations where a wall surface is so irregular that gaps inevitably occur between the casing and wall. On jobs that will be painted, you can always apply a small bead of caulk to fill any gaps. But on a job that will receive a clear finish, caulk is not an option. This is a situation where the backband can be planed to fit tightly to the wall surface. (See "Scribing a Backband to the Wall," opposite.)

Many home centers stock a backband molding that is cut in an "L"-shaped cross section, so that it wraps around the outside edge of the casing instead of just butting to it. These products are viable alternatives for your door trim; just do not feel that their offerings are your only options.

SIMPLE BUTT JOINTS are the distinguishing characteristics of traditional-style casing. The addition of a backband creates an elegant design.

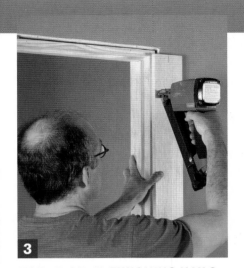

USE 4D OR 6D FINISHING NAILS to fasten the side casing to the edge of the doorjamb. Wait until the head casing is in place to nail the outer edge.

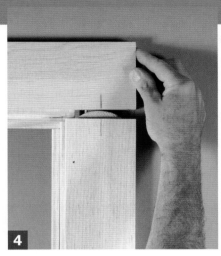

SPREAD GLUE in the plate slots and on the joining plates; then assemble the head/side casing joints. Nail the head casing to the head jamb; then nail the outer edge of the casing.

CUT THE BACKBAND STRIPS to size with appropriately beveled ends. Use 6d finishing nails to fasten the bands to the outer edge of the casing.

SCRIBING A BACKBAND TO THE WALL

If you notice that there are gaps between the wall and backband, it's a simple matter to scribe it to fit. Scribing involves marking the stock to match the wall profile and then removing material from the areas adjacent to the high points so that the molding can sit tight to the wall along its entire length.

Begin by applying a strip of masking tape to the outer surface of the backband. The tape will allow you to better see the scribed pencil lines. Next, hold the molding against the wall, in position, and set your scribers to a width that matches the widest gap between the wall and molding. Hold the two wings of the scriber parallel to the floor as you trace the wall profile onto the taped surface of the molding.

Remove the backband to a work surface, and use a sharp block plane to remove material until the pencil line is left exposed. Test the fit of the piece, and make any necessary adjustments.

If you remove stock from the top edges of a side backband, the top band will also need to be adjusted so that it does not protrude beyond the sides. If the top piece is already installed, it is a simple matter to plane the face to the required depth.

APPLY MASKING TAPE to the outside edge of backband; hold the band against the wall; and use scribers to mark the required adjustment.

USE A SHARP BLOCK PLANE to trim the backband to fit the wall profile. Plane just up to the scribed line. Test the fit, and adjust if necessary.

Neo-Classical Casing

Casing that is described as Neo-Classical includes a range of options that are appropriate for a variety of design traditions. Homes that include these details could be Georgian, Federal, or Greek Revival style, those forms that have evolved, in some measure, from the classical conventions of ancient Rome and Greece. The basic casing structure is intended to suggest the structure of a column, with base, shaft, and capital replicated in the elements of the door trim.

Within this style, there are many variations and combinations you can try. Side casings can be plain flat stock, or the edges can be rounded or shaped into a cove or ogee profile. You can use fluted material for the side casing to mimic a pilaster or column, or any custom-made profile, tapered or symmetrical.

Creating the Header. The head casing, also called a *frieze*, or an *entablature*, is usually constructed of stock that is the same thickness as the side casing. You can select a variety of molding treatments for the head casing to present

Installing Neo-Classical Casing

Difficulty Level: Moderate

TOOLS
Hammer • nail set • block plane • nail gun and nails (optional) • miter saw • table saw • square

MATERIALS
1-by casing stock • plinth blocks • lattice • crown or bed molding • finishing nails • wood glue

1 MARK GUIDELINES on the top edge and face of plinth block stock to indicate the limits of the chamfer; then use a sharp block plane to cut the chamfer.

2 HOLD THE PLINTH BLOCK flush to the inside face of the door jamb, and nail it to the jamb edge and wall framing.

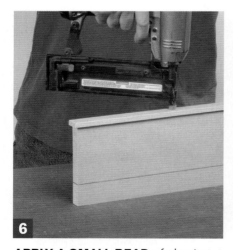

6 APPLY A SMALL BEAD of glue to the bottom edge of the head casing and then nail the crosshead strip to it. The strip should project an even distance beyond the face and both ends.

7 USE BRADS to fasten the bed molding to the head casing with its bottom edge on the previously scribed line.

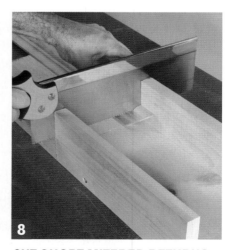

8 CUT SHORT MITERED RETURNS on bed molding stock using a simple crosscutting jig and handsaw.

a more formal or casual appearance, but the trademark of this style is a crown or cap molding at the top of the frieze and crosshead molding near, or at, the bottom edge of the frieze. The particular moldings that you use on the head can range from a specialty cap to a stock crown or bed molding.

The dimensions for the side and head casing are somewhat arbitrary. For the sides, a width of 4½ to 5 inches is typical, while head casing is often 5½ to 6 inches wide. The final decision will often depend on whether you are using stock profiles or making your own casing. Make a full-scale sketch of your trim to best judge if the proportions are correct.

Establish a Base. Most casing treatments in this style make use of a plinth. A plinth is a block that serves as a base for the casing and transition between the horizontal baseboard and vertical door trim. Plinths are typically fashioned of thicker stock than the casing and baseboard, usually 1 or 1 1/16 inches thick.

In the Neo-Classical rationale, the plinth suggests the base of a column, adding weight and a sense of grounding

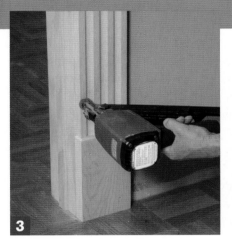

3

CUT CASING to length; set it on top of the plinth; and nail it to the edge of the doorjamb with 4d or 6d finishing nails. Use 8d finishing nails to fasten the outer edge to the wall framing.

4

USE A SQUARE to determine the "drop" of the bed molding for the head assembly. Mark the casing along the bottom edge. Scribe a line across the face and ends of the casing.

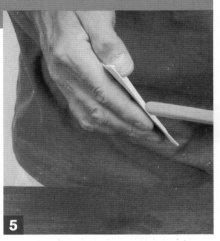

5

YOU CAN SHAPE a bullnose profile on the ends of the crosshead strip with sandpaper. If you use simple lattice instead of a bullnose molding, simply ease the sharp edges.

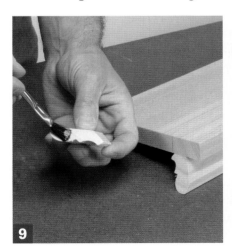

9

APPLY GLUE to the mitered return joint, and carefully place the small pieces on the head assembly. Use small brads to hold the parts in place while the glue sets.

10

INSTALL A LATTICE CAP over the top of the casing and bed molding. Use brads to fasten the part in place.

11

NAIL THE HEAD ASSEMBLY to the head jamb and wall framing.

NEO-CLASSICAL CASING designs are intended to suggest the structure of a column.

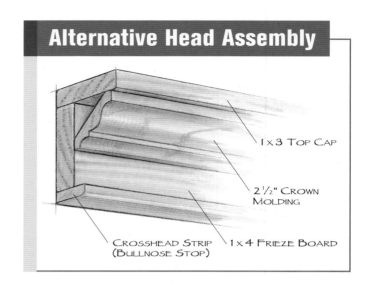

Alternative Head Assembly

1 x 3 TOP CAP

2¹/₂" CROWN MOLDING

CROSSHEAD STRIP (BULLNOSE STOP)

1 x 4 FRIEZE BOARD

to the door trim. Of course, if you wish to run your side casing directly to the floor, you should certainly do so; there is considerable precedent for that type of treatment as well. If you decide to include plinth blocks as part of your trim package, they are the first element to install. The size of a plinth is dependent on the width of the door casing and height of the baseboard.

Determine the Width of the Plinth. To determine the width, add twice the amount of your jamb reveal to the casing width; to arrive at the height, add at least ¹/₂ inch to the overall height of the baseboard—the exact height is arbitrary. Cut the blocks to size, and sand or plane a small chamfer along the exposed top edges.

As an alternative, there are commercially available plinth blocks that feature a molding profile along the top edge. If you use these, you may have to adjust the width or height of the block to suit your installation. Nail the plinth blocks to the jamb, holding the edge of the block flush to the inside surface of the jamb face. Then nail the outer edge of the blocks to the wall framing.

Fasten the Side Casing. Make a square cut on one end of each piece of side casing stock. Rest the cut end on top of a plinth block, and use the reveal mark on the head jamb as a guide to mark the casing length. Cut the casing to length, and fasten it to the jamb with 4d or 6d finishing nails. Use 6d or 8d finishing nails to fasten the outer edge of the casing to the wall framing, but take care that you do not pull the jamb out of alignment while nailing.

USING SPECIALTY MOLDING

As an alternative, you can use a specialty cap molding to create a decorative head assembly, although you may need to go to a specialty molding supplier to find it. Once again, cut the head casing to length; determine the length of the cap molding; and cut mitered returns at each end. Assemble the returns to the cap molding. While the glue sets, glue and nail the crosshead strip to the bottom edge. Use nails and glue to fasten the cap to the top edge.

SPECIAL CAP MOLDING is an alternative to creating your own design, although it may be difficult to find.

Building the Head Casing

It is much easier to add the cornice and crosshead molding to the head casing before it is installed. And, by working on these parts on a worktable or bench, you can bring some mass-production techniques to bear and construct all of the door and window head casings for a room at the same time. Just remember to mark each assembly with a code to identify the door or window to which it belongs.

To determine the length of your head casing, cut the stock a few inches long with a square cut on one end. Set the blank on top of the side casings, and align the square end with the outer edge of one of the side casings. Mark the blank at the outer edge of the opposite casing, and cut the piece to length.

Creating the Design. For the simplest head casing, such as the one shown on page 100, use ¼- to ½-inch-thick lattice for the crosshead strip and a stock bed or crown molding at the top of the head. The bed or crown molding wraps around the top of the casing, so you need to determine the

amount of vertical drop of the molding from the top edge of the casing. When installed, the top of the bed molding should be level with the top of the casing board. Use a square to help gauge the position of the bottom edge of the molding; then mark a line the appropriate distance down from the top edge of the board. (See Step #4, page 101.)

Next, rip the ⅜-inch crosshead strip to a width of 1⅛ inches (for a ⅜-inch reveal), and crosscut it to a length ¾ inch longer than the casing. Glue and nail the strip to the bottom edge of the board to expose a ⅜-inch reveal on the front and ends. If you wish, you can shape the exposed edges of the stop to a bullnose profile with router or sandpaper. Cut the bed molding to length, with mitered ends for returns, and tack it in place. Cut the short return pieces, and use glue and small brads to mount them to the assembly. Then cut a cap from ¼-inch-thick stock so that it overhangs about ¼ inch on the face and each end, apply glue, and nail it in place. Install the head casing to the door.

Neo-Classical Casing Assembly

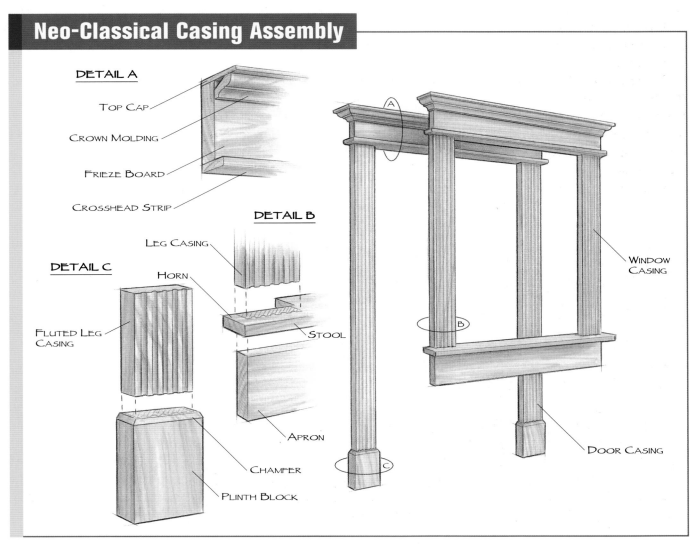

DETAIL A
- TOP CAP
- CROWN MOLDING
- FRIEZE BOARD
- CROSSHEAD STRIP

DETAIL B
- LEG CASING

DETAIL C
- HORN
- FLUTED LEG CASING
- STOOL
- APRON
- CHAMFER
- PLINTH BLOCK

WINDOW CASING

DOOR CASING

Victorian Casing

Victorian-style door trim is characterized by the use of symmetrical, rather than tapered, casing, as well as plinth blocks and rosette corner blocks at the juncture of the side and head casing. Fluted or beaded casing can certainly be used, but more common is a style called "bellyband" casing which displays a combination of bead, cove, and ogee profiles. Some home centers offer scaled-down versions of Victorian casing that measure 2⅛ to 3 inches wide, and these are certainly an option. However, true Victorian casing would tend to be made from wider stock, usually 5½ inches wide—and for that you will probably have to look to a specialty millwork supplier or make your own fluted casing.

Corner Blocks. Rosette corner blocks are also available in a variety of configurations and sizes to suit different casing widths. The most common designs are "bullseye" and "sunburst" patterns. These blocks eliminate the need for any mitered molding, and they also provide visual focal points for the door trim. Rosettes are most often square, but there are variations, called head blocks, that are larger, more highly detailed, and either rectangular or of unusual shape, with arched or scalloped tops. In most cases, rosettes and head blocks are fashioned of wood, but true Victorian ornaments were sometimes cast in soft plaster for paint-grade applications. Some suppliers, mostly those located in areas where Victorian homes abound, still offer cast ornamental blocks.

Install the Casing and Blocks. Cut, chamfer, and install the plinth blocks, using the same technique described in "Neo-Classical Casing," page 100. The width of the plinth should equal that of the rosette blocks so that the reveal around the casing is the same at the top and bottom. Next, cut one square end on each piece of side casing, and rest each one on the plinth to mark its finished length. The bottom and inside edges of the rosette block will be mounted in line with the inside faces of the jamb, so mark the end of the casing flush with the face of the head jamb. Cut the casings to length, and nail them in place. Rest the rosette blocks on the top ends of the side casings, and tack them to the wall, but do not drive the nails all the way in. Measure the distance between the blocks, and cut the head casing to length. Slide it in place between the blocks, and nail it to the jamb and wall framing. If necessary, you can pull the nails holding the rosettes and adjust their position to eliminate any gaps at the casing joints.

Installing Victorian Casing

Difficulty Level: Moderate

TOOLS
Hammer • nail set • nail gun and nails (optional) • power miter saw

MATERIALS
Casing stock • plinth blocks • rosette blocks • finishing nails

1 **CUT ONE END** of a length of casing square; then rest that end on top of a plinth block. Mark the top end flush with the inside edge of the head jamb.

2 **TACK THE ROSETTE BLOCKS** in place, resting on the top of the side casings. Leave the nailheads exposed to make adjustment easier.

3 **FIT THE HEAD CASING** between the rosette blocks. You may have to slightly adjust the relative position of casing and blocks to achieve tight joints.

Arts and Crafts Casing

The Arts and Crafts style celebrates simple, strong lines and a distinct lack of elaborate ornamentation, but at the same time, the style allows quite a bit of latitude in the particular trim details that are used. Door and window casings are often fashioned from flat, wide stock that is joined with butt joints. Some of the details of a Neo-Classical treatment can apply to the Arts and Crafts style as well. You could use a small cornice and crosshead strip on the head casing, and a gently molded, tapered profile for side casing is also appropriate. Plinth blocks are not common in this tradition; instead, carry the casing directly to the floor to emphasize the strong vertical lines. Clear wood finishes over a warm brown stain are a trademark of Arts and Crafts interiors.

Classic Arts and Crafts. One of the most characteristic Arts and Crafts details uses 1 1/16-inch-thick stock for the head casing and 3/4-inch-thick stock for side casings. The head casing overhangs the sides both on the face and at the ends, simulating the feeling of post-and-beam construction.

First, lay out the casing reveals on the edges of the door jambs. Rip head and side casing stock to a width of 4 1/2 inches. Make a square cut on one end of each piece of side casing; then hold each one in place to mark its finished length. Mark the location of a joining plate slot in the top end of each piece, and use the plate joiner to cut the slots. Then, nail the side casings to the door frame. Determine the width of the head casing by measuring the distance be-

tween the outer edges of side casings and adding 2 inches for overhangs. Lay out a 5-degree angle at each end, and use the miter saw to cut the head stock to size. Hold the head casing in place at the door frame to mark the joining plate slot locations, keeping the long edge of the casing at the top. Cut the matching plate slots. Apply glue to the slots and plates, and fasten the casing to the jamb and wall.

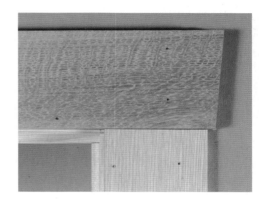

AN ARTS AND CRAFTS design uses simple, flat stock with the head casing overhanging the side casing.

Installing Arts and Crafts Casing

Difficulty Level: Easy

TOOLS
Hammer • nail set • nail gun and nails (optional) • power miter saw • angle gauge

MATERIALS
1-by casing stock • finishing nails • masking or painter's tape

USE AN ANGLE GAUGE to mark a 5-deg. angle on each end of the head casing stock. Use a miter saw to make the cuts. The short point of the angle should overhang each side casing by 3/8 in.

MARK THE LOCATIONS of joining plate centers onto the head casing, transferring them from the previously marked side casing slots. Tape protects wood that will receive a clear finish.

Window Trim

Some aspects of window trim are identical to those on door trim. Casing details, once established for any particular job, are applied equally to both types of opening. However, there are some features of each that are particular. Of course, plinth blocks are only relevant in a discussion of door casing. In similar fashion, window stool, aprons, and extension jambs are particular to window trim. And there is a particular treatment that is an option with windows that does not apply to door openings, and that is the picture-frame casing—casing that surrounds all four sides of the opening.

Before you start to apply trim to a window, you should take a few minutes in preparation. As part of most window installations, shims are placed between the jambs and rough framing to help maintain the position of the unit. Check each of these shims to make sure that they are firmly lodged in place, with nails driven either through the shim or in very close proximity. Make sure that no shims protrude beyond the wall surface. Use a sharp utility knife to

Adding Extension Jambs

Difficulty Level: Moderate

TOOLS
Hammer • nail set • measuring tape • square • drill-driver • power miter saw • table saw

MATERIALS
1-by stock • trim screws • spray foam

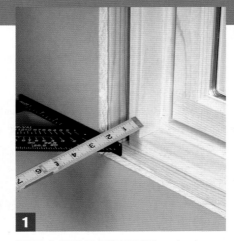

1 USE A STRAIGHTEDGE and ruler to measure the depth of required extension jambs. Check the measurements at several places around the frame, and use the largest dimension.

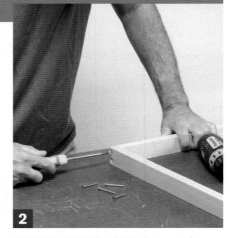

2 IF EXTENSION JAMBS are wider than 1¼ in., it is best to assemble them into a frame before installing them to the window. Drill and countersink pilot holes, and screw the parts together.

3 IF THERE IS NO INSULATION around a window, use nonexpanding foam to fill any gaps before installing the extension jambs. When the foam sets, you can easily cut off any excess.

4 PLACE THE EXTENSION JAMB assembly into the window opening, and align the inside surfaces with the factory window jambs.

5 USE TRIM SCREWS to fasten the extension jamb assembly to the factory window jambs. If you center the screws in the edge of the jambs, the holes will be covered by the casing.

Trim Tip OVERSIZED JAMBS

If the jambs protrude just a bit too far past the wall (⅛ in. or less), you can use a sharp block plane to trim them back. But if the jambs extend farther into the room, it's better to mount the casing and install a filler strip between the back of the casing and the wall to fill the gaps.

Once you determine the width of the extensions, use a table saw to rip them to width. If at all possible, maintain one factory edge on each jamb to minimize edge preparation, and mount that edge facing into the room. Jambs that are less than 1¼ inches wide can be nailed directly to the factory jambs; just drill pilot holes through the stock to keep the nails going straight, and to avoid splitting. If the extensions need to be wider than 1¼ inch, it is best to assemble them into a frame and then use long trim-head screws to fasten the entire assembly to the window. If you are concerned about keeping the extensions perfectly flush to the factory jambs, you have the option of creating a small reveal between the parts.

Troubleshooting. Sometimes, the distance varies between the factory jambs and wall surface at different spots around the perimeter of the window. If the difference is small, less than ⅛-inch, pick the greatest measurement and cut all extensions to that dimension. You can take up that discrepancy with shims and caulk or by skim-coating the wall surface. If the difference in dimension is great, you can plane the strips to follow the wall surface.

score any shim that is too long, and snap off the excess. Many installers stuff fiberglass insulation in the space between the window and framing. This practice is fine as long as the insulation is not overly compressed, which will cause it to become ineffective. As an alternative, you can purchase a can of nonexpanding foam insulation and use it to fill the spaces around the window. If you use the foam, first pry out any fiberglass insulation so the foam can completely fill the cavity.

Extension Jambs

To prepare a window for casing, the first step is to determine whether you will require extension jambs. Because exterior walls are framed at different thicknesses and receive different interior wall treatments, the finished depth of an exterior wall can vary considerably from job to job. Instead of offering windows with different jamb widths, most manufacturers rely on the trim carpenter to adapt the windows to the site by applying extension jambs to the window. Some window companies offer proprietary extension jamb stock that has an interlocking profile, but most allow for site-built extensions; most often ¾-inch clear pine is used, but hardwood extensions could also work.

Establish the Extension Size. Use a small straightedge to measure the distance between the edge of the jambs and the wall surface. Sometimes a window is installed so that it is not perfectly parallel to the wall surface, so check the dimensions at several spots around the window frame and use the largest measurement. Ideally, the jambs should be about 1/16-inch proud of the wall.

WINDOW CASINGS can follow a traditional style or be totally unique.

Stool and Apron

The traditional approach to window trim involves the installation of a wide, horizontal shelf-like member at the bottom of the window. Many people mistakenly refer to this piece as a window sill; however, the correct term is window stool. (Sill refers to the angled exterior portion of the window designed to shed water and snow.) Stools are generally cut from 5/4 stock. You can sometimes purchase dedicated stool stock from a millwork supplier; this material will usually have a molded profile along its front edge, and sometimes an angled rabbet that is designed to sit over the sloped window sill.

However, it is a simple matter to fabricate your own stool stock, either with or without a molded edge, from 5/4 lumber. The stool extends past the window jambs onto the wall surface—these extensions are known as horns. The horns support the side casings, and generally extend about 3/4 inch beyond the casing on both end and face. The gap between the wall surface and the bottom of the stool is covered by a trim piece called an apron.

Add Extensions. If extension jambs are necessary, install them first. Older windows require extensions only on the top and sides as the stool could rest directly on the interior portion of the sill. On newer windows, it is often appropriate to install extension jambs on all four sides of the window—even when a stool will be used. On these windows, the sill only extends to the exterior portion of the window, so the bottom extension provides support for the stool and eliminates the need for separate blocking.

Casing Reveals. Once the extension jambs are in place, lay out the casing reveals. Gauge the eventual position of the outside edge of the side casing by taking a piece of casing stock and holding it on the reveal mark. Place a light mark on the wall surface to indicate the outside edge of the casing; then place another mark 3/4 inch outside that line to indicate the end of the stool. Repeat this process on the opposite side of the window. Measure the distance between those marks on either side of the window to arrive at the overall stool width; then crosscut the stock to length.

Lay Out the Horns. Hold the stool blank against the wall with its ends on the outside gauge marks. Use a square and sharp pencil to mark the locations of the inside surfaces of window jambs on the stool. Then, measure the distance between the stool and the window sash. In some cases, the distance may be different at each end of the sash. In these situations, use the larger measurement and plane the leading edge of the stool to fit later.

The ends of the stool that project beyond the sides of the window and onto the wall surface are called the horns. Use a square to extend your measurement marks onto the stool surface to indicate the cuts for the horns. Calculate the overall depth of the stool by adding the casing thickness plus 3/4 inch to the horn layout line.

Trim the Horn. Use the table saw to rip the stool to the desired width. Next, use a hand saw or jig saw to make the cutouts for the horns. Test the fit of the stool in the opening. On some windows, you will need to make further notches and rabbet cuts to accommodate window stop and specialized weather-stripping. The horns of the stool should sit tight to the wall surface and there should be a

THE HORNS of a window stool extend beyond the casing.

Installing a Stool and Apron

Difficulty Level: **Challenging**

TOOLS
Basic carpentry tools • saber saw • router and bits • power miter saw • table saw • nailing gun and nails (optional)

MATERIALS
5/4 sill stock • casing and apron stock • rosette blocks • finishing nails • wood glue

1

ALIGN A PIECE of casing with the reveal mark on window jambs, and mark its outside edge on the wall. Place another mark 3/4 in. away to indicate the end of the window stool.

2

HOLD STOOL STOCK in place against the window, and use a square and sharp pencil to mark the inside dimensions of the window jambs onto the stool surface.

3

USE A COMBINATION SQUARE to gauge the depth of the notch for the horns on the window stool.

4

HOLD THE BODY of the combination square against the edge of window stool stock; then run a pencil along the end of the blade to lay out the cutout for the stool horns.

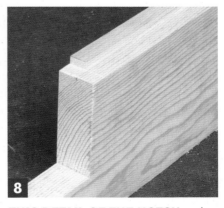

5

PLACE A PIECE of casing stock along the horn cutout line, and lightly mark along its front face. Add 3/4 in. to this dimension to determine the overall width of the window stool.

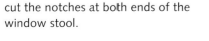

6

USE A SABER SAW or handsaw to cut the notches at both ends of the window stool.

7

PLACE THE STOOL BLANK in the window opening to mark any additional notches required to fit around window stops. Some windows may require a rabbet.

8

THIS DETAIL OF THE NOTCH and rabbet on the edge of the window stool accommodates the jamb and a stop.

Continued on next page.

Continued from previous page.

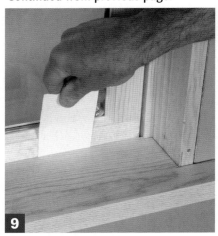

9 **TO AVOID ANY BINDING** between window sash and stool, you need to provide a gap of about ⅟₃₂ in. Use cardboard to test the gap. If necessary, trim the leading edge of the stool.

10 **SHAPE THE INSIDE EDGE** and ends of a window stool with a router and bit of your choice. It is most common to use roundover, chamfer, or ogee profiles for this part.

11 **USE 8D FINISHING NAILS** to fasten the stool to the window jamb or sill. If necessary, place shims beneath the stool to keep it level.

15 **CUT HEAD CASING STOCK** to length—it should fit snugly between the rosette blocks. Nail it to the head jamb and window header.

16 **CUT MITERED RETURNS** on the ends of apron molding stock. Apply glue to both surfaces of each miter joint before assembling the parts.

17 **IF NECESSARY,** use a sharp block plane to trim the top edge of the apron so that it fits tight to the stool. You can also drive nails through the stool into the top edge of the apron.

---

uniform gap between the sash and the stool of about ⅟₃₂ inch. You can easily gauge the gap by slipping a piece of cardboard between the sash and stool. Use a sharp block plane to adjust the fit of the stool against the sash.

Shape the Edge. Use a router to shape the desired profile along the front edge and ends of the stool. It is perfectly acceptable to use a roundover, chamfer, or ogee profile for the stool. Just select a shape that works well with the casing of the windows. If you are not comfortable cutting a profile on the relatively narrow end of the stool, you can always create a mitered return to carry the profile back to the wall

surface. And if you prefer a simpler treatment, just use a sanding block to ease the sharp edges of the stool.

Install the Stool. Place the stool in the opening, and place shims under it, if necessary, to adjust its position. The stool should be level, so use a spirit level to check it. Then, fasten the stool to the sill or bottom jamb with 8d finishing nails. It is also a good idea to nail through the horns of the sill into the wall framing, but if you do so, be sure to first drill pilot holes for the nails.

Apply the desired casing to the sides and head jamb, following the methods discussed for door trim. The casing

12

DRILL PILOT HOLES through the edge of the horns before driving 8d or 10d finishing nails to fasten the stool to the wall framing.

13

FOR A VICTORIAN-STYLE CASING, make a square cut on each side casing blank, and rest the cut on the stool to mark its length. It should be flush with the under side of the head jamb.

14

PLACE A ROSETTE HEAD BLOCK in place so that it overhangs the side casing evenly on each side. The inside corner of the block should be flush to the inside corner of the window jambs.

should rest firmly on the stool, but otherwise, the treatment is the same whether a window or door is involved.

The stock for the apron can be the same as that used for the window casing, or you can use an entirely different profile or a combination of two or more moldings. The overall length of the apron should be the same as the distance between the outside edges of the side casings—generally 1½ inches shorter than the stool. If you use flat stock for the apron, you can simply cut it to length with square cuts at the ends. If you choose profiled stock, you should cut mitered returns on the ends to continue the profile back to the wall. Hold the apron in place, and check that it fits tightly to the bottom side of the stool. If the stool is not perfectly flat or if the apron stock is not perfectly straight, it may be necessary to plane the top edge of the apron so that there is no gap between the parts. Fasten the apron to the wall using 8d finishing nails; then drive two or three nails through the stool into the top edge of the apron to lock stool and apron together.

Window Casing Assembly

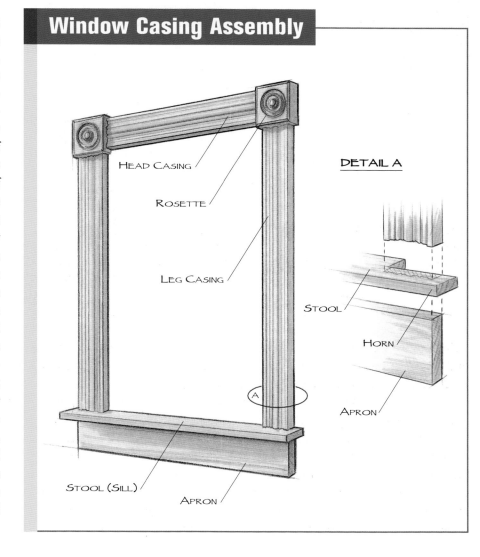

HEAD CASING

ROSETTE

LEG CASING

STOOL (SILL)

APRON

DETAIL A

STOOL

HORN

APRON

A

Troubleshooting Casing Problems

Trimwork can be challenging when everything goes according to plan, but especially so when problems arise. Unfortunately, it is relatively rare that all parts of an installation proceed without running into something unexpected, so it's good to be prepared for those situations.

Most problems with casing arise from a limited universe of causes. And although it can be tempting to lay blame on the shoulders of an errant drywall installer or previous carpenter, a problem with trim can be the result of a relatively innocent combination of small discrepancies, or oversights, that are not considered critical at that prior stage of the job. For example, a framing carpenter might reasonably assume that a small hump in wall framing would be absorbed and nullified by the drywall sheathing. Or a drywall finisher could be more concerned with creating a smooth taped joint than with the later effects of the resultant swelling in the wall surface. Of course, there is always a case when some door or window installer loses their concentration, and as a result,

Fixing Bulging Drywall

Difficulty Level: **Easy**

TOOLS
Surform or abrasive tool

MATERIALS
Casing stock

1

HOLD A PIECE OF CASING in position, and make a light pencil mark along the outside edge over the high spot. Work inside the line.

2

USE A SURFORM or similar abrasive tool to grind down the drywall surface until it is flush to the jamb.

Fixing Open Miter Joints

Difficulty Level: **Easy**

TOOLS
Hammer • nail set • block plane • caulking gun

MATERIALS
Casing stock • caulk • shims • finishing nails

1

A JAMB that protudes past the wall surface can cause an open miter joint. Be sure the joint will close by planing a back-bevel on each half of the miter.

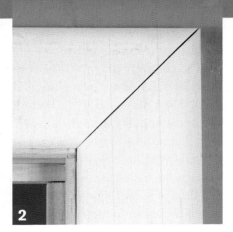

2

IF YOU STILL SEE A GAP after installing the casing, you'll need to shim the back of the casing.

the jamb does not line up properly with a wall surface. Regardless of the cause, it is important to remember that trim is the place where all problems start to surface and become visible, so learn to accept those conditions as a natural part of the process.

Bulging Drywall

It is relatively common to encounter a situation where the drywall surface has a hump, or high spot, adjacent to a door opening. This can be the result of bowed framing lumber or too much joint compound. In either case, the easiest way to remedy the situation is to grind the drywall down so that it is flush to the edge of the jamb.

Smooth the Surface. First hold a piece of casing in place, and mark the location of the outside edge so you do not damage an exposed wall surface. Then use a Surform tool or other abrasive tool to abrade the drywall surface until it is flush with the jamb. Test your progress frequently with a straightedge so that you do not remove too much material. If you inadvertently damage the adjacent drywall, either lightly sand the surface or apply a skim coat of new drywall compound to repair the damaged area.

Using Filler Strips

Difficulty Level: **Easy**

TOOLS
Table saw • hammer • nail set • nail gun and nails (optional)

MATERIALS
Filler material • finishing nails

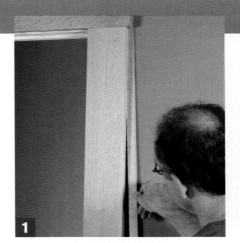

1 WHEN A JAMB PROTRUDES beyond the wall surface. Slide filler strips between the casing and wall until the edges are flush.

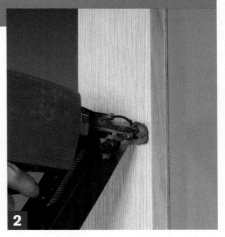

2 DRIVE NAILS through both the casing and filler strips to lock them in place. A pneumatic nail gun eliminates the need to drill pilot holes.

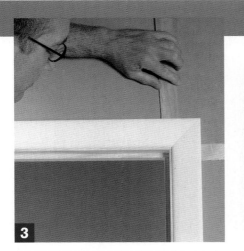

3 CAREFULLY PLACE SHIMS behind the upper portion of each casing leg to help close the miter joint. Cut away the excess shims.

4 USE A GOOD GRADE of latex painter's caulk to fill the gap between the back side of the casing and the wall surface.

Protruding Jambs

Where a doorjamb extends beyond a wall surface, you may need to place shims between the back side of the casing and wall. Some tapered casing can be nailed to the wall, but you may have to plane a bevel on the face of the miter. Or you may have to do both.

When your casing includes a backband, the strip can often cover the gap. If no backband is used and the gap is uniform in size, you can apply a filler strip behind the casing to fill the gap. If all else fails, you can caulk or apply a thin coat of drywall compound to the wall to bring the surface flush to the edge of the jamb.

DESIGN IDEAS: **CASING**

NATURAL WOOD, knots and all, creates a rustic-looking trimwork package, left.

SELECT CASING, above, that is in harmony with other trimwork elements.

CUSTOM TREATMENTS, below, can turn a window or door into the focal point of a room.

ROSETTE CORNER BLOCKS, opposite left, are popular elements in Victorian-style trimwork.

PAINTED CASING, opposite right, can complement the color scheme of a room.

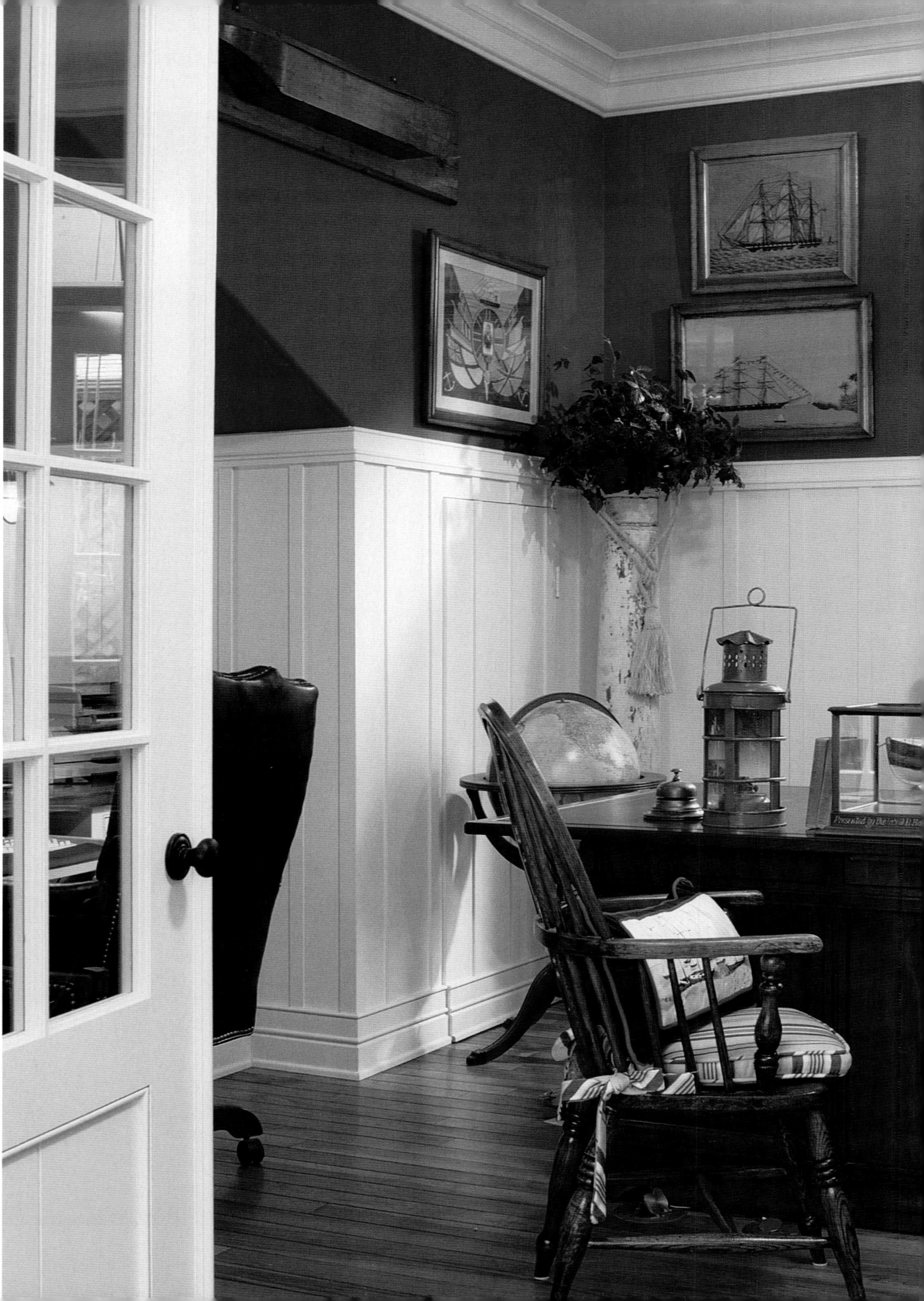

CHAPTER 5

TRIMWORK FOR
WALLS

T he walls of your home provide the opportunity to install a number of trimwork treatments, including baseboards, chair rails, wainscoting, and wall frames. Many wall treatments have their origins in practical uses—for example, chair rails were first installed to keep the backs of chairs from damaging wall finishes. A good chair rail can still fulfill that function, but today chair rails are installed more for their decorative qualities than their original use. Other elements, such as wainscoting, will occupy a great deal of space and make a definite design statement, so it is important that the design you choose complements the overall design of the house as well as the other trimwork used throughout the home.

Baseboard

Baseboard trim includes a variety of board and molding applications to the bottom of a wall. The trim serves a practical purpose in that it covers the inevitable gap between the wall surface and floor, but it also serves a design function in that it provides a strong visual line around the base of a room and acts as the foundation for the rest of the trim. Of course, the decision as to what type of baseboard you will use is tied into the trim motif of the room as a whole. Certain base treatments are more appropriate with some trim styles than others, but a few different options provide an adequate selection for most situations. If your trim package is based on stock molding profiles, there is simple, one-piece baseboard stock available. But if you are committed to a style that features wider, more complex moldings, the baseboard trim should be of taller, heavier stock—usually a three-piece assembly. Keep in mind that specialty millwork suppliers can offer a wide variety of base profiles that you otherwise will not find. So, to expand your options or just to be inspired, it is worth exploring these resources.

One-Piece Baseboard

Most lumberyards and home centers offer baseboard moldings in two different styles to match their stock casings—colonial and ranch (also called "clam-shell"). The height of these moldings can run from 3 to 5½ inches, and most are about ½ inch thick. Select a profile and size that is compatible with the rest of the trim details in the room. If the floor is to be carpeted, the simple baseboard is all you will require. But for a tile or hardwood floor, you should also plan to install a flexible shoe molding to cover inevitable gaps between the different materials.

Built-up Baseboard

Most traditional trim styles feature a three-piece baseboard assembly consisting of a flat or molded base, a decorative cap molding, and flexible shoe molding. Some elaborate styles add additional layers or embellishments to the mix, but once you understand the basic principles and techniques for the installation, you can add or subtract elements to suit your taste.

Baseboard Height. The height of the baseboard trim should be in proportion to the trim in the rest of the room, but it should relate to the size and height of the room as well. A room with 8-foot-high ceilings can accept a baseboard that is 5 inches high, but a room with 9- or 10-foot ceilings needs a more substantial base—perhaps one that is 8 or 9 inches high. If you are in doubt as to the appropriate height of the molding, cut some scrap stock to various dimensions, and place it on the floor in the room to better judge the proportions.

Covering Mistakes. Even though the central portion of a built-up baseboard is relatively rigid, the layered construction provides a means for accommodating irregularities in both the wall and floor surfaces. Both the cap molding and shoe molding are flexible enough to conform to slight dips and humps so that most gaps can be eliminated.

DETAIL OF ONE-PIECE BASE TRIM with stock Colonial door casing.

DETAIL OF THREE-PIECE BASE TRIM with traditional casing.

USE A LONG STRAIGHT 2x4 with a 4-ft. level to check that the floor in the room is level. As long as any difference is less than ¼ in. across the length of a room, you really do not need to make any adjustment. If the problem is severe, scribe the bottom edge of the baseboard to absorb the difference.

IT'S COMMON TO FIND A BUILDUP of excess drywall compound around the base of a wall or on the adjacent floor. Check the perimeter of the room, and use a putty knife to scrape off any offending pieces that might interfere with the base trim.

Evaluate Room Conditions

In most situations, baseboard can be laid with its bottom edge parallel to the existing floor. But in those situations where a floor is dramatically out of level—say by more than ½ inch in a 12-foot span—you should make an effort to install the base level. The alternative would leave you feeling as if you are walking into a fun house when you enter the room. So start by checking along each wall to see if the floor is level.

Check for Level. Select a long straight 2×4, just shy of the length of the wall, and lay it on edge in front of the wall. Place a spirit level on the top edge. If necessary, place a shim under one end of the board to bring the bubble to the center of the vial; then measure the height of the shim required. If the difference is considerable, make a notation on the wall of the amount of correction required so that you can make the adjustment during fitting and installation.

Clean Up Drywall. On newly drywalled walls, it is common to find a buildup of drywall compound around the base of the wall. Make a careful examination of the wall condition, and use a putty knife to scrape any lumps from either the wall or floor surface. Inside corners are a particularly troublesome spot in this regard, as it is difficult to finish the bottom of a corner joint without the compound trailing off into the room. Excess compound can prevent the base trim from extending fully into the corner, so scrape or sand those areas to leave a clean, plumb surface.

A MULTIPIECE BASE MOLDING can be a strong design element in a room, yet it is easy to install.

Plan the Installation. To make your job proceed as efficiently as possible, you should plan the order of installation of the baseboard pieces. The inside corners of each baseboard element need to be coped to provide tight joints, and you should minimize those situations that demand coped joints on both ends of a single piece of stock. To that end, make a simple map of each room with the order of installation noted and with the type of cut required—butt, miter, scarf, and cope. By planning ahead, your installation will go smoothly and you will end up with the neatest job.

If your room is to receive wall-to-wall carpet, it is customary to raise the baseboard up from the subfloor about ½ inch to allow the carpet installer to tuck the ends under the trim. In these situations, a shoe molding is not required, as the nap of the carpet covers any gaps caused by small dips in the floor. Cut blocks of ½-inch-thick stock (small pieces of colonial or ranch base work well) to use as temporary spacers under the baseboard. Simply place them around the room and rest the trim on them when nailing to the wall.

Base trim needs to be nailed to the wall framing. A wide baseboard is fastened with a nail driven into each wall stud and similarly spaced nails driven into the bottom plate of the wall. While typical framing dictates that there is a stud every 16 inches along a wall, this is sometimes not the case. It can save you considerable time and frustration by locating the wall studs before starting the installation. Use an electronic stud finder to scan each wall at baseboard height, and make a light pencil mark on the wall or floor to indicate stud centers. If you are working with finished wall or floor surfaces, you can place a piece of masking tape on either surface to receive the pencil marks.

TO AVOID UNNECESSARY MARKS on a finished wall surface, place a strip of masking tape on the wall just above the baseboard height to mark stud locations. Use an electronic stud finder to locate framing members.

Suggested Cutting Sequences

Rectangular Room

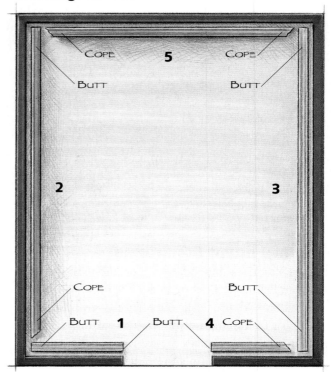

L-Shaped Room

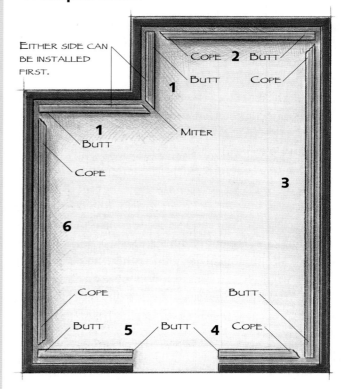

Room with Scarf Joints

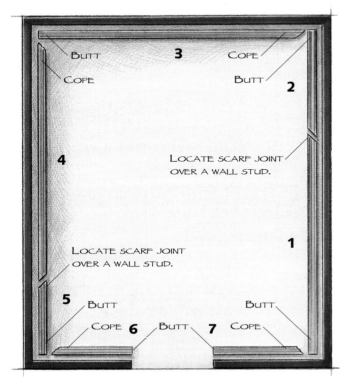

Butt
Cope
3
Cope
Butt
2
4
Locate scarf joint over a wall stud.
1
Locate scarf joint over a wall stud.
5
Butt
Cope
6
Butt
7
Butt
Cope

Room with Bay Window

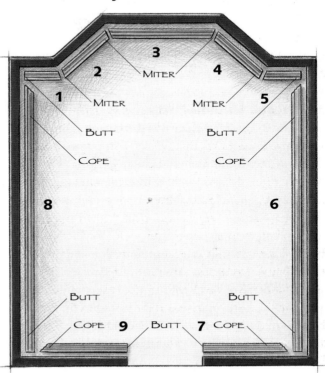

3
Miter
2
4
1
Miter
Miter
5
Butt
Butt
Cope
Cope
8
6
Butt
Butt
Cope
9
Butt
7
Cope

Double L-Shaped Room

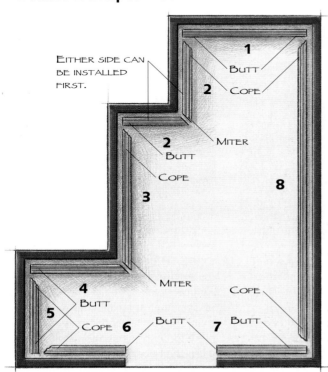

1
Butt
Cope
2
Either side can be installed first.
2
Miter
Butt
Cope
3
8
Miter
4
Butt
Cope
5
Cope
6
Butt
7
Cope
Butt

Room with Alcove

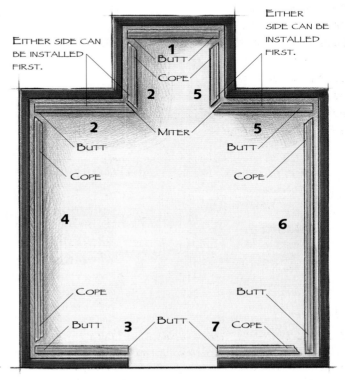

Either side can be installed first.
Either side can be installed first.
1
Butt
Cope
2
5
Miter
2
Butt
Cope
5
Butt
Cope
4
6
Cope
Butt
3
Butt
7
Cope

5

TRIMWORK FOR WALLS

Trim Tip BASEBOARD BEFORE FINISH FLOORING

A finished hardwood or tile floor can be installed either before or after the baseboard. If the baseboard will precede the floor, use small blocks of the finished floor material as spacers under the baseboard. Place an additional layer of cardboard on top of each of these spacers to provide a small margin so that the flooring can easily slip under the wall trim. The base shoe will hide any gaps between the trimwork and the floor.

Baseboard Installation

Because a one-piece baseboard is the default approach, it makes sense to start with that type of installation. It is typical to begin with the longest closed wall in a room. Of course, there are situations where this will not be appropriate, but as a general rule this is a good approach. (See "Suggested Cutting Sequences," page 120.) Professional carpenters often cut all baseboards for a room at one time, but for the amateur this can cause confusion and opens up the possibility of badly cut joints or wasted material.

The first piece of baseboard can butt squarely into the wall surface on both ends, so it is the easiest to fit. Measure the length of the wall, at baseboard height, and add 1/16 inch to that measurement. (See "Cutting Baseboard to Length," opposite.) Place the baseboard into position, and fasten it to the wall by driving a nail into each stud and one near each stud into the wall plate. If you use a pneumatic nail gun for installing the trim, the nails will automatically be set as they are driven. But if you nail by hand, you should set the nails as you finish nailing each piece of molding. If you wait until the entire room is finished to set the nails, you could cause gaps to open in some coped joints by driving one of the pieces further toward the wall surface.

Inside Corner Joints

Cut a piece of stock to about 2 inches longer than finished dimension for the next piece of baseboard. Use a miter saw to cut an open 45-degree bevel cut on the end that will receive the coped joint. (See "Coped Joints," page 56.) An open bevel has its long point on the back surface of the stock, and it exposes the profile of the molded surface. Use a coping saw to cut along the exposed profile, keeping the saw blade angled to provide a back-cut or clearance angle that is slightly greater than 90 degrees.

Installing an Inside Corner

Difficulty Level: Moderate

TOOLS
Hammer • nail set • nail gun and nails (optional) • power miter saw • files or rasps

MATERIALS
Baseboard molding • finishing nails • shim stock

AT INSIDE CORNERS, cut a square end on the first piece of baseboard and run it into the drywall corner. Because only the top portion of the molding will be visible, it does not need to be tight along its entire height. Note the use of a piece of finished flooring and cardboard as a spacer beneath the baseboard.

COPE THE END of the second piece for an inside corner joint. Test the fit. An open joint can be the result of one of a number of factors, including a wall that is not perfectly flat or straight, a piece of debris behind the molding, or a less than perfect coping job. Use a knife, rasp, file, or sandpaper to make the necessary adjustments.

CUTTING BASEBOARD TO LENGTH

Whenever you cut a piece of baseboard, it is a good practice to add an extra $\frac{1}{16}$ inch to the length to ensure a tight fit and to allow you some room to adjust the joint. When fitting a piece of base between two surfaces, an extra $\frac{1}{16}$ inch allows you to spring the molding into position, pushing the end joint closed. And when fitting an outside corner joint, the extra length gives you the opportunity to work toward a tight fit—something that does not always come automatically, especially in corners that are not perfectly square. Remember that some fitting and recutting is an expected part of trim installation.

Place the molding against the wall, and test the fit of the coped joint. If the molding is to fit against another inside wall, you will need to slightly angle the opposite end toward the center of the room to test the joint. Use a combination of knife, rasp, and file to adjust the coped profile until you have a tight fit. It is common for baseboard to be slightly tipped from a perfectly vertical plane, and when this occurs, you will need to modify the coped profile to adapt to whatever situation exists. This is often a matter of making a series of small modifications until a proper fit is achieved, so be prepared to exercise your patience and attention to detail. Once you are satisfied with the fit of the joint, measure the length of the piece, from the face of the existing molding to the opposite wall, add $\frac{1}{16}$ inch and cut the molding to length.

3

COMPLETED INSIDE CORNER JOINT on one-piece baseboard. It is not unusual for a joint to require some modification to close tightly.

COPED INSIDE CORNERS help ensure that changes in humidity or building movement will not cause the trimwork to separate and show gaps at the corner.

5

TRIMWORK FOR WALLS

Outside Corner Joints

On outside corners, the first step is to determine the angle of the corner. Drywall is not a precision material, and the combination of corner bead and layers of drywall compound can create corners that are either greater or less than 90 degrees. For this it is handy to have some scrap baseboard stock that you can use as test pieces. Of course, you can try to use an angle gauge to determine the angle of an outside corner, but these are usually too small to get an accurate reading.

Determine the Angle. Cut two pieces of scrap 1×6 stock, each about 18 inches long. Make a 45-degree bevel cut on the end of each piece, and test the fit of the parts on the corner. If the joint is open at the outside, slightly increase the angle of the cut; if it is open at the wall, try a slightly reduced angle. After just a few joints you will learn the amount of adjustment required to make a joint fit. Note that it is important that both pieces of a miter joint have the identical angle. Resist the temptation to cut one piece at a steeper angle than the other, as the result is that one piece of molding will protrude farther at the corner. The only remedy would then be to sand off the excess, leaving end grain visible at the joint.

Install the Molding. Once you are satisfied with the test joint, hold the molding stock against the wall, and place pencil marks on the floor (or on masking tape) to indicate the outside surface of the molding. You can then use those marks to directly scribe the long point of the miters on the baseboard stock. First fit the opposite end of the baseboard to its appropriate joint and hold it in place. Keep pressure on that joint while you mark the long point of the miter on the outside corner joint; then cut the joint to the previously determined angle. Cut the second half of the mitered corner using the same technique. Nail the first piece to the wall; then apply glue to the mating surfaces of the miter joint and use two 4d finishing nails or brads to pin the joint together. If you are nailing by hand, drill small pilot holes for the nails at the corner joint so the stock does not split—splits are much less likely when using a pneumatic nail gun. Note: for multipiece installations, record the actual angle of the outside corner so that you can use it for cutting the cap and shoe molding without additional trial and error.

Installing an Outside Corner Joint

Difficulty Level: **Easy**

TOOLS
Hammer • nail set • nail gun and nails (optional) • power miter saw

MATERIALS
Baseboard molding • 4d finishing nails • glue • masking or painter's tape • shim stock

1

TEST THE ANGLE of outside corners with two pieces of scrap 1x6 stock. Cut a 45-deg. bevel on each piece, and hold them together around the corner. If the joint is not tight, modify the cuts until you achieve a perfect fit.

FIGURING CORNER ANGLES

While testing an outside corner with test blocks is an efficient method of determining a workable miter angle, there is also a direct approach involving elementary geometry. Fit a sliding bevel gauge around the outside corner, and position it so that it the legs are snug to the wall surface. Take the gauge and trace the angle onto a piece of scrap lumber or stiff cardboard. Next, place the point of a compass at the apex of the angle, and scribe an equal distance along each leg of the angle. Reposition the point of the compass at each of these marks and, using the same distance setting, scribe two new intersecting arcs. Draw a line from the apex of the angle through the intersecting point to indicate ½ of the original angle. You can then use an angle gauge to measure the resulting angle, and set your miter saw accordingly.

Difficulty Level: **Easy**

TOOLS
Sliding bevel gauge • compass • straightedge • angle gauge

MATERIALS
Stiff cardboard

2

PLACE MASKING TAPE STRIPS on the floor around the corner; then mark along the outside face of the baseboard. Hold stock for each side of the joint in place; use these lines to mark the long point of each miter.

3

FOR AN OUTSIDE CORNER, cut and test the fit of the joint before nailing either piece in place. When you are satisfied with the joint, nail the first piece of baseboard to the wall.

4

APPLY GLUE to the surfaces of the miter joint, and place the second piece in position. Make sure that the joint comes together tightly before nailing it to the wall. Use 4d finishing nails or brads to pin the joint together.

1

TRANSFER THE ANGLE (left). Place a compass at the apex of the angle, and scribe an arc along each leg (right).

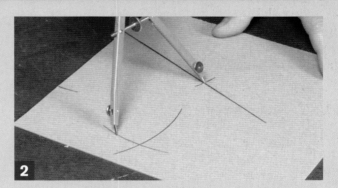

2

REPOSITION THE COMPASS at each of these intersecting marks, and scribe two new intersecting arcs.

3

DRAW A LINE connecting the intersection of the new arcs with the apex of the original angle.

4

USE AN ANGLE GAUGE to measure the resulting angle. Use that setting on the miter saw to cut the joint.

Dealing with Out-of-Level Floors

There are times when a floor is so far from level that you need to adjust the baseboard to accommodate the condition. You might also find that a run of floor has an unusual hump or dip in the surface that is too large to ignore. Small gaps between the floor and baseboard are typically covered by a flexible shoe molding, but extreme cases require that you scribe the molding to fit the contour of the floor.

First cut the baseboard to length, with appropriate joints at either end. Then place shims under the trim piece to support it in position with the top edge level. Set your scribers to a dimension equal to the largest shim dimension, and run the tool along the floor surface to mark a contour line along the face of the baseboard. Use a sharp plane or jig saw to remove stock up to the scribed line. Keep in mind that because you will install shoe molding, a ⅛- to ⅜-inch gap is perfectly acceptable. Remember, if you need to remove stock at the end of a run of baseboard, the adjacent piece will also need to be adjusted so that their top edges will align.

Three-Piece Base Trim

Using built-up base trim gives you the opportunity to personalize and customize the base treatment. In its simplest

IF THE FLOOR is dramatically out of level, you should scribe the baseboard to absorb the discrepancy. Place shims beneath the baseboard to bring it level; then use a scriber to mark the bottom face of the board for the required adjustment.

incarnation, three-piece trim involves a flat baseboard with added cap and shoe molding. The height of the baseboard and particular profile of the cap molding are yours to decide. You can shape the edge of the baseboard to a rounded or chamfered profile, or leave it square.

The heart of a simple three-piece base is ¾-inch flat stock. If you leave the outside edge of the stock square, there is no need to cope the inside corner joints. Simply run the pieces tightly together with butt joints at each inside corner. If you decide to shape a rounded or chamfered edge on the stock, use the router to mill all of the material at one time. Then treat the inside corners as you would any shaped molding, with coped joints.

Cap Molding. Once you have the initial baseboard installed around the room, you can move to the cap molding. Follow the same order of installation that you used for the baseboard, using butt, coped, and mitered joints as necessary. If you need to construct a scarf joint, make sure that the joint does not fall directly over a similar joint in the baseboard.

Shoe Molding. Wait to install the shoe molding until the finished floor surface is installed. As with the cap molding, you can either use another stock profile or fabricate your own molding. Just keep in mind that the molding should be flexible enough to conform to minor irregularities in the floor surface. Use coped joints at the inside corners and miter joints for outside corners. When the shoe molding approaches a casing, plinth block, or wall register, the normal treatment is to cut a partially open 45-degree miter on the end of the molding. Always nail shoe molding to the baseboard, not to the finished floor material.

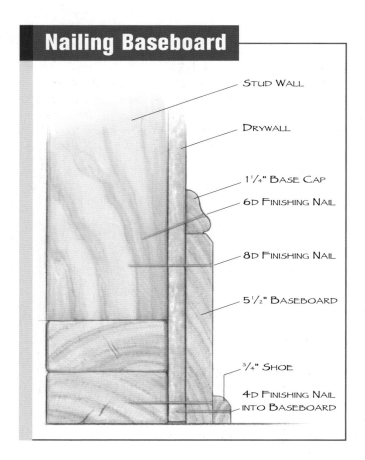

Nailing Baseboard

STUD WALL

DRYWALL

1¼" BASE CAP

6D FINISHING NAIL

8D FINISHING NAIL

5½" BASEBOARD

¾" SHOE

4D FINISHING NAIL INTO BASEBOARD

Installing Three-Piece Base Trim

Difficulty Level: Moderate

TOOLS
Hammer • nail set • nail gun and nails (optional) • power miter saw • coping saw

MATERIALS
Baseboard molding • finishing nails • glue • shim stock

1 FOR SQUARE STOCK, use butt joints for inside corner joints. Fit the first piece, and nail it in place. Cut the second piece a few inches long, and test the fit before cutting to length.

2 ONCE THE FLAT BASEBOARD molding is installed, you can move on to the cap molding. Nail the cap to the wall studs, angling the nails to draw the cap down tightly to the baseboard.

3 AT INSIDE CORNERS, cut a coped joint on the second piece of cap molding. Test each joint, and make necessary adjustments with knife, rasp, or sandpaper until you achieve a tight fit.

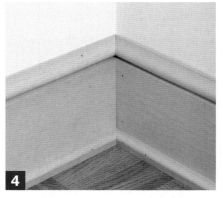

4 FINISHED INSIDE CORNER JOINT of three-piece base trim. Both cap molding and shoe molding require coped joints at an inside corner.

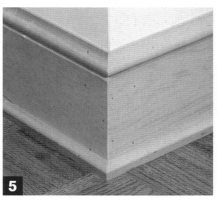

5 FINISHED OUTSIDE CORNER JOINT of three-piece base trim. Apply a small amount of glue to the surfaces of miter joints before nailing the molding to the wall.

6 WHEN A SHOE MOLDING ends at a plinth block, hold the shoe molding against the block, and place a pencil mark on the end to indicate the exposed portion of the molding.

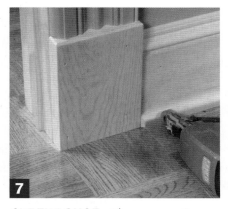

7 CUT THE SHOE with an open miter that leaves the layout line in place. Nail the shoe molding to the baseboard using 4d finishing nails. Make sure that you don't nail the molding to the flooring.

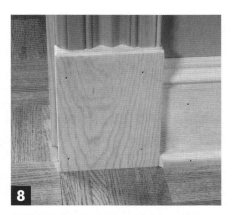

8 DETAIL OF THREE-PIECE BASE TRIM intersection with a Victorian casing and a plinth block. Three-piece base trim complements a number of trimwork styles.

Electrical Receptacles in Baseboard

Difficulty Level: Easy

TOOLS
Drywall saw • power drill and bit • saber saw • screwdriver

MATERIALS
Electrical box for template • pan-head screws

1

CUT BASEBOARD STOCK to length, and lay it on the floor in front of the wall. Transfer the position of each electrical cable to the baseboard, indicating the center of each electrical outlet.

2

CENTER each outlet box vertically on the baseboard stock, and trace around the box to mark the cutout required. Remember to leave stock to support the "ears" that hold the box in place.

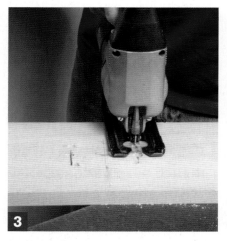

3

DRILL HOLES to start, and use a saber saw to make cutouts for electrical boxes. Keep the saw kerf just to the outside of the layout lines to provide a margin of adjustment.

4

MOUNT THE ELECTRICAL BOXES to the baseboard with small pan-head screws. Feed the electrical cable into each box; push the boxes into the previously cut holes in the wall surface.

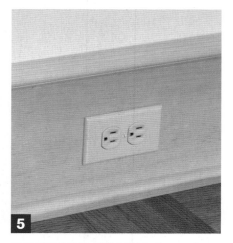

5

COMPLETED OUTLET in three-piece base trim. Some local codes require a licensed electrician make all electrical connections.

Working around Electrical Receptacles

When the height of your base trim is less than 6 inches, it is unlikely that the placement of electrical outlets will be a problem. However, taller baseboards sometimes interfere with the placement of outlets. As part of your trim project, you might also want to move existing outlets to provide uninterrupted wall space for other decorative treatments. In either case, a wide baseboard provides an excellent location to mount these outlets while maintaining their accessibility and keeping them somewhat inconspicuous.

Plan the Wiring. First, consult with your electrician to determine the difficulty of running wire to your planned outlet locations. Locate the outlets so that they fall between wall studs; that way, there will be no interference in placing the boxes. The leads of the outlet wires should be left protruding from the wall surface close to the floor. It is always a good idea to have a bit of extra wire at each outlet location to make installation easier. Make sure that the circuit to which these wires are connected is turned off until the installation is complete.

CORNER AND PLINTH BLOCKS

If you find the prospect of cutting all those coped and mitered joints less than appealing, there is an alternative approach to base trim. You can install corner blocks at either inside or outside corners and simply let the base trim end squarely against the blocks. Some millwork houses manufacture blocks designed for just this purpose, most often as part of a trim package with matching baseboard; these tend to have decoratively molded tops. However, you can certainly fabricate your own blocks if you cannot find some that you like. Blocks that are designed for outside corners should have an L-shaped cross section to wrap around both wall surfaces, while those for inside corners can be square. In all cases, the thickness of a corner block should exceed that of the base trim so that it provides a neat, finished look at the joint.

Cutting Jig for Plinth and Corner Blocks. When door trim includes plinth blocks at the base of the casing, the baseboard simply is cut to butt tightly to the block. Sometimes a plinth block can be installed so that its edges are not perfectly plumb. In this case you need to scribe the end of the baseboard to fit the angle of the block. A simple jig can be used to mark the angle. Cut a slot in a piece of scrap stock wide and tall enough to slip over the baseboard molding. Hold the length of baseboard in position so that its long end runs past the plinth block. Slide the marking jig over the base, and hold it tight to the side of the plinth. Then run your pencil along the outer edge of the jig to mark the angle on the baseboard. The same technique can be also be used to mark the intersection of a corner block and baseboard trim.

Outside Corner Block

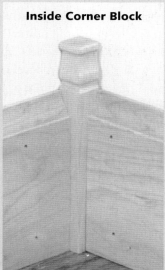

Inside Corner Block

A PLUMB COMMERCIAL PLINTH BLOCK fits tightly against colonial-style casing.

USE A MARKING JIG to scribe the length of baseboard at a plinth or corner block.

Plan for the Receptacle. Cut a piece of baseboard to length and lay it in front of the wall. Mark the center location of the outlet wires as they protrude from the wall, and then use an outlet box as a template to trace the required cutouts onto the baseboard. All outlets should be at a uniform height above the floor. Drill starter holes at the corners of each cutout, and then use a jig saw to make the cuts. Test the fit of the test box in each cutout. Also make sure that you have a clearance notch at the ends of the cutout for the outlet mounting screws.

Place the baseboard against the wall, and allow the electrical leads to extend through each hole. Trace the outline of each outlet opening onto the wall surface, and then remove the base and use a drywall saw to cut a clearance hole in the wallboard. Make each hole slightly larger than the outline.

Mount the electrical boxes to the baseboard. Hold the baseboard in front of the wall, and feed the electrical cables into the boxes before you fit the boxes into the openings in the drywall. Nail the baseboard to the wall before mounting the outlets to the boxes.

Working Around Wall Registers

Wall registers can present a challenge when installing baseboard trim. If you are installing a simple one-piece colonial or ranch-style baseboard and the register cover is of the flat style, the easiest option is to stop the baseboard on either side of the register cover. In this type of treatment, make a 45-degree open bevel cut at the end of the baseboard so that the long point of the bevel just tucks behind the cover. If you need to apply a shoe molding, cut a similar open miter and install it so that the long point of its bevel aligns with the short point of the baseboard bevel.

Protruding Registers. If your register cover is the type that protrudes from the wall, you can simply make a square cut at the ends of the base and shoe molding and let them die neatly against the sides of the register.

The most elegant option when dealing with a register cover is to carry the base trim around the sides and top of the plate, as shown in the examples below. These methods convey a sense of intention and treat the grille as a decorative feature rather than as an inconvenient annoyance.

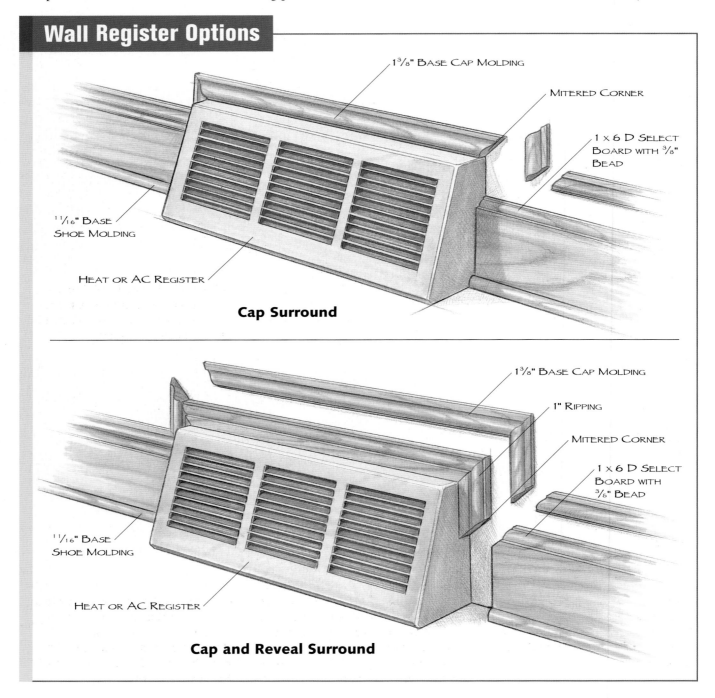

Wall Register Options

1 3/8" BASE CAP MOLDING

MITERED CORNER

1 x 6 D SELECT BOARD WITH 3/8" BEAD

1 1/16" BASE SHOE MOLDING

HEAT OR AC REGISTER

Cap Surround

1 3/8" BASE CAP MOLDING

1" RIPPING

MITERED CORNER

1 x 6 D SELECT BOARD WITH 3/8" BEAD

1 1/16" BASE SHOE MOLDING

HEAT OR AC REGISTER

Cap and Reveal Surround

Base Trim and Stair Stringers

Another spot that requires special attention is the intersection of base trim with the top and bottom ends of a stair stringer. This condition presents a number of options, depending on the particular stair construction and type of base trim you are using. Often these trim details need to be worked out on a case-by-case basis.

The most common approach involves trimming the end of the baseboard at the top of the stair so that the angle of the stringer is continued to the top edge of the base. At the bottom end of the stair, you can butt the baseboard into the plumb cut at the end of the stringer. Use a sliding bevel to gauge the angle between stringer and baseboard, and bisect the angle to determine the proper miter cuts for cap molding. (See the technique described in "Figuring Corner Angles," page 124.) Cut the cap molding at the appropriate angles to follow along the top of the baseboard and stair stringer.

Another solution is to use a modified plinth block at both the top and bottom ends of the stair stringer.

Installing Base Trim at Stairwells

Difficulty Level: Moderate

TOOLS
Sliding bevel gauge • hammer • nail set • nail gun and nails (optional) • power miter saw • straightedge

MATERIALS
Baseboard material • finishing nails • shim stock

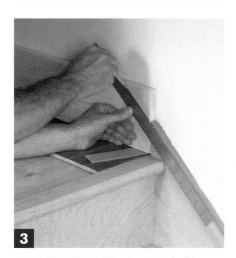

1 **AT THE BOTTOM END** of a stair, you can make a square cut on the end of the baseboard stock and butt it into the plumb cut of the stair stringer.

2 **DETERMINE THE ANGLE** between the base and stringer using a sliding bevel. Cut and install cap molding to make a smooth transition.

3 **AT THE TOP END** of a stair, hold baseboard stock against the plumb cut of the stringer, and mark the angle of the stringer onto the baseboard. Trim the baseboard to the line.

4 **USE THE SLIDING BEVEL** to gauge the angle between the stringer and top edge of the baseboard; then bisect the angle to determine the miter cuts. Install cap molding to the top edges of both stringer and baseboard.

5 **FOR AN ALTERNATIVE APPROACH,** use a plinth block to make the transition between the baseboard and stair stringer. Design the plinth to be tall enough to provide a clean terminus for both base and cap molding.

Picture Rail, Chair Rail, and Plate Rail

Picture rails, chair rails, and plate rails are all horizontal applications to a wall surface, each with a particular functional aspect. While chair and plate rails are sometimes installed as part of a wainscoting, they are not limited to that type of application. Each of these elements can be used on its own to provide a strong trim component to a room.

Picture Rail

A picture rail consists of a particular molding with a rounded top profile that projects away from the wall surface. You can use special hooks and wire to hang paintings, prints, or photographs from the rail. And depending on the height of the rail, it can also serve to delineate a frieze at the top portion of a wall surface or to suggest a small crown molding when mounted near the ceiling.

Picture Rail Height. The height you choose to mount a picture rail will depend largely on the ceiling height of your room. As a general rule, consider spacing the rail about 12 to 18 inches from the ceiling. For this type of installation, place a mark on the wall to indicate the bottom edge of the rail, and use a spirit or laser level to extend a line through the mark along the length of the wall. If you plan to run the molding only along one wall, measure the length, cut each end square, and nail it up. To wrap the room, use coped joints at inside corners and miter joints at outside corners.

1

MARK A LEVEL LINE around the room to indicate the top edge of the chair rail.

Installing Chair Rail

Difficulty Level: **Moderate**

TOOLS

Spirit level • hammer • nail set
• nail gun and nails (optional)
• miter saw • files and rasps

MATERIALS

Chair rail stock • finishing nails
• wood glue • masking or
painter's tape

PICTURE RAIL MOLDING, above, can be used for hanging pictures, or it can help delineate a frieze at the top of the wall.

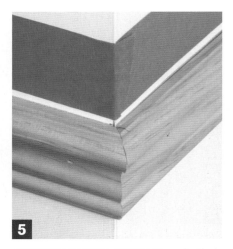

5

CUT THE MITER ANGLES on both halves of an outside corner joint to test the fit before nailing the first piece to the wall. Glue and nail the second piece in place.

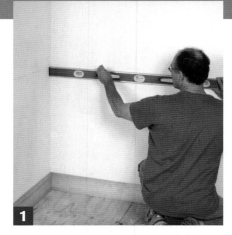

6

MAKE A SQUARE CUT on the end of a one-piece chair rail to allow it to butt into the edge of a door or window casing.

Chair Rail

Chair-rail molding can consist of a single piece of stock or a combination of profiles mounted at a height of 30 to 36 inches above the floor. Originally, chair rail was designed to protect wall surfaces. But as a decorative element in a room, the chair rail has exceeded that particular function and is used to create a strong horizontal line around a room, dividing the wall height into distinct areas.

Chair-Rail Profiles. There are moldings that are sold specifically as chair-rail stock, but you can use a wide variety of other moldings, including a flat piece of 1×3.

Some chair-rail applications feature a projecting cap that provides a flat surface on the top of the rail that returns to the wall. Whatever the configuration, it is important to consider the intersection of a chair rail with vertical trim elements, such as door and window casings. If the casing protrudes farther into the room than the rail, you can simply let the rail butt into the side of the casing. But if the rail protrudes beyond the casing, fashion it into a finished return to give a finished appearance.

2 **APPLY MASKING TAPE** to the wall just above the layout line, and mark the locations of wall studs. For an outside corner, hold the first piece in place, and mark the inside of the miter cut.

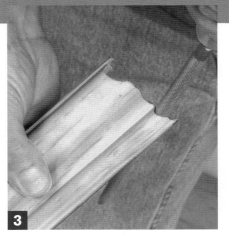

3 **FOR AN INSIDE CORNER JOINT,** run the first piece square into the corner; then cut a coped joint on the second piece.

4 **DETAIL OF COMPLETED INSIDE CORNER JOINT** on one-piece chair rail. Repeat the process for a built-up assembly.

7 **WHEN A CHAIR RAIL** includes a cap, create an elegant termination point by notching the cap around the casing. Hold the cap stock against the casing to mark the depth of the notch.

8 **CUT THE CAP STOCK** to notch tightly around a door or window casing; then shape a rounded or chamfered transition on the end of the piece.

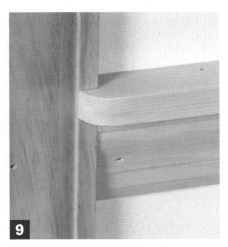

9 **DETAIL OF NOTCHED AND ROUNDED END** of chair-rail cap at door casing.

Milling and Installing a Plate Rail

Difficulty Level: Moderate

TOOLS
Router and edge guide • core-box bit • hammer • nail set • nail gun and nails (optional) • power miter saw

MATERIALS
1-by stock • apron stock • wood glue • finishing nails

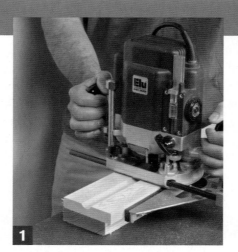

1 **INSTALL AN ACCESSORY EDGE GUIDE** to the router, and use a core-box bit to mill a groove in the top surface of the plate-rail shelf. Test the depth of cut on scrap material before approaching the actual shelf stock.

2 **MARK A LEVEL LINE** on the wall at the height of the top of the plate rail. Cut a rail to length with appropriate end joints, and nail it to the wall studs.

PLATE RAILS can be used alone or as part of a wainscoting treatment as shown above.

Plate Rail

A plate rail is a variation on the chair-rail theme, but mounted higher on the wall—normally 60 to 72 inches from the floor. Consisting of a narrow shelf with a shallow groove parallel to its front edge, the plate rail is frequently used as a cap for an Arts and Crafts-style wainscoting. Decorative plates or other types of artwork can be propped against the wall with their lower edge engaged in the groove. If you wish, you could omit the groove and use the shelf to display small collectibles or other items. A plate rail can also be used in conjunction with other styles of wainscoting, or simply as a trim element used on its own.

Plate-Rail Components. There are usually three components to a plate-rail installation. The rail is a horizontal band fastened flat against the wall to support the back edge of the shelf. If the installation is part of a wainscoting treatment, the top rail of the wainscoting forms the support rail for the shelf. The shelf is usually 3¼ to 4½ inches wide with a relatively simple edge treatment. Between the bottom face of the shelf and the rail, an apron or decorative molding provides both support for the front edge of the shelf and a graceful transition between the two perpendicular surfaces. As an alternative, you can also install individual brackets between the shelf and rail to provide support for the shelf. In that case, you have the option to provide a molded strip, between the brackets, to add another decorative element and cover the joint between shelf and rail.

3

CUT THE APPROPRIATE MITERS on shelf stock, and apply glue to the joint surfaces. Use small nails to pin the parts together while the glue sets. You can also use small joining plates to help position the parts and reinforce the joint.

4

RUN A BEAD OF GLUE along the top edge of the rail; then place the shelf in position. Use 8d finishing nails to fasten the shelf to the top rail.

5

CUT APRON MOLDING to size; then nail it to both the rail and shelf. If your plate rail has any exposed ends, construct mitered returns on the ends of the apron molding.

Create the Groove. For an independent plate rail, begin by ripping the shelf and rail stock to width. Use a router with a ½- or ⅝-inch-diameter core-box bit and edge guide to mill the groove, about ⅜ inch deep in the top of each shelf blank.

Next, use a spirit or laser level to lay out guide lines on the walls to indicate the top of the rail. Nail the rail to the wall using 8d finishing nails. If the rail is formed from flat stock, butt joints are fine at all inside corners. If the rail has a profile, you need to cut coped joints.

For the shelf, make sure that you include an appropriate overhang at an exposed end or where the shelf must return onto a casing. At an exposed outside end, you have the option of cutting the shelf square and leaving the groove exposed, or making a mitered return. (See "Making Mitered Returns," page 58.) For a mitered return, make the appropriate angled cuts, and glue the return onto the shelf. If you wish, you can use joining plates to align and reinforce the joints. Allow the glue to set before continuing with the piece.

Add the Shelf. If the shelf has a square-edge profile, use a butt joint at the inside corners. But if you decide to add a decorative edge to the shelf, you can cut an inside miter joint at the corner. Fasten the shelf to the top edge of the rail using glue and 8d finishing nails. Finally, cut the apron trim, and mount it to the rail/shelf assembly. Use coped joints at inside corners and mitered returns at any exposed ends.

Plate-Rail Construction

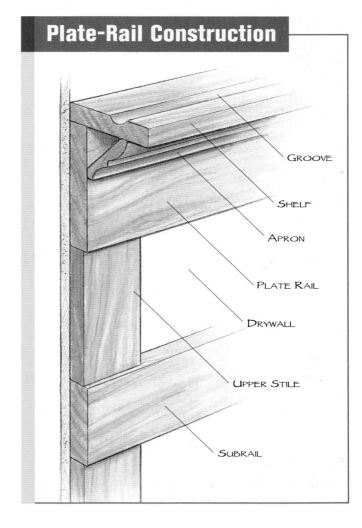

GROOVE

SHELF

APRON

PLATE RAIL

DRYWALL

UPPER STILE

SUBRAIL

Wall Frames and Wainscoting

Wall frames and wainscoting create a sense of drama and style in a room. They provide focus and a sense of order to an otherwise blank room canvas, and they offer the opportunity to use color and finish options to define the room environment.

Of the two, wall frames are the simpler option to install. They consist of some type of panel molding that is assembled into "frames" and then mounted to the wall. While the basic process is rather simple, the infinite range of frame sizes and shapes allows you the ability to create vastly different looks with the same essential material and technique. Wall frames can be made in either horizontal or vertical configurations, and they can be installed on just the lower portion of a wall, under a chair rail, or above the chair rail as well. If you add in the possible decorative painting and wallpapering options that wall frames provide, you can start to see how rich an alternative this can be.

Wainscoting Designs. Wainscoting is a more labor- and material-intensive approach to wall treatment. It involves applying either boards or frame-and-panel assemblies to the lower part of a wall and capping the installation with an integral chair rail. You can fashion a wainscoting to be compatible with almost any style decor. A simple country- or rustic-style treatment would consist of tongue-and-groove boards with a beaded or V-groove molded profile.

A room in the Arts and Crafts genre would typically feature plain-edge frame stock surrounding flat panels, often in quarter-sawn white oak, cherry, or mahogany, but this style is regularly executed in paint-grade materials as well. For a more layered decor—such as Georgian, Federal, or Greek Revival—panel molding can be added to either a flat-panel or raised-panel design.

The height of a typical wainscoting can vary from 30 to 36 inches, or extend to 60 inches in Arts and Crafts-style rooms. Try to avoid installations that divide the wall height in half, as this can appear awkward.

WALL-FRAME DESIGNS, left, often include the frame, a chair rail, and a subrail.

DECORATIVE PAINT AND PAPER FINISHES, above, are an excellent way to complete a frame design.

Wall-Frame Layout Options

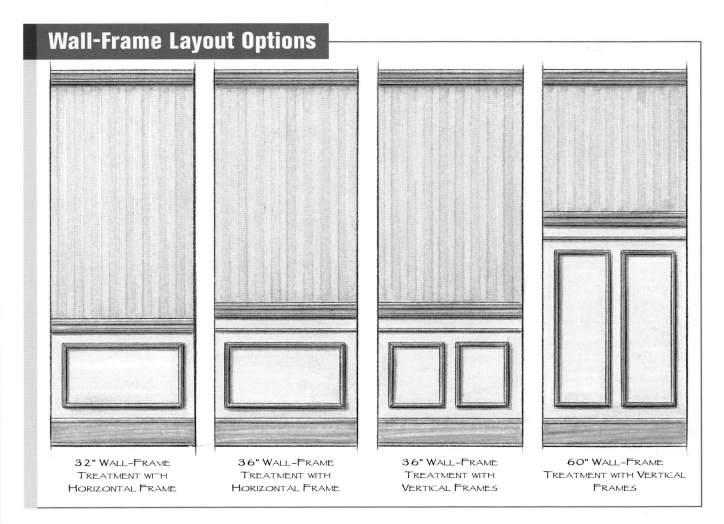

| 32" WALL-FRAME TREATMENT WITH HORIZONTAL FRAME | 36" WALL-FRAME TREATMENT WITH HORIZONTAL FRAME | 36" WALL-FRAME TREATMENT WITH VERTICAL FRAMES | 60" WALL-FRAME TREATMENT WITH VERTICAL FRAMES |

Wall Frames

Planning a room layout for a wall-frame treatment may be the most complex part of the job. Since the options are so varied, you need to focus on the ultimate look you wish to achieve and work backward toward the specific frame sizes. First decide if you want to apply frames to the entire wall or just the lower portion of the wall. Frames above a chair rail can limit or interfere with the placement of artwork and mirrors, so take these factors into account before you begin. You also have the option of adding a subrail below and parallel to the chair rail to further embellish the lower portion of a wall.

Frame Orientation. Consider the orientation of the wall frames—horizontal or vertical. It is also possible to mix a horizontal orientation below a chair rail with a vertical orientation above the rail. Mixing frames of different dimensions can also provide an intentional and defined sense of balance and proportion in a room. If you want to entertain this option, develop a pattern that can be repeated around the room. In mixing wide and narrow frames, the outside frames of a pattern should always be the narrow ones, and the grouping should be symmetrical. A short wall can feature one distinct grouping of frames, while on a long wall you can repeat the pattern two or three times.

Wall-Frame Layout. The number of vertical margins, or spaces between frames, is always one more than the number of wall frames on each wall. Position the frames so that the margins are uniform; although small discrepancies should not be noticed at either end of a wall, or where a window or door interrupts the layout.

The margins above and below the frames—for example, the spaces between baseboard and the frame or the chair rail and the frame—can also deviate from the dimension of the vertical spacing; just try to keep the difference minimal. The best way to decide on a layout is to plot each wall surface on a sheet of graph paper, with window and doors drawn to scale. Use tracing paper to experiment with different options. Draw in the baseboard, chair rail, subrail (if appropriate), and cornice molding; then try different frame layouts. If you will be placing frames below a window, the

MARGIN SPACING, the areas around the frames, should be as consistent as possible, left. Note the angled cut following the path of the staircase.

CREATE A MINIFRAME, above, to deal with electrical receptacles that fall within a frame.

outer edges of the frame should align with the outer edges of the window casing. If you place a frame above a door, the sides of the frame should align with the door casing.

Once you have determined the size of your frames, make a cut list for each of the frame parts. Use a miter saw to cut the panel molding to size with appropriate angles on the ends of each piece. For square frames, make some test cuts on scrap stock to check the accuracy of your saw settings.

Frame Cutting Jig. To simplify assembly of the wall frames, construct a simple jig to help position the parts. Cut a small piece of plywood, about 8 inches on each side, with perfectly square corners—use a try-square to check the cuts. Screw that block to a larger piece of plywood at least 2-foot square. Keep the block back from the panel edge about 1½ inches to create a lip to support the panel molding. Apply glue to the first set of mitered ends, and position them around the gauge block on the jig. Use a brad gun, or

a hammer and nail set, to fasten the joints by driving a fastener through the edges of the molding. Join the molding into two L-shaped subassemblies, and then join those to create the frame. Allow the glue to set before fastening the frames to the walls.

As an aid in laying out the frames, rip a block to the width of the top margin (for frames below a chair rail), and use it to scribe a light mark on the wall to indicate the top edge of the frames. Then use a tape measure to mark the locations of the top outside frame corners where they intersect that line. Apply a small bead of panel adhesive to the back side of the first frame, and hold it in place on the guide lines. Use 6d finishing nails to fasten the top edge of the frame to the wall. Check that the sides of the frame are perfectly plumb; then drive nails to fasten them on the remaining three edges. If you notice small spaces between the back of a frame and the wall, apply a small bead of caulk.

Trim Tip FRAME ATTACHMENT

Although you can sometimes rely on the position of wall framing to provide good nailing for trim members, for wall frames this is often not the case. The arbitrary position of frames can result in a situation where good nailing bases are absent—many frames will fall between wall studs. However, this is one case where you need not be too concerned. Because the frames are extremely lightweight and only decorative in nature, you can use a combination of adhesive and nails to safely hold them to the wall.

Installing Wall Frames

Difficulty Level: Moderate

TOOLS
Power drill with screwdriver bit • hammer • nail set • nail gun and nails (optional) • power saw • measuring tape • spirit level

MATERIALS
Scrap plywood • 1-by stock • wood glue • finishing nails • utility screws • base cap molding

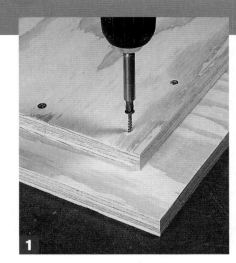

1

ATTACH A SMALL PIECE of plywood (with two adjacent factory edges) to a 2 x 2-ft. sheet. Leave a margin of 1½ in.

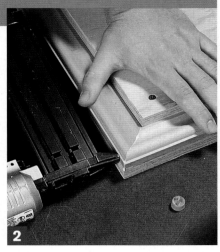

2

APPLY GLUE to the mitered ends, and fasten them using an air nailer or hammer and brads. Keep your fingers clear.

3

CUT A BLOCK the same width as the top margin; place it against the chair rail; and scribe a guideline on the wall.

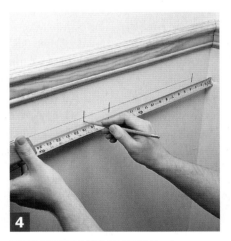

4

MEASURE AND MARK the top corners of each wall frame. Then apply adhesive to the first frame.

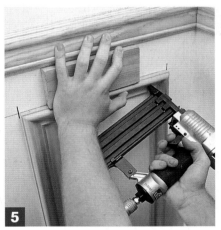

5

USING THE SPACER BLOCK from Step 3, align the wall frame with the corner marks, and fasten it in place.

6

WITH THE TOP EDGE FASTENED, plumb the vertical sides of the frame, and attach them with 6d finishing nails.

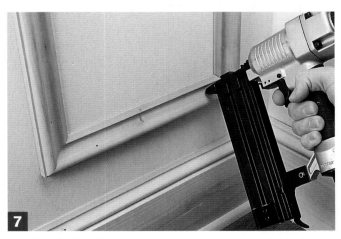

7

DOUBLE-CHECK that the bottom of the frame is level, and then fasten it. Fill all holes, and caulk all around the frame.

Tongue-and-Groove Bead-Board Wainscoting

One of the simplest and most common types of wainscoting consists of an application of tongue-and-groove boards to the lower portion of a wall. This is a popular treatment in kitchens, bathrooms, and other less-formal rooms in a home.

While the basic installation process is the same regardless of the particular material chosen, you can achieve unique results by selecting different materials for the paneling. A popular choice for this treatment is fir boards with a beaded profile milled into the surface. This material is manufactured in various thicknesses, ranging from ⅜ to ¾ inch, as well as in various width boards, usually between 3 and 5 inches. Beaded-board stock is available as random length milled stock and also in prepackaged kits. In addition, you can also find the same pattern milled into various hardwood species so that you have the flexibility to customize your installation to suit your desired decor. And to further increase your options, you can use other tongue-and-groove stock, such as ¾-inch-thick knotty pine or cedar, following the same basic installation methods.

In all cases, tongue-and-groove wainscoting features an applied base trim and chair-rail cap to complete the installation. The particular configuration of these elements is another area where you can look to personalize your installation. The examples we provide are simply a guide to basic installation techniques; you can easily use these as models for your own designs.

Install Blocking. Since this type of wainscoting requires fastening at frequent intervals along the wall, it is important that you provide blocking for nailing at all necessary points. Of course, you can apply continuous furring strips to the surface of the wall, but this would extend the projection of the wainscoting into the room and could cause problems at those points where it intersects door and window casing. To avoid this problem, determine the height of the top of the wainscoting material; subtract the thickness of the cap; and scribe a level line at that height around the perimeter of the room.

Use a utility knife or drywall saw to cut the drywall along that line, and remove the drywall down to the floor. Then rip panels of ½-inch-thick CD grade plywood to width to replace the drywall.

Nail or screw the plywood panels to the studs and soleplate of the wall. If you wish to save material, you could install three or four nailing strips instead of full panels, but the time saved and additional backing provided make the full-panel system a good approach.

Cut the Wainscoting. Cut the tongue-and-groove boards to length. For ease of installation, cut the boards about ¼ inch short of the full wainscot height. For a wall

Installing Bead-Board Wainscoting

Difficulty Level: **Challenging**

TOOLS

Hammer • nail set • nail gun and nails (optional) • power drill with screwdriver tip • power miter saw • table saw • circular saw • spirit level • block plane • drywall saw

MATERIALS

½-inch CD plywood • Tongue-and-groove wainscoting • finishing nails • wood glue • utility screws

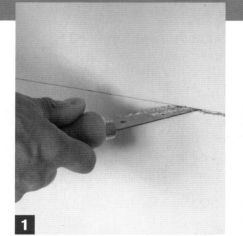

1 **MARK A LEVEL LINE** at the height of the bottom of the wainscoting cap; then use a drywall saw and utility knife to cut the drywall. Remove the drywall from that line to the floor.

2 **INSTALL ½-IN. CD PLYWOOD PANELS** in place of the drywall. Nail or screw the plywood to the wall studs and soleplate.

with two inside corners, begin the installation at one end. Hold the first board against the corner, with the groove edge toward the corner, and check that it is plumb before nailing it to the backing. If necessary, you can move the board away from the corner at top or bottom to bring it plumb. As long as the gap in the corner will be covered by the adjacent corner board, you do not need to scribe the piece.

Slide the groove of the second board over the tongue of the first strip, and then drive the nails, just above the tongue, angled to drive the boards tightly together. Proceed in this way across the wall until you approach the opposite corner. If you encounter difficulty sliding the tongue and groove joints together, you can fit a small block of the wainscoting stock over the outside tongue and tap it with a hammer.

When you reach the last board, measure the distance at both top and bottom from the V-groove to the face of the adjacent wall. Mark these measurements on the last board; connect the marks; and rip the board to width. Since the wainscoting will continue on the adjacent wall, you can cut the strip about ⅛ inch shy of the mark to make installation easier, or you can cut it for a snug fit and use the corner to wedge it in place.

TONGUE-AND-GROOVE BEADED WAINSCOTING is a popular component of casual decorating schemes.

3

TO BEGIN at an inside corner, hold the first board in place, and use a level to check that it is plumb. Make necessary adjustments to nail it to the plywood backer. Always work so that the tongue of the board is exposed and the grooved edge faces the corner.

4

USE A CUTOFF PIECE of wainscoting stock as a block to coax boards together. You can use a hammer to tap on the waste block without damaging the delicate tongue.

5

AS YOU APPROACH an inside corner, take careful measurements between both the top and bottom of the next-to-last board and the corner. Transfer these measurements to the last board, and use a saber saw to cut it to width.

Continued on next page.

Continued from previous page.

ENGAGE THE GROOVE of the last board on a run with the tongue of the previous board, and push it into place. Drive nails through the face of the board in the corner to hold it.

PLACE THE FIRST BOARD on the adjacent wall into position, and use a level to check that it is plumb. If it is, nail it in place.

THE SECOND HALF of an outside corner requires that you remove the groove plus an amount equal to the thickness of the stock to create an equal reveal on each side of the corner.

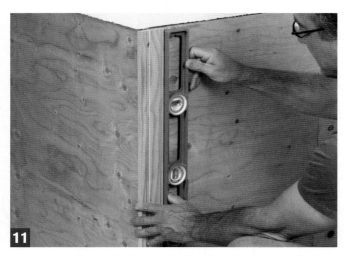

USE A LEVEL to check that the first board at an outside corner is plumb. Allow the outer edge of the board to protrude just beyond the backer so you can fashion a tight corner joint.

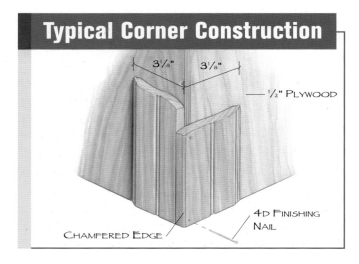

Typical Corner Construction

3⅛"   3⅛"

½" PLYWOOD

4D FINISHING NAIL

CHAMFERED EDGE

Adjoining Wall. Hold the first strip on the next wall in position, and check that its leading edge is plumb. If necessary, adjust the strip so that it is plumb; then measure the resulting gap and set a scriber to that dimension. Continue holding the strip in position as you run the scriber along the joint to mark the necessary adjustment. Remember to keep both wings of the scriber parallel to the floor as you move it down the joint. Use a sharp block plane to remove the required stock; then test the fit of the board. Once you are satisfied with the joint, nail the strip in place.

Outside Corners. If your room includes an outside corner joint, you should begin the installation there so that you can ensure a neat and balanced joint at this more visible

8

IF AN INSIDE CORNER is not plumb, hold the first board plumb, and use scribers to mark the face for the adjustment. Use a saber saw or sharp plane to remove the necessary material.

9

FOR AN OUTSIDE CORNER JOINT, create a tight butt joint by first ripping the groove off of the first board. Use sandpaper or a sharp plane to remove saw marks.

12

APPLY A SMALL BEAD of glue to the outside corner joint; then nail the two boards together.

13

USE A SHARP PLANE to shape a bevel on the outside corner of wainscoting panel stock.

point. Rip the groove off of one board to form one half of the corner joint. Next, rip the width of the groove plus the thickness of the wainscoting stock off the adjacent corner board. This detail ensures that when you assemble the two pieces at the corner you will have a symmetrical reveal on each face. (See sequence of steps 9 through 13, above, and "Typical Corner Construction," opposite.)

Install the narrower board on the corner first; once more, check that it is plumb before nailing it in place. Allow the edge of the board to extend just beyond the corner so that you can be sure of achieving a tight joint. Hold the wider corner board in place. If necessary, adjust the board so that it is plumb, and plane off the required stock so that

it does not project beyond the corner. Apply glue to the joint and install the second corner board with nails. You can later plane a new bevel on the outside edge of the corner to provide a finished appearance to the joint.

Baseboard and Chair Rail. Apply baseboard and chair-rail molding to the wall. Depending on the configuration of your window and door trim, these elements might project beyond the face of the casing. In that situation, you will need to fashion a neat return or end treatment at each opening. Since the range of possible situations is vast, examine our example for a suggested approach; then feel free to devise an appropriate solution for your own installation. (See "Adding Baseboard and Chair Rail," page 144.)

Adding Baseboard & Chair Rail

Difficulty Level: Moderate

TOOLS
Basic carpentry tools • power miter saw

MATERIALS
Baseboard stock • chair rail stock • finishing nails • wood glue • shim stock

1

NAIL BASEBOARD to the wainscoting panel stock. Remember to use appropriate spacers for carpeting, hardwood, or tile flooring.

2

CUT MITERS for the outside corners of apron molding. Test-fit the joints to check for proper fit; then apply a bead of glue; and nail the molding in place.

3

IT'S COMMON for drywall surfaces to flare out at the corners. Cut the stock to length with appropriate end joints; then use a scriber to mark the required adjustment on the face of the cap.

4

NAIL THE CHAIR-RAIL CAP to the top edge of wainscoting panels and apron molding; then pin the miter joint together with a 4d finishing nail or brad.

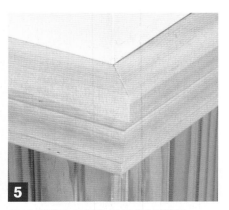

5

FINISHED OUTSIDE CORNER DETAIL of wainscoting chair rail.

6

FINISHED INSIDE CORNER DETAIL of wainscoting chair rail. Note butt joint for square-edge cap stock.

7

MARK THE END of the apron molding to indicate the depth of the casing. Then cut an open 45-deg. miter that meets the face of the casing. Nail the apron to the wainscot paneling

8

CUT A NOTCH in the chair-rail cap stock to fit tightly to the casing. Ease the edges of the cap, or shape a rounded end; then nail it to the top edges of apron and wainscot paneling.

DEALING WITH ELECTRICAL BOXES

As you proceed across the wall, it is inevitable that you will encounter electrical outlets. Make sure that the electrical circuits are turned off; then remove the cover plates and outlets. When you approach an outlet box, take careful measurements from the edge of the last strip before the box to determine its position. Mark the location of your cutout on the board and, if necessary, drill clearance holes in each corner so that you can insert a saber saw blade.

Use the saw to make the required cutout. For ease of installation, allow about 1/16 inch extra space around the box on all sides. Test the fit of the board, and make any necessary adjustments. If the electrical box straddles two boards, mark and cut the second part of the cutout, and mount the second board. Remember to provide clearance for the outlet mounting screws. Depending on the thickness of your wainscoting and local electrical codes, you might need to install extension sleeves to the electrical boxes before reinstalling the outlets.

Difficulty Level: **Easy**

TOOLS
Folding stick ruler • power drill and bit • saber saw • pencil • combination square

MATERIALS
Tongue-and-groove wainscoting • box extension

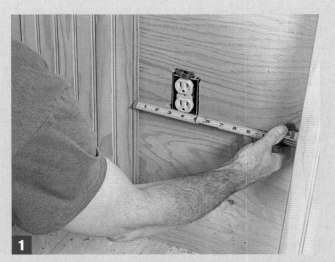

1

MEASURE THE DISTANCE between an outlet box and the nearest full board. Transfer the measurements to a piece of wainscoting stock. Allow an additional 1/8 in. for adjustments.

2

TRANSFER THE HEIGHT of the bottom and top of an electrical box directly to the wainscoting stock. Use a saber saw to make the necessary cutout. Make sure that you leave clearance for the outlet mounting screws.

3

IF REQUIRED, install an extension to the existing electrical box. Slide it into position, and make the necessary electrical connections.

Flat-Panel Wainscoting

Although the finished product may look intimidating, the application of a frame-and-flat-panel wainscoting is definitely approachable for a beginner. And this type of installation can be customized in a variety of ways to conform to many different interior design schemes.

The simplest approach is an unadorned, paint-grade wainscoting. But you can also opt for a clear or stained finish using pine lumber or one of the many domestic hardwood species that are available. Base and cap molding can be simple one-piece moldings or complex assemblies of stock or custom profiles. You can also install a molding around the perimeter of each panel to completely alter the feel of the wainscoting.

This basic system can be constructed entirely on site or prefabricated in sections in your home workshop, and it is suitable for new construction or a renovation project for an existing room. For a painted finish, your best choices are solid poplar for the frame and birch plywood for the backer and panel stock. These materials are relatively inexpensive and easy to work, providing a smooth surface to accept paint. And if you find stock pine profiles that will work with your design, you can always use them for base, panel, or cap moldings.

Lay Out the Project. Begin your project by determining the panel layout for the room. Use graph paper to make a simple scaled drawing of each wall with windows, doors, outlets, switches, and heat registers all included. Draw in a line to indicate the top of the chair rail; then determine the width of the cap and baseboard. If you have no particular preference, you can follow our design scheme shown in the

Trim Tip | FINISHES

If you are planning on a clear or stained finish for your wainscoting, install the panel stock so that the grain on the exposed face runs vertically. This may result in a less efficient use of materials, but it will greatly improve the finished look of the installation.

drawing opposite. Notice that it is perfectly fine to hold the wainscoting frame up from the floor and apply blocking at the bottom of the wall to support the base trim. Using this technique will allow you to save on material for extra-wide rail stock that would be buried behind the baseboard. Sketch in the top and bottom rails next. Make sure that your base trim overlays the bottom rail enough to provide adequate support for all trim pieces.

Doors and Windows. Anticipate how the wainscoting will intersect door and window casing. In many cases, windows do not intersect wainscoting panels at all as the stools are high enough to provide clearance for the panels. In some situations, you can modify the casing details to provide additional depth, and thereby devise a way for the wainscoting trim to simply die into the casing. This could be as simple as adding a backband to the edge of a casing or a panel molding to the face. But other times it will be necessary to provide a more intentional terminus for the wainscoting at a casing. One of the more elegant ways to solve this problem is to construct a small pilaster at the casing that extends far enough into the room to accept the wain-

Typical Frame-and-Panel Corner Joints

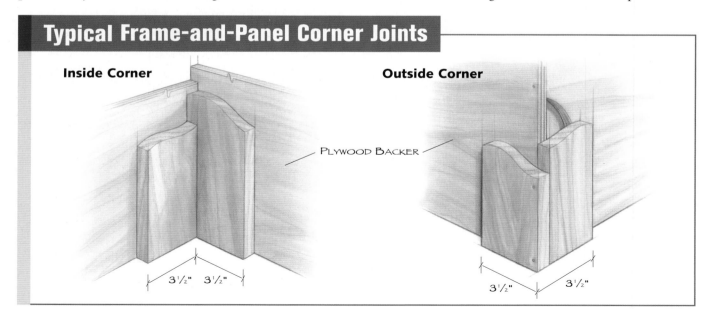

Inside Corner

Outside Corner

Plywood Backer

3½" 3½"

3½" 3½"

Flat-Panel Wainscot Construction

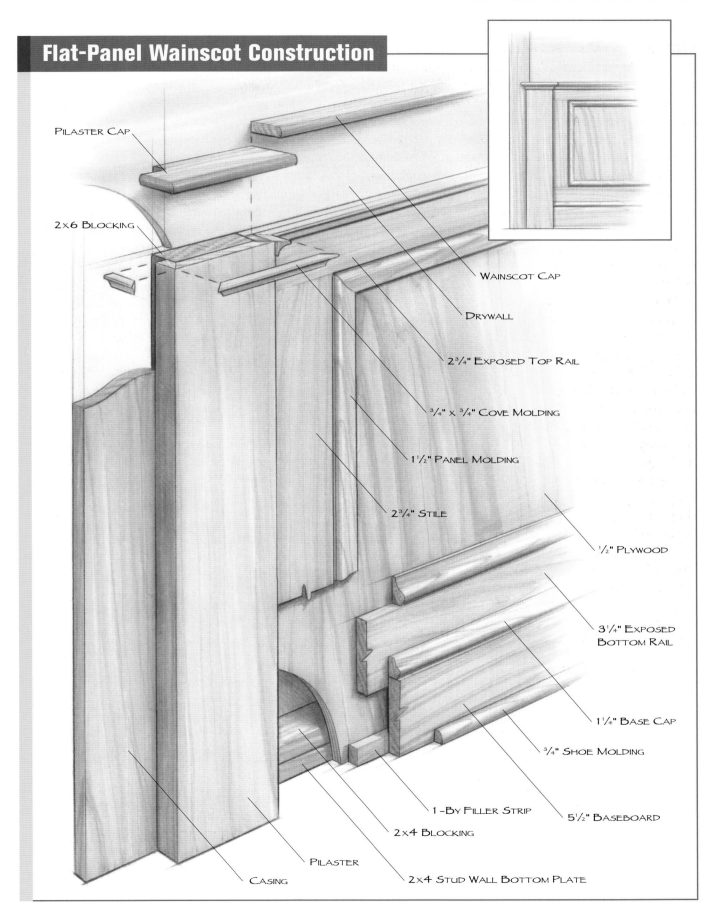

PILASTER CAP

2×6 BLOCKING

WAINSCOT CAP

DRYWALL

2¾" EXPOSED TOP RAIL

¾" × ¾" COVE MOLDING

1½" PANEL MOLDING

2¾" STILE

½" PLYWOOD

3¼" EXPOSED BOTTOM RAIL

1¼" BASE CAP

¾" SHOE MOLDING

1-BY FILLER STRIP

2×4 BLOCKING

5½" BASEBOARD

PILASTER

CASING

2×4 STUD WALL BOTTOM PLATE

scoting trim. Whatever your solution, it is always best to anticipate these details rather than find yourself stuck at an advanced part of the job.

Panel Dimensions. Experiment with the placement of frame stiles to achieve a pleasing division of space across the wall. The width of your panels does not need to be identical on each wall; however, the general proportions of the panels should be close. Once you have determined the layout for the room, plan the size of the plywood panels so that seams will be covered by the stiles.

If you are working in a newly constructed room, apply ½-inch-thick plywood to the wall studs up to the height of the top rail to serve as both the panel faces and frame backer; then apply drywall to the remaining sections of the wall. If you are renovating an existing room, remove the drywall up to the rail height, and install the plywood in its place.

Attach the panels with finishing nails, about 8 inches on center along the studs and soleplate. Set the nailheads slightly below the panel surface. Any fasteners that remain

Installing Flat-Panel Wainscoting

Difficulty Level: **Challenging**

TOOLS
Hammer • nail set • nail gun and nails (optional) • spirit level • saber saw • power miter saw • plate joiner • power drill and bits • clamps • square

MATERIALS
1-by stock • ½-inch birch plywood • wood glue • finishing nails • joining plates

1 **IF YOU MUST** deal with electrical receptacles, mark the outline of the boxes on the plywood panels before installing the panels. Allow ⅛ in. on each side for ease of installation and adjustment.

2 **DRILL CLEARANCE HOLES** for the saw blade; then use a saber saw to make the cutout for electrical outlet boxes. Attach the panels to studs up to rail height.

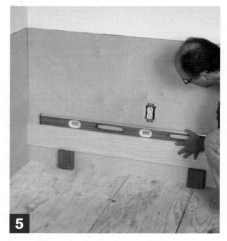

5 **CUT BLOCKS** to support the bottom rails at the proper height. Use a 4-ft. level to check for level. If necessary, place shims below one or more of the blocks to adjust the position of the rail.

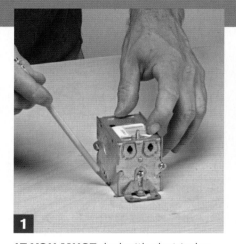

6 **NAIL THE BOTTOM RAIL** to the plywood panel. Place two nails every 16 in. along the length of the rail.

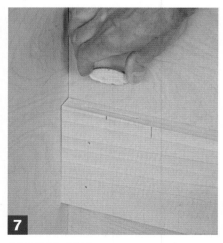

7 **SPREAD GLUE** on a joining plate as well as in the matching slots. Place the plate into the slot in the rail before installing the first stile.

visible after applying the frame parts can easily be filled prior to finishing. If you wish to reduce the number of nails, you can apply a bead of panel adhesive to each stud before placing the panel. With adhesive, you can fasten the panels only at the top, bottom, and center. Remember to cut the panel stock so that the seams between adjacent panels fall behind a frame stile.

Electrical Boxes. Once again, you will need to make provisions for electrical outlets as you apply the plywood backer. Carefully measure the locations of outlet boxes and

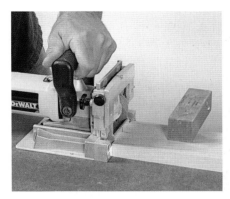

CLAMP A STILE to the worktable before using the plate joiner to cut slots in the end-grain. End-grain cuts are particularly liable to kick back, and this technique keeps hands far from the spinning blade.

3

CLAMP A BOTTOM AND TOP RAIL together to mark the locations of the frame stiles. Place a mark to indicate the center of each stile to use when cutting slots for joining plates.

4

USE THE PLATE JOINER to cut slots in the top and bottom rails. Firmly press both the joiner and rail stock to the table top to accurately register the slots.

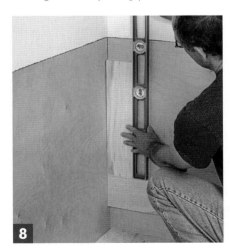

8

USE A SHORT LEVEL to check that the first stile is plumb before nailing it. Since the adjacent corner stile will cover the inside edge, a small gap at top or bottom will not be visible.

9

APPLY GLUE to joining plates and matching slots before installing the top rail to the ends of stiles.

transfer them to the first panel. Use a drill to bore clearance holes for the saw blade; then use a saber saw to make the cutouts. Allow an ⅛-inch margin around the box for adjustment.

Depending on your situation, you may need to install box extensions to comply with local building and electrical codes. In some cases you may have to move the boxes so that they are flush with the new finished wall surface. If possible, it is best to lay out the stiles so that they do not fall over an outlet, but sometimes this cannot be avoided. In those cases, you will definitely need to move the box so that it comes flush with the face of the frame. For challenging electrical adaptations, it is always best to call an electrician.

Use a similar approach for heating and air conditioning registers. You can generally treat them in the same way you would when running simple baseboard. Duct extensions are available for almost any type of duct, so you can adapt your installation for registers that fall either in the panel or base trim.

Cut the Rails. Determine the length of the rails for your first wall and crosscut the stock to length. If you need to splice two pieces together to span the wall, use a scarf joint where the sections come together. Temporarily clamp the top and bottom rails together, with their face sides up,

Continued on next page.

Continued from previous page.

10

IF THE JOINTS between the top rail and stiles are reluctant to close, you can use a clamp to pull the rail into position before nailing it to the plywood backer.

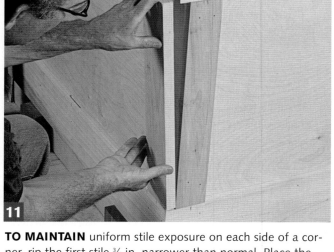

11

TO MAINTAIN uniform stile exposure on each side of a corner, rip the first stile ¾ in. narrower than normal. Place the second stile in position, and nail the corner joint together.

14

CUT COVE APRON MOLDING to size with appropriate end joints; then nail it to the top rail. Keep the top of the molding flush with the top edge of the rail. Add the cap.

15

TO ADD MOLDING to wainscoting panels, first cut the molding to length with 45-deg. miters at each end. Test fit all four pieces; then nail them to the plywood panel.

and mark the position of the frame stiles. If you wish to avoid pencil marks on parts that will receive a stained or clear finish, apply some masking tape to the faces, and place your marks on the tape. Also place a light mark to indicate the center of each stile. Use these marks to cut joining plate slots in the rail edges for the stile joints. Repeat the process for the rails for each wall section.

If your room includes one or more outside corners, you should cut miter joints on the rails to avoid exposing end grain. These joints can be made using the same techniques you would employ for baseboard stock.

Cut the Stiles. Next, cut stock to size for the stiles. As a general rule, the exposed width of all stiles should be the

same. This means that at inside corners, the first stile to be installed will need to be ¾ inch wider than a normal stile. At an outside corner, the first stile installed will need to be ¾ inch narrower than a normal stile. The length of all stiles should be identical, so you can speed the task by putting a stop on the miter saw stand to eliminate the need to measure each piece. Mark a line to indicate the center of each stile, at both top and bottom, and use the plate joiner to cut the slots.

Install Bottom Rail. Cut small blocks from scrap stock to support the bottom rail at the predetermined height. Place the first rail on top of the blocks, and check it with a 4-foot level. If necessary, place shims under one or more

RIP NARROW STRIPS to act as backers to support the bottom edge of base trim. Nail the strips to the plywood panel at floor level.

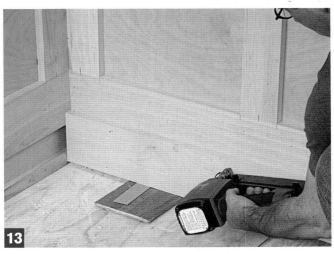

PLACE BASEBOARD in position, and nail it to both the bottom rail and backer strip. After all baseboards are installed, run the cap molding around the room.

of the block to level the rail. (See steps 5 and 6, page 148.)

Then begin at one corner and install the first stile. Spread a bit of glue in the mating plate slots and on the joining plate and assemble the stile to the bottom rail. Use a level to check that the stile is plumb, and apply pressure to the rail/stile joint to keep it closed while you drive nails to lock the stile in place. Repeat the procedure for each stile. When you have installed all the stiles on one wall, apply glue to the slots in the top rail and stiles, install joining plates to the slots in the stiles, and position the rail. Once again, apply downward pressure to close the joints while you nail the rail to the backer panel. If the rail is bowed and you have trouble closing a joint, you can use a clamp to pull the parts together.

Proceed around the room, installing the panel frames on one wall at a time. To fashion an outside corner joint, you can miter the rails and stiles together, but it is difficult to achieve good results in the field. A perfectly respectable alternative is to lap the second side over the end of the first one applied. Remember to apply a bead of glue to the joint; then use 4d finishing nails to pin the joint together.

Base Trim. Install strips of continuous blocking to the bottom edge of the plywood backer to support the base trim. Then install base trim using the same techniques you would use if there were no wainscoting.

Cove Apron Molding. Install the apron molding flush with the top edge of the top rail; miter outside corner joints; and cope inside corner joints. Rip stock to width for the wainscoting cap. The cap should be wide enough to cover the top rail and apron molding plus an overhang of about ¾

inch. If you wish to put a profiled edge on the stock, use the router table to cut the profile before you rip it from a wider board. For inside corners on the wainscoting cap, you can use either a coped, butt, or inside miter joint, depending on the cap profile.

Apply a bead of glue to the top rail, and place the cap in position. Nail the cap to the top edge of the rail and apron molding. Continue around the room, installing one piece at a time, fitting the joints carefully.

Complete the Panels. If you want to further embellish your wainscoting, you can install molding around the perimeter of each panel. The specific molding which you select should be in keeping with the overall design scheme for your room. For a simple treatment, a cove, beaded, or chamfered molding might be appropriate, while a more formal design might call for an elaborate panel molding.

Installing these moldings is not difficult, but it is labor intensive. Each piece must be either measured or scribed individually, and you must take the time to make accurate miter cuts or the results will reflect shoddy workmanship. If you have installed the panel frames accurately, the corners of each panel should be a 90-degree angle, and your miter cuts can all be 45 degrees. Measure, cut, and, install the molding pieces for one panel at a time to reduce confusion. It is always best when cutting to err slightly on the long side and have to trim a piece to fit, rather than cut a part too short. Always test the fit of all four pieces for each panel before nailing any one of them in place. When you are satisfied with the fit, use brads or 4d finishing nails to fasten the molding to the plywood backer.

Modular Construction of Wainscoting Panels

If you have a home workshop, or can set aside a space as a temporary shop, you can also prefabricate wainscoting panels in wall-length units. Then you can bring these panels to the site and install them in sections. In addition to minimizing installation time, this system has two other notable advantages. First, you can clamp the frame parts to pull the joints tight and ensure no gaps. And, second, you can fasten the plywood panel backer to the frame by screwing it through the back side, eliminating the need to fill nailholes in the face of the frame. Of course, you still will need to apply the cap, apron, and base molding after the panels are installed. If you find the calculations for a complicated room too difficult, you can combine prefabricated panels for the simple walls with some that are built on site for the more complex areas.

Begin by taking careful measurements of your room. Create a detailed drawing for each wall which includes all window and door openings, outlets, and registers. You will

COMBINE WAINSCOTING and plate rail, left.

PLAN WHERE PANELS meet casing, above.

PANELS, below, complement other finishes.

CREATE LAYOUTS, opposite top, for custom looks.

PANEL DESIGNS, opposite bottom, fit any decor.

plywood panels to extend below the bottom rail the appropriate amount.

Build the wainscoting frames first. Apply glue to the joining plate slots and on each joining plate; then assemble the rails to the stiles. Use bar clamps, positioned at each stile, to draw the joints tight, and leave the clamps in place until the glue sets—at least one hour. For an alternative construction technique, you can use pocket screws to join the stiles and rails. Use the jig to drill two pilot holes at the ends of each stile; then temporarily clamp the stiles to the rails while you drive the screws to assemble the frames.

Cut the plywood panels to size. Lay one of the assembled panels, face side down, on a worktable or cleared floor surface and position a plywood panel over it. Drill and countersink pilot holes; then fasten the panel to the frame with 1-inch flat-head screws. Repeat this process for each panel assembly.

Follow your installation plan, installing one wall of paneling at a time. Check each panel to make sure that it is level; place shims beneath the bottom edge of the assembly to hold it in place while you fasten it to the wall. Screw the panels to the wall with long screws driven into the studs. Bore and countersink pilot holes for all screws so that the heads sit slightly below the rail surface. If you place the screws at the top and bottom edges of the panel, the apron and base molding will cover the screw heads.

need to plan the order of installation for each wall section because it is necessary to account for the thickness of the adjacent frames when calculating panel size. When laying out panel size and stile locations, remember that joints in the plywood panels will need to fall behind stiles. Depending on the amount of space available for your work space, you can fabricate a continuous panel assembly for an entire wall or two or three subassemblies that can be joined on site.

The basic layout for prefab panels is the same as for site-built panels. As a general rule, it is wise to design the panels to be slightly long to allow for some adjustment and scribing in corners that are not perfectly plumb—in most cases, an extra ½ inch per unit is sufficient.

You can use the same layout described above for constructing the frames; this includes the use of a backer strip at the bottom edge to carry the base trim. Simply size the

DESIGN IDEAS: **WALL TREATMENTS**

PLATE RAILS, above left, can be used to display items.

HEATING REGISTERS and receptacles, above right, can be made to blend in with the trimwork package.

WALL FRAMES, right, can add distinction to any room.

WALL TREATMENTS, opposite, can set the design tone for an entire room.

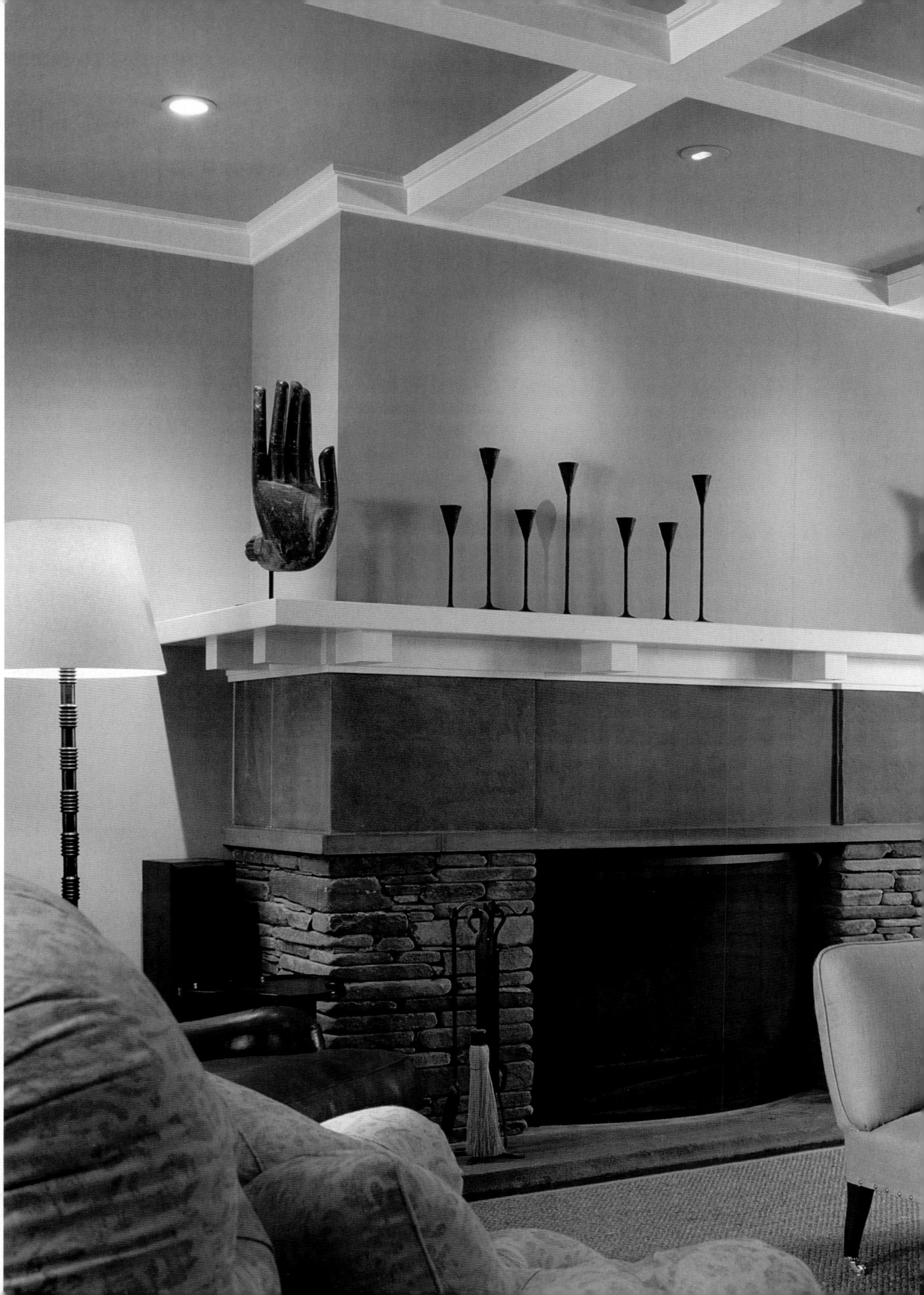

CHAPTER 6

CROWN MOLDING & CEILING TREATMENTS

A *cornice* is the name for a single molding, or combination of moldings, that serves as ornamentation at the junction of the wall and ceiling. Most people associate cornice trim with the application of a *crown molding.* A crown is a single piece of trim that is designed to sit at an angle and spans the joint between wall and ceiling; it can be as narrow as 1¾ or as wide as 8 inches. While most cornices include some type of crown molding, it is not a required element, and many treatments feature a combination of molded and flat stock applied to the wall, the ceiling, or both to create an elegant transition between the two planes. It is also common to use molding profiles that are designed for other uses as a part of a cornice.

Distinctive ceiling treatments, such as beamed and coffered ceilings, incorporate some of the same installation techniques as cornice molding. These present a wide range of options—from formal to rustic.

Cornices & Crown Molding

While it is not necessary that a cornice be part of a comprehensive trim upgrade in a particular room, whatever design you plan should be in keeping with the prevailing spirit of a room. For example, an elaborate Victorian-style treatment would be inappropriate in an Arts and Crafts-style dining room. In addition, the size of the cornice should be in proportion to the ceiling height in the room. Ceilings that are 8 feet high or less cannot support an extremely wide molding, so try to keep the trim from extending more than 4 inches from the ceiling. On the other hand, rooms with ceilings over 9 feet high need wider and more substantial moldings. In these cases, aim for a cornice that drops at least 5 inches from the ceiling surface.

For the novice, installing cornice trim is definitely more involved, and justifiably more intimidating, than any other trim element. However, if you take the time to understand the basics of cutting the joints and installing these elements, there is no reason to shy away from this job.

Cornice Materials

Like other millwork items, cornice trim is available in a variety of materials—some for paint-grade work and some that can receive a clear or stained finish. For trim that is to be painted, the most common options are clear or finger-jointed pine and poplar. However, a wide range of profiles are also manufactured in MDF, resin, and polystyrene foam. Each of these materials has its advantages and limitations, but it is certainly worth considering these options before selecting your trim stock.

MDF Cornices. MDF moldings are manufactured from a mixture of finely ground wood fibers and glue and are shaped under heat and pressure to various profiles. The resulting product is stiff and flat, without defects, and it machines very easily. This is an excellent choice for paint-grade work since it features a very smooth surface with no discernable grain. It can be drilled, nailed, and glued much like wood, and it accepts both latex and oil–based paints. If you will be nailing by hand, you should plan on drilling pilot holes for finishing nails, but pneumatic nail guns will easily drive fasteners through it.

Polyurethane Cornices. Resin moldings are available in an increasing number of profiles and sizes, and in rigid and flexible formulations. It is especially valuable for situations where you need to trim a curved wall surface—either concave or convex. Some manufacturers will provide flexible resin moldings to match stock profiles that they offer in wood trim, so you can mix materials for different parts of a job.

Polystyrene Cornices. Plastic, or polystyrene, molding is a choice that appeals to many do-it-yourselfers. This material is manufactured in a variety of simple and intricate profiles that can mimic vintage plaster moldings at a fraction of the cost of the real thing—if you could even find the real thing. In addition, plastic moldings are extremely light

Installing Plastic Molding

Difficulty Level: Moderate

TOOLS
Miter saw • pencil • hammer • nail set • sanding block • caulking gun • drywall taping knife • paintbrush

MATERIALS
Crown molding • finishing nails • joint compound • construction adhesive • paint

1 **WITH A SECTION OF MOLDING** held in place, mark guidelines along the top and bottom.

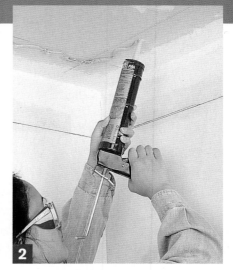

2 **AFTER CUTTING** and test-fitting the trim pieces, lay a bead of adhesive just inside your guidelines.

Trim Tip | DECORATIVE CORNER BLOCKS

If the prospect of cutting all those coped and mitered joints is just too overwhelming, there are fittings available that eliminate the need for those demanding joints. Much like plinth and corner blocks for baseboard, there are also decorative blocks that can be used for cornice trim. These elements are available in wood, resin, and polystyrene, and it is not even necessary that you use the same material for the blocks as for the rest of the trim members—as long as everything will be painted. Blocks are available for inside and outside corners, and also as connectors to be used in place of scarf joints.

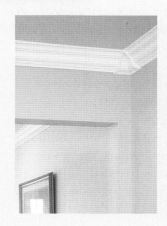

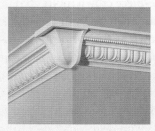

ELIMINATE CUTTING by using decorative corner blocks for cornice applications. Those shown here are made of resin.

weight, and you can install them easily and quickly without the necessity of cutting fancy joints. Plastic molding is typically available with matching corner and connecting trim blocks that will allow you to limit your cutting to square butt joints. And for those situations where you do not want to use those blocks, gaps in both inside and outside miter joints can easily be filled with caulk or joint compound.

Wood Cornices. Of course, for stained or clear-finished trim, your most widely available choices are clear pine or red oak moldings. These species are usually stocked at lumberyards and home centers. And specialty millwork houses offer a much wider selection of profiles that can be pro-

duced in any species that you choose. If you are thinking about a clear or stained finish for your cornice trim, however, keep in mind that the level of execution needs to be extremely high, and the time involved to do the job will be proportionate to those demands. While caulk and filler can be used to correct many faults on a paint-grade job, these solutions are not available for clear-finished trim. As a result, the fit of each coped and mitered joint must be tight all along the profile, and gaps between a molding and the wall or ceiling must often be scribed rather than filled. You can reasonably expect that the time required will be two or three times that for a paint-grade job.

6

CROWN MOLDING & CEILING TREATMENTS

3 **PRESS THE MOLDING** into the adhesive, and attach it with finishing nails. Sink the nailheads just below the surface.

4 **USE A SMALL TAPING KNIFE** and some joint compound to fill any gaps in the corner and to cover all nailheads.

5 **AFTER THE JOINT COMPOUND,** apply a coat of primer. When the primer dries, follow with one or two finish coats.

wn Molding

ornice treatment involves installing a
ding. These profiles are designed to sit
he wall and ceiling, and that angle is
angle. Most crown molding falls into
one of two spring angle categories—45/45-degree moldings and 52/38-degree moldings. These descriptions correspond to the angles the molding forms with the ceiling and
wall. It is important that you determine the spring angle for
your molding, as it affects not only how you mount the
molding between wall and ceiling, but how you position it
in the miter box to cut the joints.

Cutting with a Miter Saw. If you will be using a simple
miter saw to cut crown molding stock, the basic technique
involves holding the molding upside down against the saw
or miter box fence. The concept to keep in mind is that the
saw fence is acting as the wall and the saw table is acting as

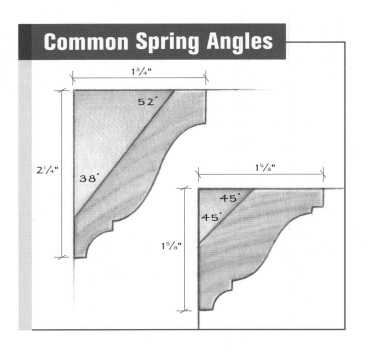

Common Spring Angles

BASIC MITER SAW CUTS

INSIDE CORNER, LEFT SIDE COPE
Place the molding bottom up on the saw's table. (Note that the cove detail is at the top.) Position the molding so that the excess will fall to the left.

INSIDE CORNER, RIGHT SIDE COPE
With the molding bottom up, reposition the miter gauge to the left 45-deg. mark. The excess falls to the right.

OUTSIDE CORNER, LEFT SIDE MITER
With the gauge set on the left and the molding bottom up, cut so that the excess falls on the left.

OUTSIDE CORNER, RIGHT SIDE MITER
Move the gauge to the right. Turn the bottom of the molding up, and cut so that the excess falls on the right.

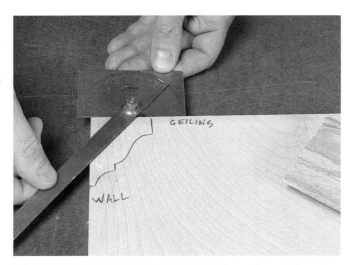

TO DETERMINE SPRING ANGLES, trace the outline of a piece of crown molding on a square panel corner. Make sure that the edges of the molding sit flush to the panel edges. Then use an angle gauge to measure the spring angle.

the ceiling, and when making a cut you need to hold the molding at the appropriate spring angle between the two registration surfaces. In order to cut an accurate miter angle, you must take care that the spring angle is maintained in every case, with the edges of the molding sitting squarely against both the fence and table, before making the cut. Until you become comfortable with the orientation of the molding in the saw, it is easy to get confused. To avoid mistakes in cutting, it is a good idea to take some extra molding stock and cut test joints on four pieces—a left and right outside miter for outside corner joints, and a left and right inside miter, which will be used to cope inside corner joints. Then you can refer to the proper sample piece to ensure that your saw and molding setup are correct.

Cutting with a Compound Miter Saw. When using a compound miter saw, the technique is different because you can make the cuts with the stock held flat on the saw

Text continues on page 164.

6

CROWN MOLDING & CEILING TREATMENTS

COMPOUND MITER SAW CUTS

INSIDE CORNER, LEFT SIDE COPE
Tilt the saw to the correct angle, and set the miter gauge to the right. Place the molding so that the top faces the fence and the excess falls to the right.

INSIDE CORNER, RIGHT SIDE COPE
With the saw tilted, set the miter gauge to the left. Place the molding so that the bottom faces the fence and the excess falls to the right.

OUTSIDE CORNER, LEFT SIDE MITER
With the saw tilted, set the miter gauge to the left. Place the molding so that the bottom faces the fence and the excess falls to the left.

OUTSIDE CORNER, RIGHT SIDE MITER
With the saw tilted, set the miter gauge to the right. Place the molding so that the top faces the fence and the excess falls to the left.

COMPOUND MITER SAW SETTINGS FOR CUTTING CROWN MOLDING

Corner Angle	52/38 Spring Angle		45/45 Spring Angle		Corner Angle	52/38 Spring Angle		45/45 Spring Angle	
	Miter Angle	Bevel Angle	Miter Angle	Bevel Angle		Miter Angle	Bevel Angle	Miter Angle	Bevel Angle
179°	0.31	0.39	0.35	0.35	134°	14.7	17.9	16.7	16
178°	0.62	0.79	0.71	0.71	133°	15	18.3	17.1	16.4
177°	0.92	1.18	1.06	1.06	132°	15.3	18.7	17.5	16.7
176°	1.23	1.58	1.06	1.06	131°	15.7	19.1	17.9	17.1
175°	1.54	1.97	1.41	1.41	130°	16	19.5	18.3	17.4
174°	1.85	2.36	2.12	2.12	129°	16.4	19.8	18.6	17.7
173°	2.15	2.75	2.48	2.47	128°	16.7	20.2	19	18.1
172°	2.5	3.2	2.8	2.8	127°	17.1	29.6	19.4	18.4
171°	2.8	3.5	3.2	3.2	126°	17.4	21	19.8	18.7
170°	3.1	3.9	3.5	3.5	125°	17.8	21.3	20.2	19.1
169°	3.4	4.3	3.9	3.9	124°	18.1	21.7	20.6	19.4
168°	3.7	4.7	4.3	4.2	123°	18.5	22.1	21	19.7
167°	4	5.1	4.6	4.6	122°	18.8	22.5	21.4	20.1
166°	4.3	5.6	5	4.9	121°	19.2	22.8	21.8	20.4
165°	4.6	5.9	5.3	5.3	120°	19.6	23.2	22.2	20.7
164°	5	6.3	5.7	5.7	119°	19.9	23.6	22.6	21
163°	5.3	6.7	6	6	118°	20.3	23.9	23	21.4
162°	5.8	7.1	6.4	6.4	117°	20.7	24.3	23.4	21.7
161°	5.9	7.5	6.6	6.7	116°	21	24.7	23.8	22
160°	6.2	7.9	7.1	7.1	115°	21.4	25.1	24.3	22.3
159°	6.5	8.3	7.5	7.4	114°	21.8	25.4	24.7	22.7
158°	6.8	8.7	7.8	7.8	113°	22.2	25.8	25.1	23
157°	7.1	9	8.2	8.1	112°	22.6	26.2	25.9	23.6
156°	7.5	9.4	8.6	8.5	111°	22.9	26.5	25.9	23.6
155°	7.8	9.8	8.9	8.8	110°	23.3	26.9	26.3	23.9
154°	8.1	10.2	9.3	9.2	109°	23.7	27.2	26.8	24.2
153°	8.4	10.6	9.6	9.5	108°	24.1	27.6	27.2	24.6
152°	8.7	11	10	9.9	107°	24.5	28	27.6	24.9
151°	9.1	11.4	10.4	10.2	106°	24.9	28.3	28.1	25.2
150°	9.4	11.8	10.7	10.6	105°	25.3	28.7	28.5	25.5
149°	9.7	12.2	11.1	10.9	104°	25.7	29	28.9	25.8
148°	10	12.5	11.5	11.2	103°	26.1	29.4	29.4	26.1
147°	10.3	12.9	11.8	11.6	102°	26.5	29.7	29.8	26.4
146°	10.7	13.3	12.2	11.9	101°	26.9	30.1	30.2	26.7
145°	11	12.7	12.6	12.3	100°	27.3	30.4	30.7	27
144°	11.3	14.1	12.9	12.6	99°	27.7	30.8	31.1	37.3
143°	11.6	14.5	13.3	12.9	98°	28.2	31.1	31.6	27.6
142°	12	14.9	13.7	13.3	97°	28.6	31.5	32	27.9
141°	12.3	15.3	14.1	13.7	96°	29	31.8	32.5	28.2
140°	12.6	15.6	14.4	14	95°	29.4	32.2	32.9	28.5
139°	13	16	14.8	14.3	94°	29.9	32.5	33.4	28.8
138°	13.3	16.4	15.2	14.7	93°	30.3	32.9	33.9	29.1
137°	13.6	16.8	15.4	15	92°	30.7	33.2	34.3	29.4
136°	14	17.2	15.9	15.4	91°	31.2	33.5	34.8	29.7
135°	14.3	17.6	16.3	15.7	90°	31.6	33.9	35.3	30

To set the miter angle, adjust the miter gauge on the saw. The bevel angle is set by adjusting the tilt of the saw blade.

Corner Angle	52/38 Spring Angle		45/45 Spring Angle		Corner Angle	52/38 Spring Angle		45/45 Spring Angle	
	Miter Angle	Bevel Angle	Miter Angle	Bevel Angle		Miter Angle	Bevel Angle	Miter Angle	Bevel Angle
89°	32.1	34.2	35.7	30.3	44°	56.7	46.9	60.3	41
88°	32.5	34.5	36.2	30.6	43°	57.4	47.2	60.9	41.1
87°	33	34.9	36.7	30.9	42°	58.1	47.4	61.5	41.3
86°	33.4	35.2	37.2	31.1	41°	58.7	47.6	62.1	41.5
85°	33.9	35.5	37.7	31.4	40°	59.4	47.8	62.8	41.6
84°	34.4	35.9	38.1	31.7	39°	60.1	48	63.4	41.8
83°	34.8	36.2	38.6	32	38°	60.8	48.2	64	42
82°	35.3	36.5	39.1	32.3	37°	61.5	48.4	64.7	42.1
81°	35.8	36.8	39.6	32.5	36°	62.2	48.5	65.3	42.3
80°	36.3	37.1	40.1	32.8	35°	62.9	48.7	66	42.4
79°	36.8	37.5	40.6	33.1	34°	63.6	48.9	66.6	42.5
78°	37.2	37.8	41.1	33.3	33°	64.3	49.1	67.3	42.7
77°	37.7	38.1	41.6	33.6	32°	65	49.2	67.9	42.8
76°	38.2	38.4	42.2	33.9	31°	65.8	49.4	68.6	43
75°	38.7	38.7	42.7	34.1	30°	66.5	49.6	69.2	43.1
74°	39.3	39	43.2	34.4	29°	67.2	49.7	69.9	43.2
73°	39.8	39.3	43.7	34.6	28°	68	49.9	70.6	43.3
72°	40.3	39.6	44.2	34.9	27°	68.7	50	71.2	43.4
71°	40.8	39.9	44.8	35.2	26°	69.4	50.2	71.9	43.5
70°	41.3	40.2	45.3	35.4	25°	70.2	50.3	72.6	43.7
69°	41.6	40.5	45.8	35.6	24°	71	50.4	73.3	43.8
68°	42.4	40.8	46.4	35.9	23°	71.7	50.6	73.9	43.9
67°	42.9	41.1	46.9	36.1	22°	72.5	50.7	74.6	44
66°	43.5	41.4	47.4	36.4	21°	73.2	50.8	75.3	44
65°	44	41.7	48	36.6	20°	74	50.9	76	44.1
64°	44.6	41.9	48.5	36.8	19°	74.8	51	76.7	44.2
63°	45.1	42.2	49.1	37.1	18°	75.6	51.1	77.4	44.3
62°	45.7	42.5	49.6	37.3	17°	76.4	51.2	78.1	44.4
61°	46.3	42.8	50.2	37.5	16°	77.1	51.3	78.8	44.4
60°	46.8	43	50.8	37.8	15°	77.9	51.4	79.5	44.5
59°	47.4	43.3	51.3	38	14°	78.7	51.5	80.1	44.6
58°	48	43.6	51.9	38.2	13°	79.5	51.5	80.8	44.6
57°	48.6	43.8	52.5	38.4	12°	80.3	51.6	81.5	44.7
56°	49.2	44.1	53.1	38.6	11°	81.1	51.7	82.9	44.8
55°	49.8	44.3	53.6	38.8	10°	81.9	51.7	82.9	44.8
54°	50.4	44.6	54.2	39.1	9°	82.7	51.8	83.6	44.8
53°	51	44.8	54.8	39.3	8°	83.5	51.8	84.4	44.9
52°	51.6	45.1	55.4	39.5	7°	84.3	51.9	85.1	44.9
51°	52.2	45.3	56	39.7	6°	85.1	51.9	85.8	44.9
50°	52.9	45.6	56.6	39.9	5°	85.9	51.9	86.5	44.9
49°	53.5	45.8	57.2	40	4°	86.8	52	87.2	45
48°	54.1	46	57.8	40.2	3°	87.6	52	87.9	45
47°	54.8	46.3	58.4	40.4	2°	88.4	52	88.6	45
46°	55.4	46.5	59	40.6	1°	89.2	52	89.3	45
45°	56.1	46.7	59.6	40.8	0°	90	52	90	45

6

CROWN MOLDING & CEILING TREATMENTS

table. First, determine the spring angle of your particular crown molding. To cut a 90-degree corner on 45-degree molding, tilt the saw to a 30-degree bevel angle and set the miter angle to either 35.3 degrees left or 35.3 degrees right. To cut a 90-degree corner on 52/38-degree molding, tilt the saw to a bevel angle of 33.9 degrees and set the miter angle to either 31.6 degrees left or 31.6-degrees right.

Saw settings for joints that occur at angles other than 90 degrees can be found in the chart "Compound Miter Saw Settings for Cutting Crown Molding," on pages 162–163. You can use an adjustable angle gauge to determine the angle of any corner. Just keep in mind that the reading is not guaranteed to be accurate, due to flared corners or dips in the wall surface. Use the angle reading as a starting point for cutting the joint and always test the angle with scrap stock before cutting expensive moldings. Orient the molding on the saw table according to the photos on page 161 to make the appropriate cuts for miter and cope joints. Once

again, it is a good idea to make sample cuts on some short pieces of crown molding. Label these for each type of joint, and use them to test your setup when readjusting the saw.

Evaluate the Room. Before starting your installation, it is important that you examine both the walls and ceiling for any potential problems that could affect the molding. The most common difficulty that you will find is a dip in the ceiling. Hold a long straight 2×4 or 1×4 against the ceiling, near the wall, to test for straightness. If the surfaces are without serious defect, you can install the molding without making any major adjustments, but if bumps or dips are present you have three options to consider.

Fixing Problems. If the irregularities are minor, you can usually bend the molding to conform to the shape of the ceiling. And if small gaps exist, you can caulk them after priming the trim. Keep in mind, though, that bending the crown too severely may result in a visible distortion of the molding, and this might be more distracting than other op-

CUTTING CROWN MOLDING USING A HAND MITER SAW

When using a hand or power miter saw, it is critical to hold a crown molding at the proper spring angle for accurate miter cuts. One way to ensure that the molding sits at the right angle is to create a jig to support the stock. First, fashion an auxiliary table and fence for the saw by screwing together two pieces of 1-by pine stock. Clamp this assembly to the saw, and use a small cut-off piece of the appropriate crown molding as a guide to mark lines on the saw table. Place wooden strips in po-

sition, on the outer side of those lines, and screw them to the table.

Difficulty Level: **Easy**

TOOLS
Hand miter saw • screwdriver • clamps

MATERIALS
Molding • 1-by fence stock • wooden strips • screws

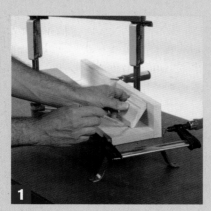

1 **USE A SHORT PIECE** of crown molding as a guide to mark lines on the miter saw table for placement of support strips.

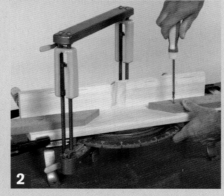

2 **SCREW SUPPORT STRIPS** to the auxiliary miter saw table to hold crown molding at the proper spring angle.

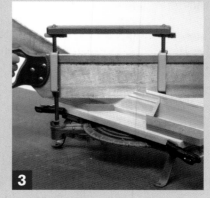

3 **PLACE A LENGTH** of crown molding in the miter saw with its top edge resting on the saw table against the support strip.

Nailing Crown Molding

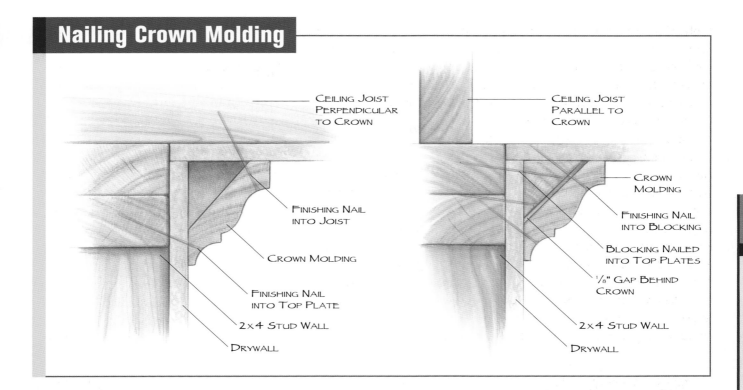

CEILING JOIST PERPENDICULAR TO CROWN

CEILING JOIST PARALLEL TO CROWN

CROWN MOLDING

FINISHING NAIL INTO JOIST

FINISHING NAIL INTO BLOCKING

CROWN MOLDING

BLOCKING NAILED INTO TOP PLATES

FINISHING NAIL INTO TOP PLATE

1/8" GAP BEHIND CROWN

2 x 4 STUD WALL

2 x 4 STUD WALL

DRYWALL

DRYWALL

6

CROWN MOLDING & CEILING TREATMENTS

tions. Too much stress on a molding can also cause problems at the corner joints because the spring angle can be difficult to maintain.

A second approach is to hold a length of molding in place at the most extreme defect, and mark the bottom edge on the adjacent wall surface. Use that mark as a reference in establishing a level line around the room, and set the crown to that line. This will result in gaps at certain points between the crown and ceiling, but if they are not too large, you can fill them with caulk or joint compound.

Another option, and the most difficult, is to scribe the crown to fit around any dips or bumps in the walls or ceiling. If your crown molding is to be stained or will receive a clear finish, this is the best approach. First, cut the molding to length with appropriate joints at either end; then have a helper assist you in holding the molding in place against the wall and ceiling. Mark the areas that need to be adjusted, and use a sharp block plane to remove the necessary stock. Proceed slowly, testing the fit of the molding frequently so that you do not remove too much material.

Installing Blocking. Because crown molding spans the joint between wall and ceiling, it must be fastened to both surfaces to maintain its position. While you can rely on having studs and a top plate to accept nails on the wall side of the molding, you can only count on ceiling joists running perpendicular to half of the walls in a room. On the remaining walls, where the joists run parallel to the wall

surface, there is often no framing member where you require one for nailing at the ceiling. You can easily solve this problem by installing backer blocks around the room to accept nails wherever necessary. Cut 2-by stock to form blocks, at the appropriate spring angle, that you can nail to the wall studs and top plate. Cut the blocks to allow a space of about 1/8 inch between the molding and block so that you have some room to adjust the molding during installation.

Plan the Layout. As with base trim, it is important to plan the order of installation of crown molding. The primary difference with ceiling trim is that there are generally no doorways or other room openings to consider. For wooden crown molding, the convention of using coped joints at inside corners and miter joints at outside corners is one to take seriously. Inside miter joints are extremely likely to open over time, if not directly upon installation. In a basic installation—a rectangular room with four walls—the first piece of crown can be installed with two square ends which butt tightly to the wall surfaces. Thereafter, you should proceed around the room with the next two pieces having one coped end and one square end. The final piece of molding will require two coped ends. Because it is difficult, even for a professional carpenter, to carefully fit a piece of molding with coped joints on both ends, you can fit each corner on separate pieces and then cut a scarf joint to join the two pieces into one continuous length.

Text continues on page 168.

Installing Crown Molding

Difficulty Level: **Challenging**

TOOLS

Hammer • nail set • measuring tape • chalk-line box • power drill and bits • power miter saw • coping saw • files • caulking gun

MATERIALS

Crown molding • blocking material • wood glue • caulk • finishing nails

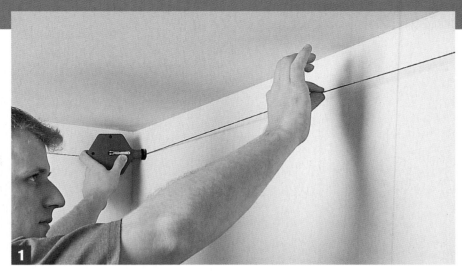

1

ONCE YOU'VE ESTABLISHED your guideline location, snap a chalk line for the molding.

4

INSTALL the full-length square-cut cornice, fitting it into the corner. Don't nail within 3 or 4 ft. of the corner yet.

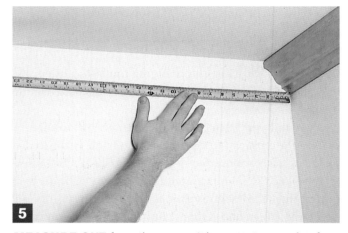

5

MEASURE OUT from the corner (plus an extra couple of inches) to find the rough length of the coped molding.

8

ROTATE THE SAW as needed to maneuver the thin blade along the profile of the miter.

9

USE AN OVAL-SHAPED FILE (or a round file in tight spots) to clean up curved sections of the profile.

MATCH THE ANGLE of the molding installation to the angle of the nailers, and cut them on your power miter saw.

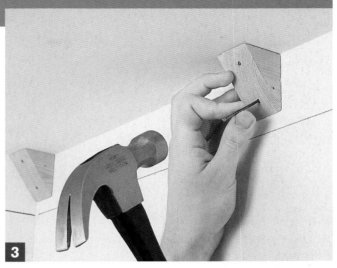

NAIL OR SCREW the support blocks to wall studs and the wall top plate every 16 inches.

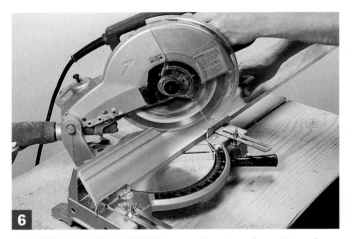

CUT THE COPING MITER on another board, and transfer the dimension from Step 5, measuring from the miter tip.

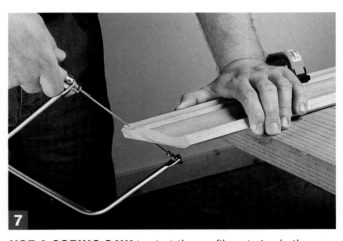

USE A COPING SAW to start the profile cut. Angle the saw to back-cut the coped piece.

USE A FLAT RASP as needed to clean up the upper section of the coped cut or to increase the back-cut angle.

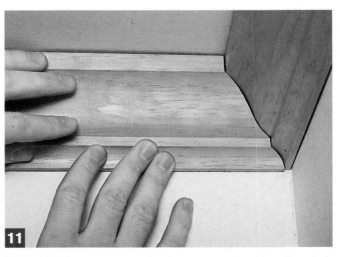

TEST-FIT the coped piece in place, supporting the other end to be sure the board is level.

Continued on next page.

CROWN MOLDING & CEILING TREATMENTS

6

Continued from previous page.

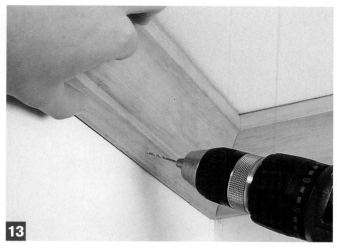

DOUBLE-CHECK your measurements, and trim off any extra wood from the rough measurement.

ADJUST AND FIT the pieces, support the coped piece in place, and drill near the coped end to prevent splitting.

Trim Tip   INSIDE CORNERS

It can be difficult to achieve tight inside corner joints even when all conditions are perfect. And since those conditions rarely exist, expect that some fussing and refitting will be necessary, especially when you first begin a job. Corners that are not perfectly square, and walls and ceilings that are not absolutely flat can modify the spring angle and change the profile of the required cope. To make your life easier, it's worth doing all you can to allow some flexibility in the joint. One technique you can employ is to refrain from nailing within 2 feet of the corner on the first piece of molding that you install on an inside corner joint. Then when you test the fit of the coped joint, the first piece is not secured fast to the wall, and you have the ability to adjust the position of that piece to better correspond to the coped profile.

For pieces that require a coped joint, cut the stock a few inches longer than the wall, then fashion and test the fit of the coped end before laying out the finished length. This provides you with some latitude to get the coped joint right without worrying about the overall length of the section of molding.

If the molding must fit between two walls, you will have to hold the opposite end away from the wall to test the fit. Of course, molding that ends at an outside corner should be held in place to be carefully marked for exact length.

Outside Corners. In rooms that include an outside corner joint, you can often avoid the necessity of having to cut coped joints on both ends of a length of molding. In this case, you can save the outside corner to be the last joint which you fit, and because it is an open-ended joint, you can fit the coped corner first and then hold the molding in place to mark the final length of the outside miter.

When cutting molding that fits between two walls, add at least $\frac{1}{16}$ inch to the measurement before cutting the stock to length. The additional length will ensure a tight joint at the ends of the molding, but it will require you to "spring" the molding into position. As a general rule, follow this technique when cutting pieces that fit between two surfaces as the additional tension can help close joints that are otherwise a bit open, or keep well-fitting joints from opening in the future.

CROWN MOLDING is often used as a cornice treatment, but it can also add a distinctive look to cabinetry.

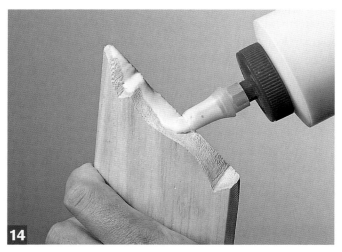

14 APPLY WOOD GLUE to sections of the coped end that will make contact with the square-end piece.

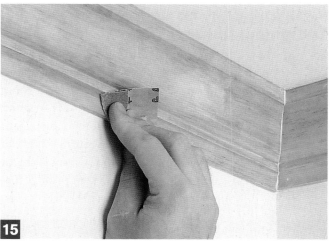

15 TO FINISH, drive and set finishing nails to secure the corner pieces, and sand or caulk the joint as needed.

Installing Outside Corners

Difficulty Level: Moderate

TOOLS
Hammer • nail set • measuring tape • chalk-line box • power drill and bits • power miter saw

MATERIALS
Crown molding • blocking material • wood glue • caulk • finishing nails

1 CUT AND FIT the coped joint first, and then hold the section in place and mark for cutting.

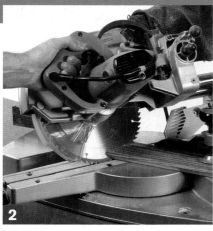

2 TRIM THE MOLDING, and cut a miter joint on the end. Do the same for the adjoining piece.

3 INSTALL THE PIECES by applying a bead of carpenter's glue to the joint and securing with finishing nails.

4 SMOOTH THE JOINT so that the molding appears to be a continuous piece. Use a nail set to knock down the edge.

Installing Built-up or Compound Cornice Trim

For rooms with high ceilings, or for any situation where you want a more elaborate ceiling molding, consider a built-up or layered approach to the cornice. Even a room with an 8-foot ceiling can accept this type of treatment, providing the cornice is in proper proportion to the scale of the room. The cornice can be as simple as pairing a frieze of inverted baseboard or 1-by pine with a crown molding, or complex, such as combining several different profiles that complement each other. A built-up cornice does not need to include an angled crown molding. It can include two or more types of flat molding stock applied to just the wall or both wall and ceiling.

Profile Choices. Common elements that are used in built-up cornices include dentil, egg and dart, cove, bead, bed, and crown molding, although your actual choices are certainly not limited to those options. The best way to proceed in developing a design is to study available molding profiles and draw full-scale cross sections of different com-

Installing a Built-Up Cornice

Difficulty Level: **Challenging**

TOOLS
Power drill and bits • hammer
• nail set • measuring tape
• nail gun and nails (optional)
• miter saw • spirit level
• screwdriver

MATERIALS
Cornice molding stock • 1-by backing stock • wood glue • hollow-wall anchors • finishing nails

1 **HOLD THE BACKER** in place against the ceiling to drill pilot holes for screws. Drill through backer and into the ceiling to mark the location of spiral anchors where necessary.

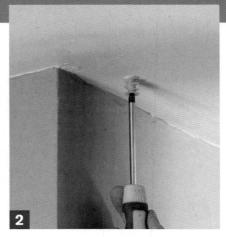

2 **INSTALL SPIRAL ANCHORS** wherever you cannot locate a ceiling joist for blocking attachment.

6 **CUT FLAT MITERS** for outside corners of the soffit trim, and nail the soffit to the backer. Fashion coped joints for inside corners. Adjust the fit as required. Cut miter joints for outside corners, and nail the crown to both the soffit and frieze.

7 **NAIL THE FASCIA** to the soffit and backer boards. Position the fascia so that it projects ¼ in. below the soffit.

binations so that you can better envision them. You can use the samples in the drawings on pages 172–173 as a guide in designing your cornice. When you arrive at a prospective design, purchase short sections of each molding, and assemble a sample block of the cornice that is 1 or 2 feet long—you can use nails or even hot glue to hold the parts together—and hold it up to the ceiling. This will allow you to best judge whether the proportions and particular moldings are correct. While this may seem excessively cautious, remember that the investment in both materials and time

for a cornice of this type is considerable. The worst case scenario has you completing the job only to realize that the trim seems totally out of place in the room. An additional bonus to making the sample cornice is that you actually go through the assembly process. This can be very helpful in planning the sequence of steps you will go through when installing the molding.

Blocking and Backing. In some cases, you will need to provide blocking to support a built-up cornice, and in other situations none will be required. In more elaborate

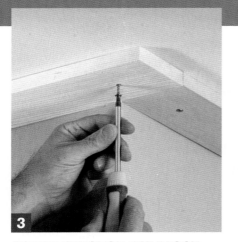

SCREW THROUGH THE BLOCKING to fasten it to the ceiling. Drive the screws into ceiling joists or spiral anchors to form a base for cornice trim.

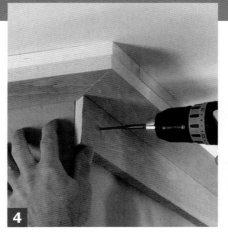

MARK A LEVEL LINE to indicate the bottom edge of the frieze. Use screws to fasten the frieze to wall studs or top plate. Locate the screws in the area that will be covered by subsequent trim.

CUT AN OPEN MITER to prepare for cutting the coped profile at an inside corner. Test the fit, and make necessary adjustments.

INSTALL BED MOLDING between the fascia and ceiling. If necessary, you can caulk any gaps between the molding and ceiling or wall surfaces.

COMPLETED built-up cornice. The goal is to make the multiple components look like one piece of molding.

6

CROWN MOLDING & CEILING TREATMENTS

Typical Built-Up Cornice Profiles

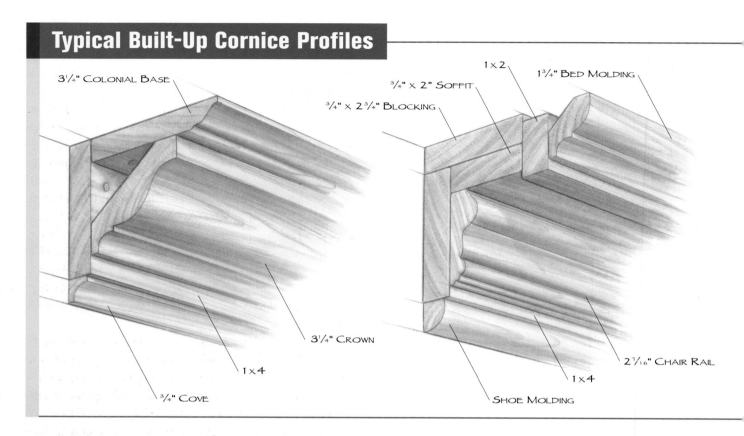

3¼" COLONIAL BASE

¾" X 2¾" BLOCKING

¾" X 2" SOFFIT

1 x 2

1¾" BED MOLDING

3¼" CROWN

1 x 4

¾" COVE

2⁷⁄₁₆" CHAIR RAIL

1 x 4

SHOE MOLDING

designs, continuous backing is often the best choice because it is good practice to stagger scarf joints, and the backer allows you to locate these joints at any convenient spot.

In a built-up cornice, it is always best to establish a level line to define the bottom edge of the trim element against the wall. Then if you encounter deviations in the height of the ceiling from that line, you can take up the difference between two or more molding elements and make the discrepancy less visible. As a general rule, those viewing a finished cornice installation tend not to notice small variations in the reveals between profiles from one part of a room to another—things that can seem quite problematic, and obvious, to the installer.

Most built-up cornices involve some type of frieze that is mounted to the wall and serves as the base for other profiles. The frieze serves as a decorative element as well as blocking to accept the nails to hold them in place. It can be made from 1×4 stock, either with or without a molded edge, or a piece of inverted baseboard molding. Once you have established your level line, it is a simple matter to install the frieze to the wall. If you are using stock without a molded edge, inside corners can be treated with simple butt joints; otherwise coped joints are required. Outside corners should be treated with miter joints, just as if installing baseboard—only upside down. Whenever possible, use screws

to fasten the frieze to the wall studs and top plate as they provide more strength and less trauma to the wall than nails. Locate the screws where they will be covered by the next layer of molding, and use nails at those spots that will be exposed.

If your design requires further blocking, install it next. The specific configuration will depend on the moldings you have chosen. Often 2×4 stock can be ripped at the required angle to form continuous backing for a crown or bed molding. Nail or screw the backer to the frieze board. For those situations that demand blocking on the ceiling, methods of fastening can be a problem. On those walls that run perpendicular to ceiling joists, you can use nails or long screws for fastening. However, on walls parallel to the joists, there are often no framing members where you need them. The easiest solution is to get an assistant to help hold the blocking in place on the ceiling and drill pilot holes for screws through the blocking and into the drywall surface. Then remove the blocking to install spiral anchors in the pilot holes in the ceiling. You can then replace the blocking and use long screws to attach it.

Place marks on the frieze to act as guides in positioning the next layer of molding. Install that layer, nailing it to the frieze and appropriate backing. Proceed with each layer in similar fashion until the cornice is complete.

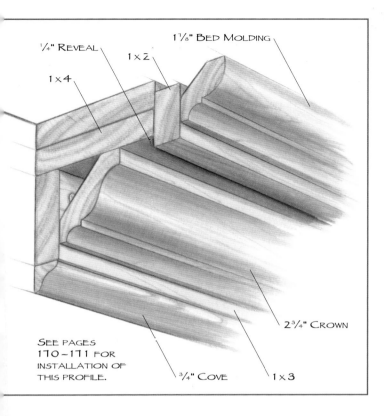

¼" REVEAL

1⅛" BED MOLDING

1 × 2

1 × 4

2¾" CROWN

¾" COVE

1 × 3

SEE PAGES
170–171 FOR
INSTALLATION OF
THIS PROFILE.

Beamed & Coffered Ceilings

Although they appear to require a high degree of skill, the assembly of a beamed ceiling is no more complex than that of a built-up cornice—in fact, many of the techniques are identical. A ceiling beam usually consists of a long U-shaped structure that is fastened to strategically located blocking on the ceiling. Beams run parallel to one another and can be spaced evenly or irregularly across a room. Rooms with tall ceilings can generally tolerate larger beams and closer spacing than rooms with lower ceilings. This type of treatment is not limited to rooms with flat ceilings; some of the most dramatic applications of a beamed ceiling are found in spaces with soaring cathedral ceilings. You can orient beams parallel to the rafters or position them so that they run parallel to the ridgeboard to suggest structural purlins.

Coffered ceilings add another level of complexity to the mix. Coffers are recessed areas on a ceiling that are the result of intersecting beams, turning the ceiling surface into a virtual grid. Most often coffers are square or rectangular, but they can be diamond shaped as well—if the beams run diagonally across a room. The ceiling surface of a coffer can be painted, wallpapered, or covered with boards or veneered panels. This treatment is most appropriate in the more formal rooms of a house, such as a library or dining room.

Beam Materials. Like all interior trim, beamed and coffered ceilings can be constructed with either paint- or stain-grade materials. Pine and poplar are the logical choices for work that will be painted, as they are easy to work and are relatively inexpensive. If painted the same color as the ceiling, the beams become more restrained details, and if given a complementary or contrasting color, they become dominant features in the room. Otherwise, native hardwood species such as oak, cherry, maple, and walnut are popular choices—each contributing its own particular character and associations. Oak makes a strong statement in a room; it accepts stain well, and draws your attention with bold open-grain patterns. Cherry and maple are more subtle choices, contributing warmth and character without overpowering other architectural features. Walnut is associated with elegance and formality; it is a good choice for a more formal public room.

COFFERED CEILINGS are usually ornamental, but they remind us of an earlier, more substantial type of design.

Installing a Beamed Ceiling

Study our drawings to consider some options for ceiling beam construction. Once you have decided on a design, draw a full-scale cross section of a typical beam so that you have a clear plan indicating the sizes of each required part, including the blocking. As an example, if your beam is to be 5 inches wide, you can use 2×4 stock for the interior blocking. Whether your beams are 5 inches or some other width, nominal 2-by material is best to use for blocking because it provides a full 1½ inches of nailing surface for hanging the beams. You can always rip the material to an odd width if the stock size does not suit your plan. If you use ¾-inch-thick stock to construct the beams, the edge of the blocking must be located ¾ inch inside the finished beam wall.

Beam Locations. In planning the locations of beams, it is helpful to note the direction and location of the ceiling joists in the room. Use an electronic stud finder to locate the joists, and place a light pencil mark on the ceiling, adjacent to the wall, to indicate the centerline of each joist. If your beams will run perpendicular to the ceiling joists, your task will be simple as you can screw the blocking directly to each joist. If the beams will run parallel to the joists, you can either decide to locate each beam directly under a joist, use spiral anchors to accept screws, or open the ceiling to install solid blocking between the joists to carry the beams. Unless your beams are to be extremely large and heavy, tearing into the ceiling should not be necessary—spiral anchors or toggle bolts are easy to use and will support the weight of a decorative beam.

In most cases, it is easiest to construct the beams in a workshop (or any spare room), and install them in one piece or in sections. Then you can apply molding at the ceiling and wall joints, if that is part of your design. It is also possible to build them in place—although the job becomes much more awkward because you must work overhead.

Beam Designs. Beams can be built using several different techniques to join the sides to the bottom. The simplest way is to use butt joints and glue and nail the parts together. This system can be used whether the bottom is recessed from the sides or held flush. Of course, you can use joining plates to align and reinforce the joints. If you use plates, you can still nail the parts, but if you have enough clamps, it is possible to eliminate the nails and the need to fill all those extra holes. Miters are also an option for these joints, however it is quite challenging to fashion a tight joint over the long distances required for a beam, and a less than perfect miter is not an attractive detail.

If you would like a beam to run along a wall, the most common treatment is to construct a partial beam that is approximately half as wide as the beams in the rest of the room.

Decorative Beam Construction

Traditional Box Beam

CEILING JOIST

COVE MOLDING

Mitered Box Beam

CROWN MOLDING

CEILING JOIST

CHAMFERED EDGE

This is a detail that can be used both parallel to the rest of the beams in the room and, on the perpendicular walls, as a way to resolve the intersection of the beams with the wall.

Termination Points. While in the planning stages of your job, give some thought to how you plan to treat the intersection of the beam ends with the wall surface. You can, of course, just let the beams die into the drywall. However, another option, and one which provides some distinct advantages, is to mount a frieze along the wall to accept the beams. If you size the frieze to be wider than the depth of the beams, it can provide a nice clean transition between the elements. It also provides you with an easier installation by removing the necessity of fitting the beams tightly between the drywall surfaces. You can also use the partial beams, discussed above, as a way to treat the beam ends. These provide a convenient way of ending the beams and also create the illusion that the deeper partial beams are supporting those that die into them.

Begin your installation by laying out the position of the blocking for the beams, including partial beams. Place light pencil marks on the ceiling surface, adjacent to each end wall, to indicate the outside edges of each piece of blocking; then strike chalk lines between the marks. Cut the blocking to length; then have an assistant help you to hold it in place along the chalk lines while you drill pilot holes for screws through both blocking and ceiling. If necessary, install spiral anchors in the pilot holes. Screw the blocking to either the ceiling joists or anchors. Repeat the process at each beam location.

Stagger Joints. Take careful measurements for the length of each beam because room dimensions can vary, and then rip and crosscut the parts to size. If you plan to assemble the beams in sections, rather than full length, lay out the joints in sides and bottom so that they are staggered. This will allow you to easily join the sections on site into a continuous straight unit. For a design that includes joining plates, lay out the location of the slots, and cut them with the plate joiner. Assemble the beams in the longest manageable sections using glue, joining plates, and nails, as appropriate.

If your plan includes either a frieze or partial beams as end details, begin your installation there. When a crown or other type of ceiling molding will be used along the beams, you can use screws to hold the beams to the blocking, and the screw heads will be covered by the molding. This is a nice option because it provides another level of detail and can also cover gaps between the beam and an uneven ceiling. In addition, the use of screws eliminates the need for pounding against the blocking. If no molding is included in your plan, use finishing nails to mount the beams. For this

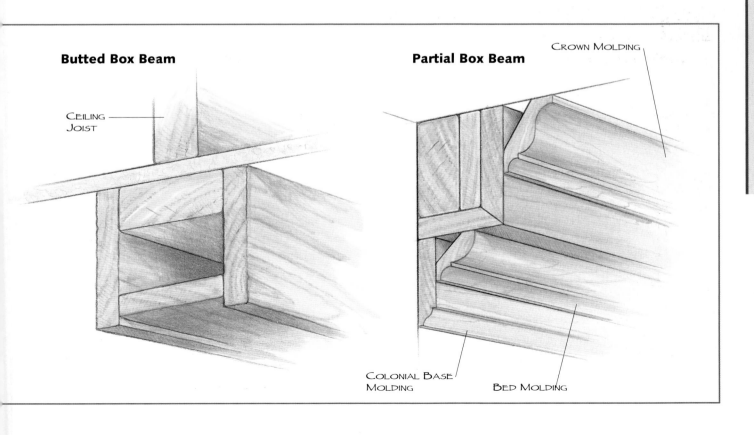

Butted Box Beam

CEILING JOIST

Partial Box Beam

CROWN MOLDING

COLONIAL BASE MOLDING

BED MOLDING

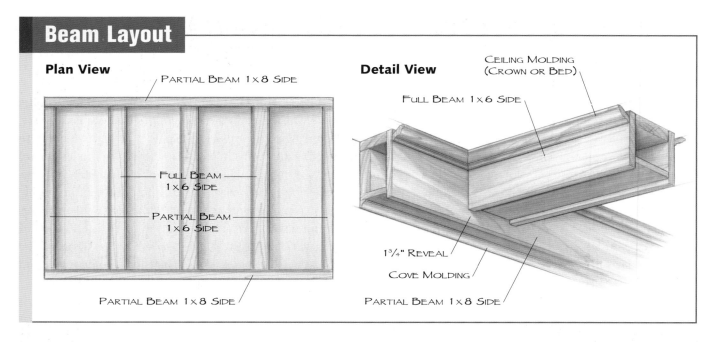

Beam Layout

Plan View

PARTIAL BEAM 1 X 8 SIDE

FULL BEAM
1 X 6 SIDE

PARTIAL BEAM
1 X 6 SIDE

PARTIAL BEAM 1 X 8 SIDE

Detail View

CEILING MOLDING
(CROWN OR BED)

FULL BEAM 1 X 6 SIDE

1³/₄" REVEAL

COVE MOLDING

PARTIAL BEAM 1 X 8 SIDE

job, it is best to use a nail gun, as it will easily and quickly sink the fasteners without beating on the blocking, and it allows you to hold the beam in place with one hand and drive nails with the other.

BEAMS OF DIFFERENT SIZES create an interesting ceiling design. The larger beams appear to support the smaller.

After you hang all the beams, install the ceiling molding. Treat the beams as you would any wall surface, and cope all inside joints where the beams meet the wall.

Coffered Ceiling Construction

Because a coffered ceiling is defined by intersecting beams, the basic construction techniques are the same as for a beamed ceiling. Beams can be designed to all be the same size, but it is also common to have deep and relatively wide beams running in one direction and shallower, narrow beams intersecting them. This type of layout emphasizes the structural reference, as the larger members appear to be carrying the smaller ones.

You can use any of the beam construction techniques previously described, and the same considerations apply. The easiest way to proceed is to install all beams running in one direction first, and then to layout and install the blocking and beams for the intersecting sections.

While it is not necessary, it is most common to wrap the interior sections of each coffer with at least one layer of ceiling molding. And for a more elaborate treatment, you can apply a built-up cornice around the coffers. If you want to include veneered panels as the surface of the coffers, cut and install them before the ceiling molding. You can use ½-inch-thick hardwood plywood for the panels. Fasten the panels to the ceiling around the edges, next to the beams, so that the fasteners will be covered by the molding.

While this type of project is definitely a labor- and material-intensive endeavor, the results of your efforts can be a spectacular transformation of your room.

Installing a Beamed Ceiling

Difficulty Level: Moderate

TOOLS

Hammer • nail set • plate joiner • power miter saw • power drill with screwdriver tip • spirit level • nailing gun and nails (optional) • clamps

MATERIALS

1-by stock • finishing nails • joining plates • wood glue • screws

1

CLAMP A FENCE to the worktable to support beam sides for cutting joining plate slots. To recess the bottom panel for the beam, support the plate joiner on a spacer.

2

SPREAD GLUE in joining plate slots and also on the plates; then place the plates into the slots in beam sides and assemble the beam.

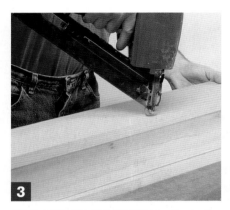

3

NAIL THE BEAM SIDES to the bottom to hold the parts together while the glue sets.

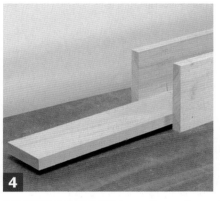

4

TO BUILD A BEAM in sections, stagger the end joints. Extend the bottom panel by about 12 in. on one section and recess it by the same amount on the adjacent section.

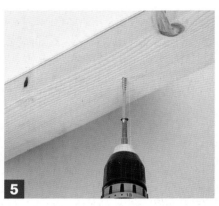

5

HOLD THE BLOCKING in place against the ceiling; then drill pilot holes through both the blocking and ceiling. If necessary, install spiral anchors in the drywall.

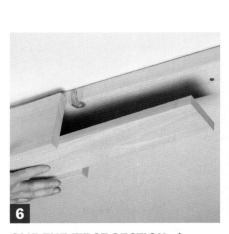

6

SLIP THE FIRST SECTION of a beam over the blocking and push it tight to the ceiling.

7

IF YOU PLAN to install a ceiling molding, use screws to fasten the beam to the blocking as the molding will cover screw heads. Another option is to use a nail gun to fasten the beam.

8

INSTALL THE CEILING MOLDING between the beams and ceiling. The molding detail can be the same as that used around the room perimeter, or it can be a complementary design.

6

CROWN MOLDING & CEILING TREATMENTS

DESIGN IDEAS: CORNICE & CEILING TREATMENTS

ROOMS WITH HIGH CEILINGS, left, can accommodate deep crown or cornice moldings.

FORMAL ROOMS, such as the dining room above, are prime candidates for elaborate cornice treatments.

IS IT REAL? The molding components used above right are real, but they are made of polyurethane rather than wood.

PARTIAL BEAMS, right, provide a termination point for beams that span the room.

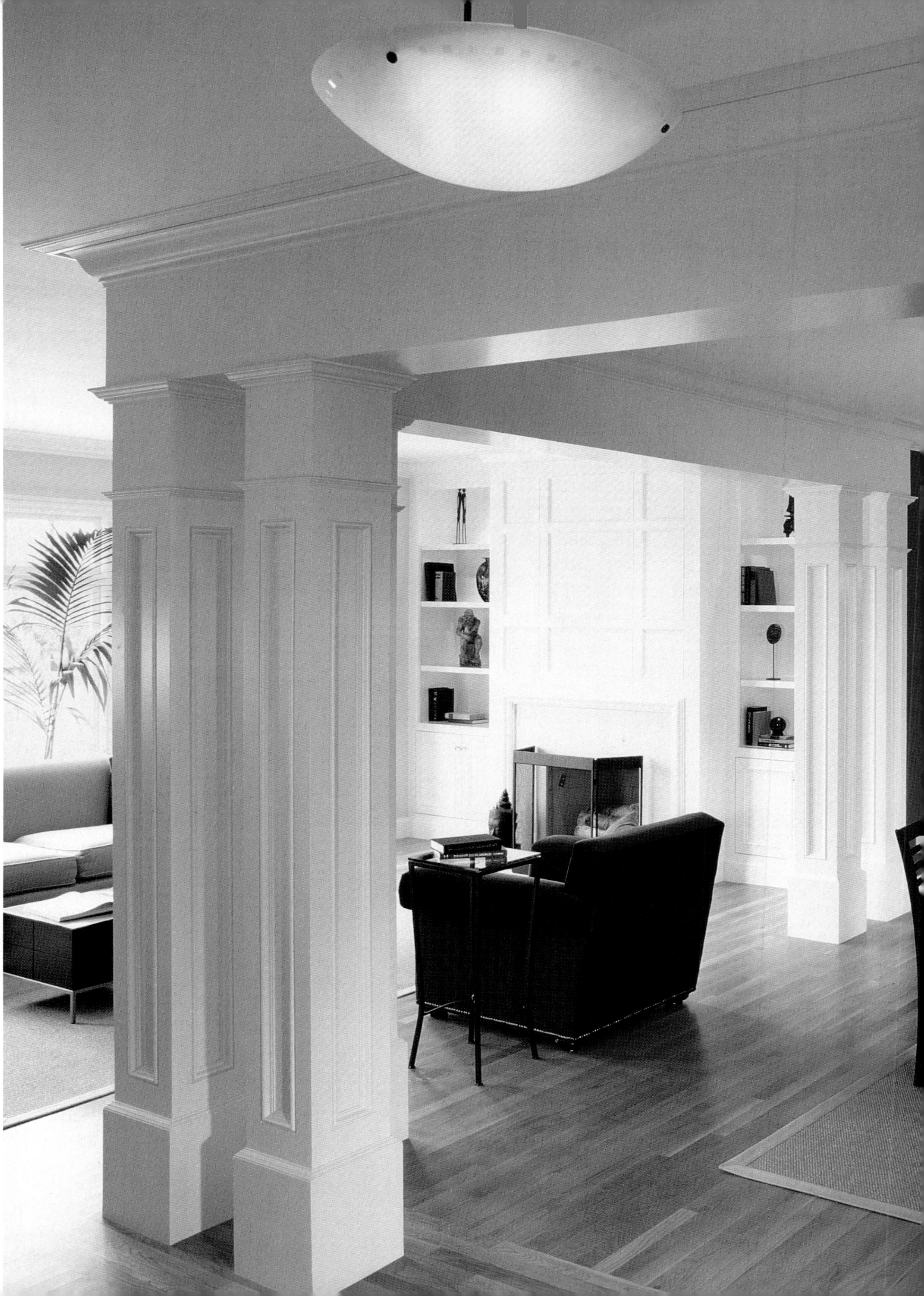

CHAPTER 7

COLUMNS & PILASTERS

A decorating challenge arises when trying to define the transition between rooms—especially those that have no clear demarcation. In newer homes, it is common to have large open areas that can serve multiple functions. Combination living/dining rooms or kitchen/family rooms are regularly included in modern floor plans. Wide hallways and entries can open into adjacent rooms without archways or doors. And while these features are attractive for their flexibility and feeling of spaciousness, they often lack the sense of place and style that only architectural features can impart. There are also many situations where we are simply seeking to make a strong design statement or add a bit of drama to an area of our homes. The answer to any of these needs might be found in the use of columns and pilasters.

Columns

Columns have been used as both structural and decorative elements in buildings since ancient times. And their clear reference to those classical traditions makes them very effective in creating a sense of elegance and dramatic flair when used in a home environment. Columns are powerful elements, though, and their use must be considered carefully so that they do not become an unwelcome and overly dominant feature in a room. The scale, style, particular detailing, and finish of a column all contribute to the overall effect.

Column Materials. While the columns of antiquity were carved from stone, today you have a choice of a wide variety of materials. Of course, stone columns are still available, and for interior use, shorter stone columns might be appropriate

Trim Tip — VISUAL BALANCE

Historically accurate columns incorporate a feature called *entasis*. From the time of ancient Greece, it was noted that if the sides of a column are straight, they have the tendency to appear concave. To counter this illusion, they modified their columns to include a slight bulge in the length of the shaft, and this is known as entasis.

as stands for plants or sculpture. However, the expense of stone columns, as well as the difficulty in moving and installing them, makes them an unlikely choice for most homes. For columns that will be painted, the selection of materials includes wood, MDF, fiberglass, polyurethane, concrete, aluminum, and polystyrene foam. These can be treated with a variety of finishes, including faux-painting techniques that mimic marble or other stone surfaces. You can also purchase stain-grade wooden columns that are designed to take a clear finish. There are suppliers that offer a variety of stock column designs and those that specialize in custom items. You can specify the material, height, diameter, and style for the particular column that will fit your situation.

Column Styles. Many people tend to think of columns as round, but square wooden columns also have a long history; they are appropriate for use in many situations, including contemporary, traditional, and Arts and Crafts interiors. These can be constructed entirely from solid wood or a combination of solid wood and veneered panels. And while round columns must be purchased from a manufacturer, you can easily construct square columns in your home shop using basic trim techniques.

SQUARE PANELED COLUMNS add distinction to an upstairs hallway. Note the arch to the right.

Although most interior columns are purely decorative, there are situations where load-bearing capability is important. For example, if you want to replace a weight-bearing post or support wall with a header and column, it is critical that the column be rated to carry the appropriate load—and that the entire alteration conforms to local building codes. In these cases, consult with an architect or structural engineer. You might also seriously consider having a contractor make the structural changes to your home, reserving the decorative projects for yourself. Columns that are rated for load-bearing applications are available in limited material choices.

Parts of a Column. There are three primary parts to a column—base, shaft, and capital. Most manufactured columns provide these parts separately to simplify installation and give you maximum flexibility in selecting individual parts. Bases and capitals for columns can be relatively simple or extremely ornate. They can be constructed to strictly follow a classical order, or they can be of a more free-form derivative design. Round column shafts can be either smooth or fluted, and most taper from bottom to the top.

Prefabricated Columns. Column manufacturers vary their construction methods depending on the materials used as well as proprietary considerations that make their operation more efficient. The particular installation procedure you must follow will depend on the column you purchase, so it is important to read and follow any instructional material that comes with your column. The instructions should advise as to the best method of fastening the parts together as well as what type of fasteners are recommended between column parts and the building structure.

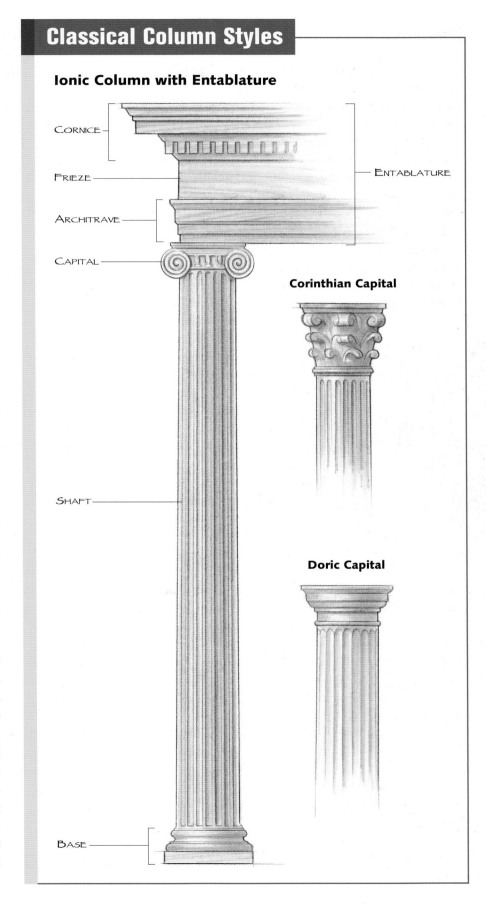

Classical Column Styles

Ionic Column with Entablature

CORNICE

FRIEZE

ENTABLATURE

ARCHITRAVE

CAPITAL

Corinthian Capital

SHAFT

Doric Capital

BASE

7

COLUMNS & PILASTERS

Building a Square Column

If you are interested in constructing your own columns, square designs are quite simple to build. The most basic approach would entail nailing four flat pieces of stock together to form a long box and then applying base and crown molding to the assembly. (See "Simple Column Construction," right.) A more involved design, but still not too difficult, is shown in our plan, and is easy to modify to suit your own particular needs. (See "Paneled Column Construction" and "Building a Paneled Column," page 186.) The basic shaft is constructed from hardwood-veneered plywood with applied frames and molding of solid stock. Base and crown molding can be designed to be consistent with your decor.

If you build your own columns, it is a simple matter to build the shaft about ¼ inch shy of the full length of the span between floor and ceiling (or beam). You can then easily slip it in place, and place shims under the bottom end to make up the additional height and bring it tight to the ceiling. To hold the top of the column in position, you can screw a block that is sized to fit inside the column to the surface of ceiling or arch; then slip the column over the block; and nail or screw it in place, much as you would install a beam. Or you can toenail the column into the ceiling or arch to secure the top. Use a spirit level to check that the shaft is plumb in both directions; then fasten the bottom end by toenailing the shaft to the floor. Finally, install the base and crown molding around the column—just as you would install any baseboard and cornice. If possible, use molding profiles that match others used in the room.

Room Dividers. One effective way to define the entrance to a room is to combine a partial wall, or raised platform, with a short column or pillar. (See "Building a Column and Pedestal Roof Divider," opposite.) This type of treatment can be designed to tie into a wainscoting that lines the room walls, or it can be an independent element in a room. The partial wall can be constructed with traditional framing methods and sheathed with drywall, or you can build it using cabinet-making techniques from veneered panels and solid lumber. In the latter case, the construction method of the platform is very similar to that used to build a square column. Simply add a top of solid wood that you notch to fit around the adjacent jamb or drywall surface.

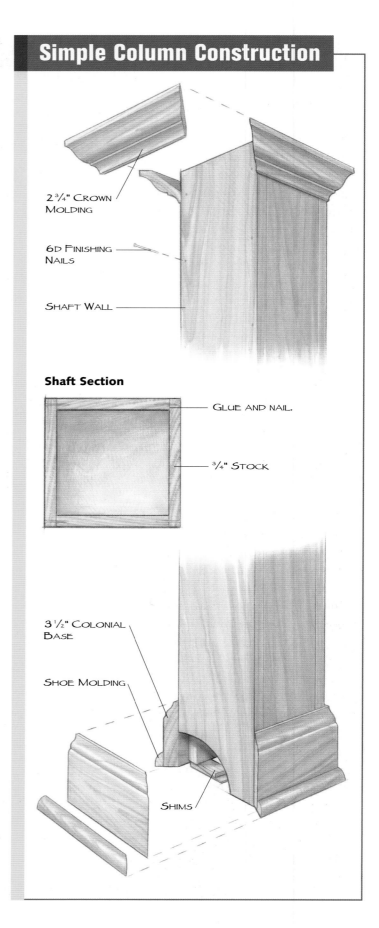

Simple Column Construction

2¾" CROWN MOLDING

6D FINISHING NAILS

SHAFT WALL

Shaft Section

GLUE AND NAIL.

¾" STOCK

3½" COLONIAL BASE

SHOE MOLDING

SHIMS

BUILDING A COLUMN AND PEDESTAL ROOM DIVIDER

To ensure that everything will fit properly, select the columns and all the trimwork before framing the pedestals. If you are building square columns, construct them before building the pedestal. Build the pedestal frames with 2x6 lumber,

and attach them to the side walls of the opening. For slimmer pedestals, you can rip the 2x6s down to match the width of the side walls. Sheathe the pedestal frames with plywood; then add rails and stiles to create recessed panels. Install a shelf and molding to cap the pedestals, notching one end of the shelf to fit around the wall to create horns that extend beyond the trim.

Install one-by jambs under the header and at the sides of the opening. Make sure the columns fit between the pedestal and the header. Install the columns so that their bases are aligned with the inside faces of the pedestals and the shelf ends overhang the bases.

Column & Pedestal Construction

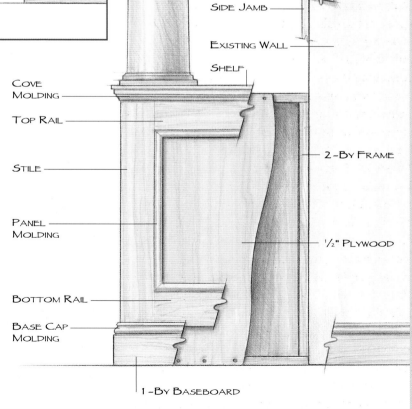

HEADER ASSEMBLY

HEAD JAMB

COLUMN

CASING

SIDE JAMB

EXISTING WALL

SHELF

COVE MOLDING

TOP RAIL

STILE

PANEL MOLDING

BOTTOM RAIL

BASE CAP MOLDING

2-BY FRAME

½" PLYWOOD

1-BY BASEBOARD

Paneled Column Construction

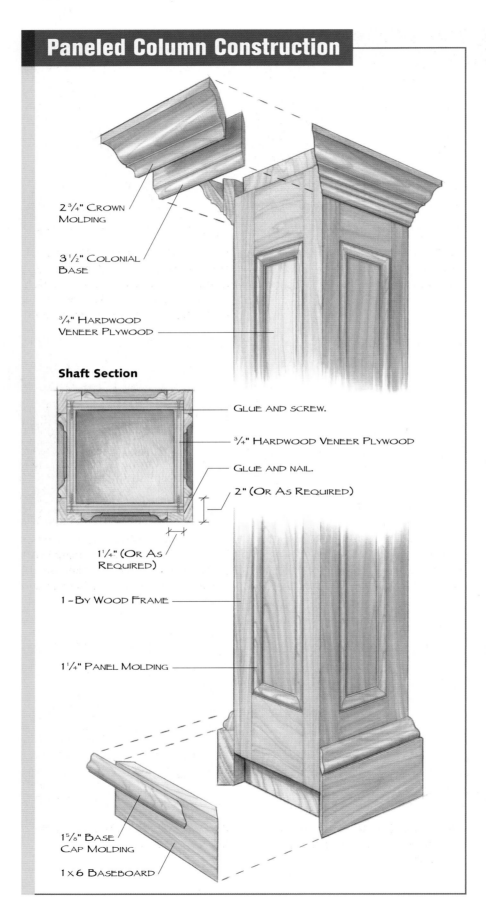

2 ¾" Crown Molding

3 ½" Colonial Base

¾" Hardwood Veneer Plywood

Shaft Section

Glue and screw.

¾" Hardwood Veneer Plywood

Glue and nail.

2" (Or As Required)

1 ¼" (Or As Required)

1 – By Wood Frame

1 ¼" Panel Molding

1 ⅝" Base Cap Molding

1 x 6 Baseboard

Building a Paneled Column

Difficulty Level: *Moderate*

TOOLS
Hammer • nail set • table saw • power miter saw • nailing gun and nails (optional) • plate joiner • clamps • power drill and bits

MATERIALS
Stock for frames • molding stock • finishing nails • wood glue • joining plates

4

APPLY CLAMPS to pull the frame joints tight. Leave the clamps in place until the glue sets—at least one hour.

8

POSITION THE COLUMN; then use a pry bar to lift it to bring its top tight to the ceiling or beam. Place shims under each corner to support the column. Use utility knife to trim.

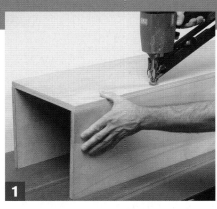

1

USE NAILS OR SCREWS to assemble plywood panels to form the shaft for your column.

2

TAKE CARE when positioning plywood panels to keep the edges perfectly flush.

3

CUT SLOTS for joining plates in the edges of frame stiles and rails. Apply glue to both the slots and plates before assembling the parts. Allow for the proper exposure above the base trim.

5

NAIL A NARROW FRAME to one side of the plywood column shaft. Keep the edges of the frame flush to the box edges all along its length.

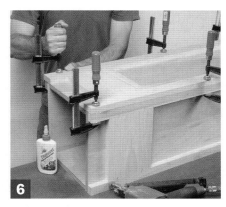

6

AFTER FASTENING the two narrow frames to the shaft, apply the wider frames. Spread glue along the joints, and use clamps to hold the parts while you nail the frames together.

7

CAREFULLY MARK panel molding to length, and cut to size with miter joints at the ends. Use brads to fasten the molding to the plywood column shaft.

9

DRILL ANGLED PILOT HOLES into the bottom of the shaft for toenailing it to the floor. Use finishing nails to lock the column in position. Set the nailheads below the wood surface.

10

APPLY BASE TRIM to the column using the same techniques you would for a wall.

11

APPLY CORNICE TRIM around the top of the column.

Pilasters

A pilaster is a vertically oriented molding assembly that is applied to a wall surface in the form of a column. In fact, the design of a pilaster is meant to suggest that it is embedded in the wall and performing a structural function. It normally features both plinth base and molded capital details and can extend from floor to ceiling or only part of the way up a wall. Pilasters can be used alone or in combination with other architectural features, such as doors or mantles, and they are often employed as part of a wainscoting installation to create a transition between the paneling and door or window casings. You can place two pilasters on the same wall, flanking a door, window, or fireplace, or locate them on opposite walls in a hallway to create a colonnade.

Types of Pilasters. The most common design for a pilaster includes a fluted shaft. You can purchase material that already has a fluted profile, or use your router and a core-box bit to make your own stock. If you choose to shape your own stock, you have the advantage of being able to customize the size and frequency of the flutes. You can design a shaft with larger but fewer flutes, or smaller flutes that are spaced close together. If you have a plunge router, you can cut flutes that stop shy of the board ends, or stagger the end points of the flutes. With a fixed base you need to gradually tip the bit into the stock to achieve a stopped flute.

PILASTERS LOOK LIKE COLUMNS embedded in a wall. They are designed to convey a structural function.

Routing Flutes

Difficulty Level: Moderate

TOOLS
Combination square • plunge router and bit • clamps

MATERIALS
Knot-free 1-by stock

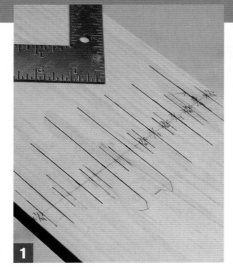

ONCE YOU MARK the locations of the flutes, split each one with a centerline to guide your router alignment.

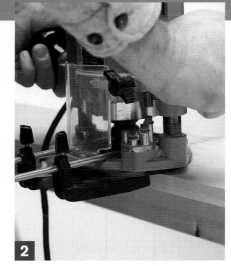

ADJUST THE GUIDE, which travels on a pair of small rails so that the bit point lines up with the flute centerline.

Keep in mind that you are not limited to using fluted material for your pilaster shaft. Almost any wide, symmetrical casing stock can be an appropriate choice; you could also use a plain flat board for a shaft or apply a surface molding to give it another level of detail.

Creating a Pilaster. Building a pilaster involves the same techniques used in installing base trim, cornices, and casing, only applied in a different context. Typically, you will begin by installing a plinth block of ¾ material that is high enough to allow the adjacent base trim to neatly die into it on either side. You could also decide to make the plinth an extension of the base trim. In this case, miter three pieces of baseboard to form a column base, and install them around the shaft. If you are fortunate to have a wall stud directly behind the shaft, you can nail the shaft to the framing. However, a wide shaft should be fastened along each edge to keep it tight to the wall. So, where necessary, use panel adhesive or hollow-wall anchors and screws to fasten it. Make sure to counterbore pilot holes for the screws, and plug the holes over any screw heads.

If you plan to install a chair rail in the room, you can add a pilaster block at chair-rail height to provide a way to terminate the adjacent molding. The block divides the length of the shaft into discrete upper and lower sections. You can fashion these blocks from solid ¾ stock, or you can miter 1-by stock to assemble a block. Chair rail or panel moldings make a nice transitional detail between the block and pilaster shaft.

To complete the pilaster, install crown molding or a built-up cornice around the shaft, just as you would any cornice trim.

THE BASE OF A PILASTER is often simply a continuation of the baseboard trim surrounding it.

7

COLUMNS & PILASTERS

3

WITH A FIRM GRASP on the router, plunge the bit just enough to make contact and leave a mark on the line.

4

SCREW A STOP BLOCK at each end of the board to limit the travel of the router and the length of the flutes.

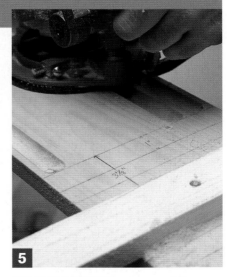

5

WITH PRACTICE you can get the knack of gradually plunging the router to create a tapered end to the flutes.

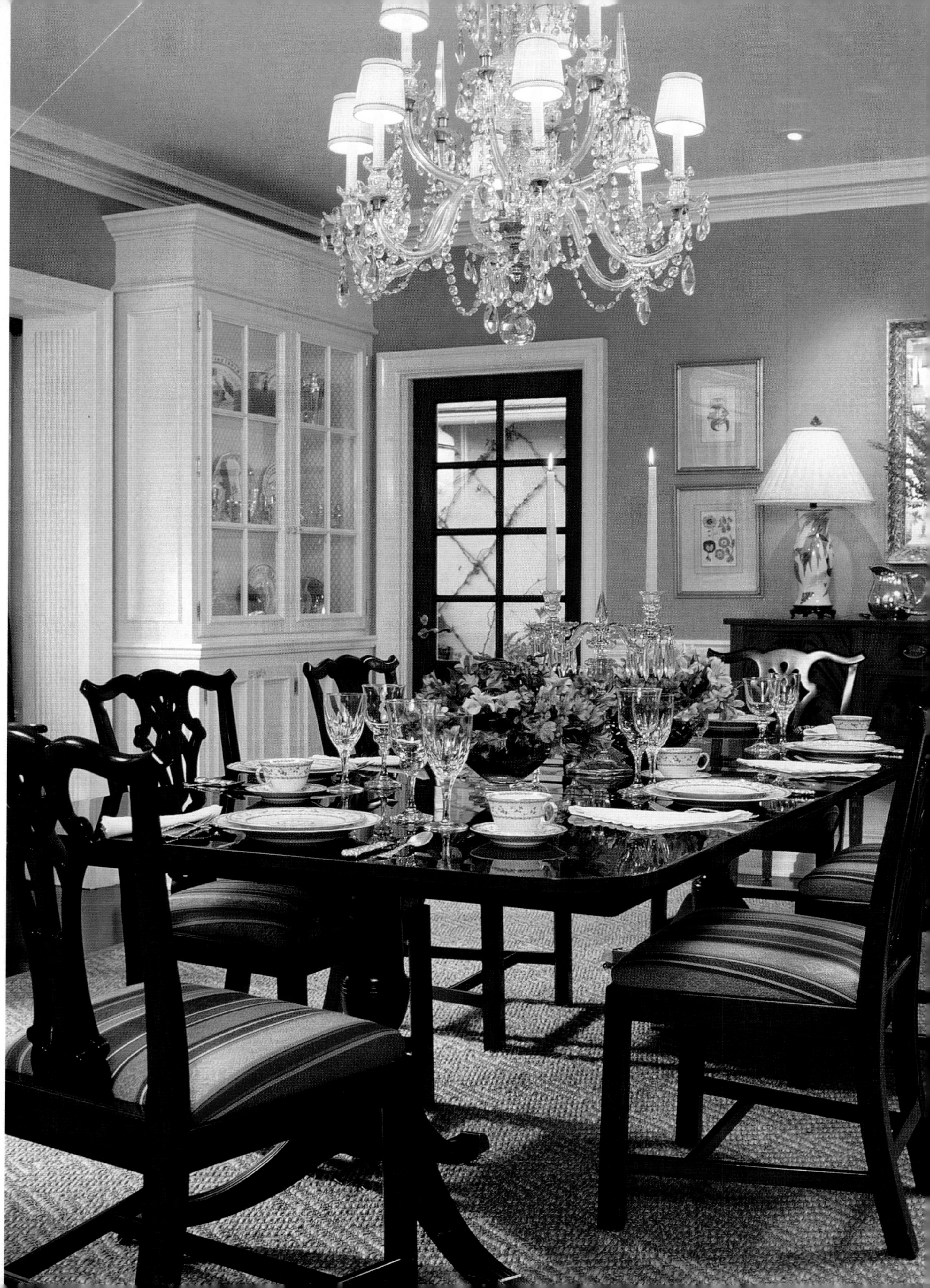

CHAPTER 8

TRIMWORK FINISHES

While the basic steps of trim installation are generally the same regardless of the type of finish that will be applied, there are a few specific considerations for particular types of finish that do not relate to others. The primary divisions in types of finish are painted and clear coatings. Within those categories, there are subclasses of finish type—for example, paint can be a latex or oil-based formula, available in a variety of sheens; clear finishes cover a range of materials, including oil, shellac, varnish, and lacquer, and with these too there are both water- and solvent-based products.

Painted Finishes

Because paint is an opaque coating, it makes sense that it is the more forgiving category of finish. You can fill and sand small smooth gaps in joints and defects in the trim surface prior to applying the final coats of paint, and if well executed, they will not be visible. As mentioned in earlier chapters, a painted finish allows you to select from a wider choice of trim materials. You can use finger-jointed or select pine, poplar, MDF, resin, plaster, or polystyrene foam trim elements, and you can mix materials as well. It is important to remember, though, that paint is not an opaque curtain that will hide a poor installation; sloppy ill-fitting joints and carelessness in implementing your design will still be apparent. And you may be surprised to see how paint will make some problems visible that you do not even notice in the raw wood surface. So do not approach a paint-grade job as an opportunity to relax your high standards of workmanship. Painted finishes, especially those with glossy sheen levels, can telegraph irregularities in a surface much more than you might expect.

Inspect Surfaces. Use a bright light to illuminate the wood surfaces as you inspect them for defects and mill marks. Even though most boards and molding feel rather smooth if you run your hands over the surface, it is common for there to be parallel knife marks left from the manufacturing process. In some cases, these marks are so subtle that a painted finish will make them invisible. But sometimes, they are readily visible and will telegraph through the finish. If you have some doubt as to how the finish will appear, apply a test finish on scrap material. Examine the finished sample in bright light to judge whether the stock requires sanding before applying the paint.

Removing Hammer Marks

Trim that has been hand nailed will usually show some hammer marks from slips or misses when striking nails. Even professional carpenters will occasionally miss the

mark, so don't look at this as an inevitable sign of inexperience. However, you do not want to leave these marks on the wood because they will telegraph through any type of finish and can ruin an otherwise excellent job. Fortunately it's not hard to eliminate hammer marks and other dents.

First, make sure that the nailhead is properly set about ⅛ inch below the wood surface. Use a small brush to spread water on the surface of the hammer mark. Then place a clean cotton cloth over the dent, and heat the area using a household iron on the highest setting. The heat of the iron will cause the water to turn to steam, swelling the wood fibers and raising the dented area. For severe defects, you might need to repeat the process two or more times. The water will cause tiny fibers in the grain of the wood to stand up. Smooth the raised grain by lightly sanding.

SOLVENT-BASED PAINTS

In response to pressures to reduce VOC's (volatile organic compounds), which contribute to ground-level ozone, several states—California, New York, New Jersey, Pennsylvania, Delaware, Maryland, and the District of Columbia—now have regulations in force that limit the content of VOC's in household paints. Similar legislation is being considered in a number of other states. As a result, in these areas most solvent-based coatings will likely disappear from the market and be replaced by waterborne products. Traditionalists may be dismayed by this prospect, as oil-based paints have long had the reputation of better appearance and performance when compared with latex formulas. However, paint manufacturers are quick to assure the consumer that water-based coatings have greatly improved over the last few years and will perform as well, or better, than their solvent-based equivalents.

FOUR TYPES OF PAINT FINISHES from left to right—flat, eggshell, semi-gloss, and gloss. They range from matte to shiny.

Removing Dents

Difficulty Level: **Easy**

TOOLS
Hammer • nail set • household
iron • small brush

MATERIALS
Cotton cloth • sandpaper

1

A HAMMER MARK will stand out on
a piece of newly installed trim. This
mark will telegraph through the finish.

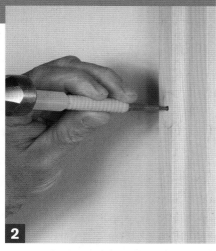

2

MAKE SURE that the nailhead is set
about ⅛ in. below the wood surface
before beginning the repair.

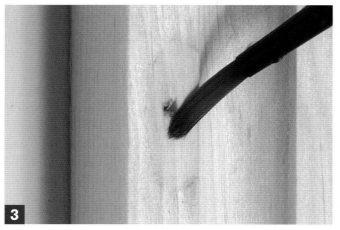

3

USE A SMALL ARTIST'S PAINTBRUSH to spread water on
the surface of the dent, covering the entire area. Let the water
soak in for just a minute, and then repeat the application.

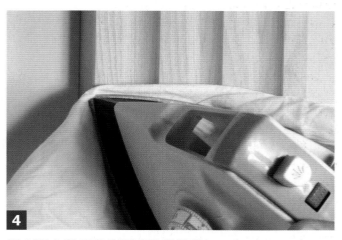

4

PLACE A CLEAN COTTON CLOTH over the dent, and use
a household iron on the highest setting to heat the dented
area. The steam will force the wood cells to swell.

5

USE SANDPAPER and a block to remove the raised grain
from the area of the repair.

6

REPEAT THE PROCESS if necessary. The nailhole is now
ready for filling.

Trim Tip   CAULKING INSIDE CORNERS

To fill gaps in inside corners, use a good-quality acrylic latex caulk—one that contains silicone—to fill the spaces in the joint. Remember, though, that caulk is not effective as a remedy for large gaps, those larger than 1/16 inch. Immediately after you fill a joint, use a wet finger or putty knife to smooth the surface of the caulk and remove excess material. You can also use caulk to fill gaps between trim and the wall or ceiling surface. Fill and tool one joint at a time before the caulk starts to form a skin on its surface.

Filling Nailholes. Because trim relies primarily on nails, and lots of them, to hold the individual elements in place, one of your main concerns will be to fill the holes over the nailheads. If you used a nail gun for installation, the nails should all be properly set. If you have been nailing by hand, go over your work to check that all heads are set. In order for filler to hold well in a hole, the nail should be set about 1/8 inch below the wood surface.

For paint-grade work, fillers come in two primary types—drying and flexible putty varieties. Of the two types, drying filler will do the better job, but it also requires more work because it must be sanded after application. Drying fillers come in one and two-part formulas. For trimwork, the one-part product is fine and simpler to use. Use a small putty knife or a finger to fill each nailhole. For best results, slightly overfill each hole, because most fillers shrink slightly as they dry. Let the product dry according to the directions on the package; then use sandpaper and a backer block to level the filler flush to the surrounding wood surface. You can also use a drying filler to repair scratches, dents, or natural defects in the wood surface. If the defect is large, you should plan to use two layers of filler, allowing the first layer to dry completely before applying the second.

If you want to use flexible painter's putty to fill nailholes, it is best to prime the wood first. When the primer is dry, lightly sand it to remove any roughness. Knead a golf-ball sized piece of putty until it is soft and pliable; then apply the putty using a knife or your finger. Wipe any excess putty from the surrounding wood surface with a clean rag before applying the first coat of paint.

For filling nailholes in polystyrene molding, the best material to use is drywall compound. Slightly overfill the holes to allow for shrinkage, and when dry, sand off the excess.

STAINED FINISHES, left, allow the natural beauty of the wood to show through.

USE CLEAR LUMBER, opposite, for any type of clear finish, as defects will become apparent.

Clear or Stained Finishes

Trim that will receive a stained or clear finish requires a different level of care. With a clear finish, even small gaps in joints are hard to hide, so it is inevitable that the installation process will be slower and more demanding. Whether your trim is pine or one of the hardwood species, you should keep in mind that the application of stain will emphasize any defect in the wood surface. Scratches or dents act as magnets for stain, and it will settle in these areas and inevitably draw your eye. Mill marks and cross-grain sanding scratches are also areas that will be accentuated by stain.

Trim Prep. If you're putting a stained or clear finish on your trim, lightly sand the material before you install it to remove many manufacturing defects. As a general rule, 120-grit sandpaper is appropriate for this type of sanding. Use a backing block for the sandpaper whenever possible. Always move the sandpaper parallel with the wood grain. Avoid cross-grain scratches, as they are particularly visible in stained finishes. Power sanders may be useful for sanding flat stock, but if you use an orbital sander, always follow up by hand sanding. Orbital sanders leave small swirl marks on the wood surface, and these can become visible when you apply stain. To remove these marks, use the same-grit paper to give the surface a light sanding, working parallel with the wood grain.

Finishing. You can fill nailholes either before or after you apply the first coat of finish. If you want to use drying filler under a clear unstained finish, you should find one that closely matches the color of the wood. It is best to make up a finished wood sample and use it when selecting the color of the filler because all woods change color when a finish is applied—and various finishes will color the wood differently. Solvent-based finishes tend to lend a warm amber cast to the wood tone, while water-based finishes are clear. Nondrying fillers are available in two types, both intended for use after the finish has been applied. Soft, putty-type fillers are available in a wide variety of colors to match different species and stains. Knead the filler until it is soft, and work it into the holes. Crayon and pencil-style fillers are waxy and quite hard. Rub the stick over the nailhole until it is filled, and then wipe away the excess. Some of these colored fillers will accept a top coat of finish; others are intended for use after the final coat.

For final touchup after the last coat of finish has cured, use colored markers that are matched to different color finishes. These are handy for small scuffs and scratches that might result from routine life around the house.

8

TRIMWORK FINISHES

RESOURCE GUIDE

The following list of manufacturers and associations is meant to be a general guide to additional industry and product-related sources. It is not intended as a listing of products and manufacturers represented by the photographs in this book.

A & M Wood Specialty
357 Eagle St. N.
P.O. Box 32040
Cambridge, Ontario N3H 5M2
Canada
800-265-2759
www.forloversofwood.com
Domestic and exotic hardwood lumber—shipping available. Offers jointing, planing, and ripping services.

Alexandria Moulding
300 Lasley Ave.
Wilkes-Barre, PA 18706
800-841-8746
www.alexandriamoulding.com
Manufacturer of pine, cedar, hardwood, and MDF moldings.

Architectural Distributors, Inc.
162 Center St.
Grayslake, IL 60030
800-729-4606
www.archdist.com
Wood moldings, wood and fiberglass columns, and pilasters.

Architectural Ornament, Inc.
55 Bradwick Dr.
Concord, Ontario L4K 1K5
Canada
905-738-9459
www.architectural-ornament.com
Polyurethane moldings.

Balmer Architectural Mouldings
271 Yorkland Blvd.
Toronto, Ontario M2J 1S5
Canada
800-665-3454
www.balmer.com
Polyurethane moldings, medallions, door surrounds, and mantels.

Block Industries
140 Commerce Dr.
Rochester, N Y 14623
585-334-9220
www.blockindustries.com
Stock and custom molding profiles and solid wood doors.

Chadsworth, Inc.
277 North Front St.
Historic Wilmington, NC 28401
800-265-8667
www.columns.com
Wood, composite, and PVC columns.

Fypon

960 W. Barre Rd.
Archbold, OH 43502
800-446-3040
www.fypon.com
Urethane millwork in hundreds of profiles.

Moulding & Millwork

1578 Sussex Turnpike
Randolph, NJ 07869
973-584-0040
www.mouldingandmillwork.com
Pine, hardwood, and MDF moldings.

Ornamental Mouldings

3804 Comanche Rd.
P.O. Box 4068
Archdale, NC 27263
800-799-1135
www.ornamental.com
Wood moldings and architectural ornaments.

San Francisco Victoriana, Inc.

2070 Newcomb Ave.
San Francisco, CA 94124
415-648-0313
www.sfvictoriana.com
Architectural ornament for traditional and contemporary buildings. Traditional Victorian trim elements and custom molding services.

Vintage Woodworks

Hwy. 34 S
P.O. Box 39
Quinlan, TX 75474
www.vintagewoodworks.com
Wood moldings and architectural ornaments.

West Penn Hardwoods

117 South 4th St.
Olean, NY 14760
716-373-6434
www.westpennhardwoods.com
Domestic and exotic hardwood lumber—shipping available.

White River Hardwoods Woodworks, Inc.

1197 Happy Hollow Rd.
Fayetteville, AR 72701
800-558-0119
www.mouldings.com
Hardwood and resin moldings, including flexible moldings. Carved architectural ornaments.

Windsor Mill

8711 Bell Rd.
Windsor, CA 95492
888-229-7900
www.windsorone.com
Wood and MDF moldings.

GLOSSARY

Apron A piece of trim that covers the gap between a window stool and the wall surface below.

Backband A narrow molding applied to the outside edge of a casing that adds a square edge and increases the overall thickness of the assembly.

Back cut The technique of removing stock along the rear surface of a piece of molding to reduce the contact area of the joint. Back cuts are recommended in coped joints to allow maximum flexibility in fitting difficult joints.

Backsaw A hand saw with a rectangular blade that is stiffened by a reinforcing metal spine along the top edge of the blade. Available in a variety of sizes, these saws are used to cut precision joints and are the saw of choice for hand miter boxes.

Baseboard Trim members mounted to the bottom of a wall that cover the gap between the wall and floor.

Base cap Molding that covers the top edge of a baseboard.

Beam A horizontal structural member, typically used to support a floor or ceiling. Beamed ceilings are decorative features meant to mimic the appearance of structural beams.

Bevel An angled cut, other than 90 degrees, into the thickness of a piece of stock

Casing A flat or profiled piece of trim that is used to surround a door or window opening.

Caulk A flexible material that is used to fill gaps and seams between adjacent materials. Caulk is supplied in tubes that require an inexpensive gun applicator to transfer it to the target area.

Chair rail A horizontal band of trim, usually located between 30 and 36 inches from the floor. Chair rails were originally intended to protect the wall surface from damage, but now function more as a decorative feature.

Chalk line A string covered with powdered chalk used to mark a straight line between distant points. A chalk-line box opens to accept the powdered chalk and has a reel inside that allows you to automatically spread chalk on the line as it extends from the box.

Chamfer A shallow, angled cut along the edge or end of a board that is used as a decorative detail.

Coffer A recessed area in a ceiling that is defined by intersecting beams. The surface of a coffer can be painted or covered with wallpaper or a veneered panel.

Column A vertical support member with a cylindrical or square shaft that also features base and capital molded details. Decorative columns need not provide actual support but are suggestive of true structural columns.

Coped joint A wood joint in which the end of one piece is cut to match the face profile of the adjacent stock.

Coping saw A handsaw with a thin blade held taut between the ends of a C-shaped frame. The saw is used to make the intricate cuts required for inside corner joints on molding stock.

Corner block   A square block, often with turned center profile, used at the junction of side and head casing in Victorian trim. Corner blocks eliminate the need for mitered joints between casing parts.

Cornice   A molding or assembly of moldings at the junction of walls and ceiling.

Cove   A concave profile on a molding.

Crosscut   To cut a board perpendicular to the direction of the wood grain.

Crown molding   A molding designed to sit at an angle between the wall and ceiling. Crown moldings can also be used as capitals on square columns or to wrap around the head casing of a traditional door trim.

Dentil molding   A molding detail that includes alternating blocks and spaces—suggestive of a row of teeth.

Dowel   A wooden cylinder or peg used to join two individual pieces of wood by fitting tightly into matching holes in the parts. Typically, glue is applied to the dowels to make the joint permanent.

Drywall   A sheet composed of a gypsum core covered with heavy paper on either side that is used to form the interior surface of walls and ceilings.

Entablature   A molded, decorative horizontal band that forms the crowning feature at the top of a building wall or other architectural element, located above a column, pilaster, or casing.

Finger-joint   A means of joining short lengths of lumber together to form a long board or piece of molding stock. Interlocking "fingers" are cut in the matching ends, and the parts are glued together. Finger-jointed stock is suitable only for paint-grade applications.

Flat-sawn   A description of lumber or veneer that is cut parallel to one side of a log. Flat-sawn stock often displays cathedral-shaped grain patterns.

Frieze   A horizontal band of decoration that runs along the wall of a room, usually just under the ceiling. A frieze can also be the area of a wall between the picture molding and cornice.

Grain   The pattern of the fibers in wood that is a result of the growth of the tree. Typically, the grain direction runs along the length of a board. The appearance of grain in a board is largely determined by the way it is cut relative to the annual growth rings of the tree.

Hardwood   Wood that comes from a deciduous tree—one that loses its leaves in winter. Common species include oak, maple, cherry, birch, and walnut.

Head block   A rectangular decorative block used in similar fashion to a corner block in Victorian trim. Head blocks can be manufactured in various shapes and are often cast in plaster. They often feature unusual shapes and elaborate detail.

Header   A horizontal, weight-bearing support over a room opening such as a door, window, or archway.

Jambs   The visible inside frame member of a finished door or window opening. The top horizontal piece is called the "head jamb" and the vertical pieces are called "side jambs."

Joining plate   Football-shaped wafers of compressed wood that fit in matching semicircular slots in a wood joint. Plates are available in a range of sizes for different applications.

Joist   A horizontal member in house framing that supports a floor or ceiling.

Kerf   The width of a saw-blade cut.

Level A term used to describe a perfectly horizontal surface. Also a tool used to determine whether a surface is perfectly horizontal.

MDF Medium density fiberboard. A manufactured material consisting of fine wood fibers bonded with glue under heat and pressure. MDF is used for panel stock as well as moldings and columns.

Millwork A descriptive term used to describe various manufactured wooden trim components such as lumber, moldings, doors, railings, columns, and architectural ornaments.

Miter An angled cut into the face of a piece of stock for a woodworking joint. Typically, the angle of a miter cut is equal to one-half of the total angle of the joint.

Miter saw A saw used to make angled cuts for woodworking joints. Hand-operated and power models are available, as well as models with sliding heads for wide compound angle cuts.

Molding Decorative strips of wood, composite, or synthetic material that are used in various trim applications.

Nail set A pointed metal tool used to drive the heads of finishing nails below the wood surface. Sets are available in various sizes to match nailhead diameter.

Picture rail A molding with rounded, protruding top edge designed to be mounted high on the walls of a room. The edge accepts hooks for hanging pictures.

Pilaster A vertical application that projects from a wall surface to suggest the structure of a column. In most cases, base and capital moldings are part of the installation.

Plate joiner A power tool that cuts semicircular slots in wood to accept compressed wood plates for joining parts. A plate joiner has an adjustable fence that aids in positioning the slot relative to a board surface, as well as various depth stops for different size joining plates.

Plate rail A shallow shelf mounted on the wall to display decorative plates or other small items. Often the rail

acts as the cap of a tall wainscoting installation, but it can also be a stand-alone trim item.

Plinth A block that functions as the base for a traditional door casing or pilaster.

Plumb A term used to describe a perfectly vertical surface.

Purlin A horizontal roof beam that supports the rafters.

Quarter-sawn A description of lumber or veneer that is cut parallel to the radius of the log. Quarter-sawn stock displays grain lines that are parallel to the long edge of the board.

Rabbet An open groove cut along the edge or end of a piece of wood. Rabbets are often used to join two pieces of stock at a right angle.

Rail The horizontal member of a wooden frame.

Rasp A metal tool with rough, toothed surface used for rapid removal of wood. Rasps are available in flat and shaped models, as well as various size tooth configurations.

Rip To cut a board parallel to the direction of the wood grain.

Router A power tool that consists of a motor with tool-holding collet held in a portable base. Various cutting tools can be mounted to the end of the rotating shaft for grooving and shaping wood.

Sandpaper A paper or cloth that is coated with an abrasive grit that is used to smooth wood surfaces. Sandpaper is graded by the size and type of grit, and also the weight of the backer. Higher numbers indicate finer abrasive—lower numbers mean coarser grit.

Scarf joint A joint that is used to join two boards or moldings end to end. Overlapping miter cuts are made in the two parts so that, when assembled, the joint appears invisible.

Scribe To mark and shape a trim member to fit against another irregular surface.

Shim A strip of wood that is used to fill a gap behind a structural or trim item. Most often, narrow tapered shingles are used for this purpose.

Shoe molding A narrow, flexible molding that is used to cover the gap between a baseboard and finished flooring material.

Spring angle A pair of angles that explains the way that a crown molding intersects the planes of ceiling and wall. The first number corresponds to the angle between ceiling and the back of the molding, and the second is the angle between the wall and back of the molding.

Softwood Lumber from a coniferous tree. The most common species are pine, hemlock, spruce, cedar, and fir.

Square A primary concept in carpentry—that two surfaces are perpendicular, or at 90 degrees to one another. Also, the steel tool used to test that two surfaces are perpendicular.

Stile The vertical member of a wooden frame—found on doors, cabinet faces, wainscoting, or square columns.

Stop A strip of wood that abuts a door or window to keep it aligned and operating properly. Stops can have square or shaped edges.

Stud Vertical structural members in house framing, typically of 2×4 or 2×6 lumber.

Toenail To drive a nail at an angle, through one framing member and into another, to lock the parts together.

Veneer A thin layer of wood that is sawn or sliced from a log. Inexpensive veneers can be glued together to form plywood, with a valuable lumber species displayed on the outer surfaces. Veneers can also be applied to composite cores such as MDF and particleboard.

Wainscoting Wooden paneling or boards applied to the lower portion of a wall.

Wall frames Assemblies of panel molding applied to a drywall or plaster wall for decorative purposes.

Warp A descriptive term indicating that a board is not flat.

Window stool A narrow horizontal shelf installed adjacent to the window sash as an interior trim member. The stool acts as a base for the side casings and is supported from below by an apron.

INDEX

A

Acrylic latex caulk, 85
Adjustable sliding bevel, 34
Alcove, baseboard cutting sequence for
    room with, 121
Aliphatic resin glue, 84
American Colonial style, 20
Angle gauge, 34, 105
Angle guides, 34
Apron, 13. See also Stool and apron
Apron molding, 151
Apron panels, 26
Arched entry, 12
Architectural embellishments, 16–17
Architectural styles
    American Colonial, 20
    Arts and Crafts, 28, 105, 134, 136,
        158, 182
    Chippendale, 22
    Colonial, 18–21, 92–94, 118
    Craftsman, 28
    craftsman, 28
    Eastlake, 26
    Farm-style Country, 21
    Federal, 24, 25, 136
    Georgian, 20, 22, 25, 136
    Gothic revival, 25
    Greek Revival, 25, 26
    Hepplewhite, 22
    Italianate, 26
    Mission, 28
    National, 25
    Neo-Classical, 100–103
    Queen Anne, 26
    Sheraton, 22
    Shingle, 26
    Stick, 26
    Victorian, 26
Arts and Crafts style, 28, 158
    for casing, 105
    for columns, 182
    for plate rail, 134
    for wainscoting, 134, 136

B

Backband
    installing, 94
    scribing, to wall, 99
Back priming, 73
Backsaw, 36
Bark inclusions, 74
Base, 69
Baseboard, 12, 20, 21, 116, 118–131
    built-up, 118
    cutting
        to length, 122, 123
        sequences for, 120–121, 122
    dealing with out-of-level floors, 126
    electrical receptacles in, 128–129
    evaluation of room conditions,
        119–121
    figuring corner angles, 124–125
    height of, 118, 126
    inside corners, 122–123
    installation, 120
    nailing, 126
    one-piece, 118
    outside corners, 124–125
    stair stringers and, 131
    three-piece, 118, 126–127
    for wainscoting, 143–144
    wall registers in, 130
Bay window, baseboard cutting
        sequence for room with, 121
Bead board, 78
Bead-board wainscoting
    installing, 140–142
    tongue-and-groove, 140–145
        adjoining wall, 142
        baseboard and chair rail for, 143,
            144
        corner construction, 142
        cutting, 140
        electrical boxes and, 145
        installing, 140–142
        outside corners, 142–143
Beamed ceiling, 14, 29, 157, 173
    beam designs, 174–175

beam layout, 176
beam location, 174
installing, 174–176, 177
stagger joints, 175–176
termination points, 175
Beams
    decorative, 174
    designs, 174–175
    exposed, 21
    location of, 174
    materials for, 173
    mitered box, 174
    rustic, 21
    traditional, 174
Belt sanders, 40
Bench-top planer, 49
Bench-top tools, 49
Block plane, 99
Brads, 82, 100
Built-ins, 29
Built-up baseboard, 118
    covering mistakes, 118
    height of, 118
Built-up cornices
    blocking and backing, 171–172
    installing, 170–172
    profiles, 172
Built-up moldings, 66, 67

C

Cap molding, 118, 126
Casing reveals, 108
Casings, 12–13, 19, 21, 69
    door and window, 87–115
        Arts and Crafts, 105
        casing drywall opening, 90–91
        Colonial, 93–95
        Neo-classical, 100–103
        prehung doors, 88–89
        routing a molding profile, 96–97
        scribing backband to wall, 99
        stool and apron, 108–111
        traditional-style, 98–99
        troubleshooting problems,

112–113
Victorian, 104
wainscoting and, 146
flat, 29
Caulk, 85
latex, 85, 194
Ceiling treatments, 14, 15, 19, 178–179.
See also Beamed ceiling; Coffered
ceilings
Chair rail, 14, 15, 19, 22, 68, 116, 133,
189
baseboard and, 143–144
coping, 56
installing, 132–133, 134
milling, 134
profiles, 133
for wainscoting, 143–144
Chalk line, 34
Checking, 74, 75
Cherry, 173
Chippendale style, 22
Circular saw, 37, 50–51
Clamping worktables, 45
Clamps, 45, 149
Clam-shell, 118
Classical motifs, 22
Classic wainscoting, 79
Clear finishes, 195
finishing, 195
trim prep, 195
Closed-grain wood, 71
Coffered ceilings, 19, 157, 173
construction of, 176
Coffers, 14, 173
Colonial style, 18–21
casing, 118
built-up, 94
simple, 92, 93
Columns, 14, 15, 16–17, 22, 182–187
bases, 183
capitals, 183
construction of, 184
Corinthian, 183
Doric, 183
Ionic, 183
materials for, 182
paneled, 186–187
parts of, 183
prefabricated, 183
rating for load-bearing, 183
shafts, 183

square, 182, 184
styles of, 182–183
visual balance and, 182
Compound cornice trim, 170–172
Compound miter saws, 39
cutting crown molding with,
161–164
Compressor, 46, 47
Construction adhesive, 85
Construction-grade plywood, 79
Contraction, lumber, 73
Coped joints, 56–57, 122
cutting, 56–57
Coping miter, 167
Coping saw, 36, 57, 122, 167
Corinthian column, 183
Corner angles, figuring, 124–125, 131
Corner bead, exposing, 90
Corner blocks, 26, 104, 129, 159
cutting jig for, 129
decorative, 159
Cornice molding, 13, 68
Cornices, 20, 22, 157, 178–179
built-up, 170–172
compound, 170–172
decorative corner blocks with, 159
installing crown molding, 160–172
MDF, 158
polystyrene, 76, 158–159
polyurethane, 158
wood, 159
Cove molding, 21
Craftsman style, 28
Crayon fillers, 195
Cross-grain scratches, 195
Cross-linking PVA, 84
Crown molding, 13, 157
blocking, 165
cutting with miter saw, 160–161
basic cuts, 160
compound, 161–164
hand, 164
evaluating room, 164
fixing problems, 164
inside corners, 168
installing, 160–172
nailing, 165
outside corners
installing, 169
planning layout, 165
Custom jambs, 90–91

Custom profiles, 66, 68–69, 114
Cutoff jig, making simple, 59
Cutting tools, 36–39
miter saws, 37
power, 37, 39

D
Decorative beams, construction of, 174
Decorative corner blocks, 159
Door(s)
with flat-panel wainscoting, 146,
148–149
interior, 88
prehung, 88–89
Door casings, 87–115
Arts and Crafts, 105
casing drywall opening, 90–91
Colonial, 93–95
Neo-classical, 100–103
prehung doors, 88–89
routing a molding profile, 96–97
scribing backband to wall, 99
stool and apron, 108–111
traditional-style, 98–99
troubleshooting problems, 112–113
Victorian, 104
wainscoting and, 146
Doric column, 183
Double L-shaped room, cutting baseboard for, 120, 121
Doweling jigs, 48
Dowels, 83
Drills, power, 46
Drywall
casing opening, 90–91
fixing bulging, 112, 113
Drywall compound, cleaning up, 119
Drywall saw, 140

E
Eastlake style, 26
Electrical boxes, 149
dealing with, 145
Electrical receptacles, 128
working around, 128–129
End nippers, 44
Engineer's precision square, 33
Entablature, 100
Entasis, 182
Entry, arched, 12
Epoxies, 84

Expansion, lumber, 73
Extension jambs, 107
    adding, 106

F
Farm-style Country aesthetic style, 21
Fasteners, 82–83
Federal style, 24, 25
    wainscoting in, 136
File card, 44
Files, 44, 166
Finger-jointed molding, 62
Finishing nails, 82, 93
Fireplaces, 20
    decorations around, 20
    open, 21
Flat panels, 79
Flat-panel wainscoting, 146–151
    apron molding for, 151
    base trim for, 151
    completing the panels, 151
    construction of, 147
    cutting rails, 149–150
    cutting stiles, 150
    doors and windows, 146, 148
    electrical boxes in, 149
    finishes for, 146
    installing, 148–49
    installing bottom rail, 150–151
    lay out for project, 146
    panel dimensions, 148–149
Flat-sawn lumber, 72
Floors
    dealing with out-of-level, 126
    installing baseboard with hardwood
        and tile, 122
Folding stick rules, 32
Framing square, 33
Frieze, 13, 17, 22, 100, 172, 175

G
Gaps, closing, 95
Garnet paper, 85
Georgian style, 20, 22, 25
    wainscoting in, 136
Glue and construction adhesives,
    84–85, 101
Gothic Revival style, 26
Greek Revival style, 25, 136

H
Hammer, 46
Hammer marks, removing, 192
Hand chisels, 37
Hand miter saw, 37
    cutting crown molding with, 164
Hand sanding, 40
Hardwood, 65, 173
    open- and closed-grain, 71
    thickness chart, 65
Hardwood floor, installing baseboard
        with, 122
Hardwood plywood, 79
Head casing
    attaching, 93
    building, 103
    cutting, 94
Heating registers, 154
Hepplewhite style, 22
Hollow-wall anchors, 83
Honeycombing, 74
Housing, changes in, 18–19

I
Improper drying, 74–75
Inside corners, 122–123, 168
    caulking, 194
Installation tools, 46–47
Instant-bonding adhesives, 84–85
Interior doors, 88
Ionic column with entablature, 183
Italianate style, 26

J
Jack stud, out-of-plumb, 89
Jambs, 12, 88
    adding extension, 107
    assembling, 90–91
    custom, 90–91
    oversized, 107
    protruding, 113
Joining plates, 83
Jointer, 49

K
Kerf, 36
Knots, 74

L
Laser level, 34, 135
Latex caulk, 85, 194

Lattice cap, 101
Levels, 34, 35, 149
Locking pliers, 44
L-shaped room, cutting baseboard for,
    120
Lumber
    characteristics of, 72–75
    defects in, 74
    grades of, 62
    matching, 70
    for trimwork, 62–71
Lumber-core panels, 80–81

M
Maple, 173
Marking, 34, 93
Marking jig, 129
Masking tape, 99
MDF cornices, 158
Measuring and layout tools, 32–35
    angle guides, 34
    chalk line, 34
    folding stick rules, 32
    levels, 34, 35
    measuring tapes, 32
    squares, 33
    steel rulers, 32–33
    stud finder, 35
Measuring jig, making, 35
Measuring tapes, 32
Medium density fiberboard, 76, 80
Mill marks, 195
Millwork, 11
Mission style, 28
Miter box, 37
Mitered box beam, 174
Mitered returns, 58
Miter joints, fixing open, 112
Miter saws, 37, 38, 52–53
    basic cuts, 160
    compound cuts, 161
    cutting crown molding with,
        160–164
    hand, 37
    power, 39, 53
    stand for, 38
Modern design, 17–19
Molder marks, 75
Moldings
    back side of, 64
    distinctive, 21

installing plastic, 158–159
making narrow, 77
making own, 77
painted, 17
routing profile, 96
types of, 62
Morris, William, 28

N

Nail guns, 47, 176, 194
Nailholes, filling, 194, 195
Nailing
baseboard, 126
crown molding, 165
Nails
finishing, 82, 93
sizes of, 82
Nail sets, 46
National style, 25
Natural wood, 29, 114
Neo-Classical casing, 100–103
installing, 100–101
Non-drying fillers, 195

O

Oak, 64, 159, 173
One-piece baseboard, 118
Open-grain wood, 71
Orbital sanders, 40, 195
Out-of-plumb jack stud, 89
Outside corner joints, 124–125, 168
installing, 169

P

Painted casing, 114
Painted finishes, 71, 192–194
inspecting surfaces, 192
removing hammer marks, 192–194
types of, 192
Painter's putty, 194
Paint-grade work, 158, 159, 194
Paneled columns
building, 186–187
construction of, 186
Panel faces, 81
Panel materials, 80–81
Parallel lines, 33
Particleboard cores, 80
Pencil-style fillers, 195
Picture-frame style, 13
Picture rail, 14, 132

height of, 132
installing, 132–133
Pilasters, 14, 15, 22, 188–189
base of, 189
creating, 189
routing flutes for, 188–189
types of, 188–189
Pillars
fluted, 19
painted, 17
Pine, 62, 159, 173
finger-jointed molding, 62
lumber grades, 62
molding types, 62
Pitch pockets, 74
Plain-sliced veneers, 81
Planer, 49
marks from, 75
Plaster ceilings, 20
Plastic molding, 76
installing, 158–159
Plate joiner, 41, 54, 149
Plate rails, 14, 134–135, 154
adding the shelf, 135
in Arts and Crafts style, 134
components of, 134
creating groove, 135
Plinth blocks, 26, 100, 101–102, 129, 159
cutting jig for, 129
Plumb bob, 34
Plywood, construction-grade versus
hardwood, 79
Plywood cutting jig, 51
Plywood panels, 78
standard dimensions of, 80
Pneumatic nail gun, 47, 124
Pocket screw jigs, 48
Polystyrene moldings, 76, 158–159
filling nail holes in, 194
Polyurethane adhesives, 84
Polyurethane moldings, 76
Polyvinyl acetate adhesives, 84
Popular, 64, 173
Portable jig saw, 37
Power cutting tools, 37, 39
Power drills, 46
Power miter saws, 39, 53
setup, 52–53
Power nailers, 47
Power sanders, 195
Power screwdrivers, 46

Prefabricated columns, 183
Prehung doors, 88–89
installing, 88–89
Protractor, 34
Pry bars, 44
Putty knives, 44, 119

Q

Quarter-sawn lumber, 72, 105
Quarter-sawn veneer, 81
Queen Anne style, 26

R

Ranch casing, 118
Random orbital sanders, 40
Rasps, 44, 167
Rectangular room, cutting baseboard
for, 120
Red oak, 64, 159
Resin moldings, 76
Reveal, 92
Rip guide, 50
Rip saws, 36
Room dividers, 184
building column and pedestal, 185
Rosette corner blocks, 114
Rotary-cut veneers, 81
Routers, 42–43, 94
bits for, 43
fixed base, 42
plunge base, 42–43
setting up, 42
Router tables, 41, 77
Routing
flutes, 188–189
molding profile, 96
Ruskin, John, 28
Rustic beams, 21
Ryoba, 36

S

Saber saw, 37, 145
Safety equipment, 48
Sanders, 40
Sandpaper, 85
Saw guides, 51–52
Saw horses, 45
Scarf joints, 55
baseboard cutting sequence for room
with, 121
Screwdrivers, power, 46

Screws, 82–83
  types of, 82
Shaping and finishing tools, 40–43
  plate joiner, 41
  routers, 42–43
  sanders, 40
Sheraton style, 22
Shims, 95
Shingle style, 26
Shoe molding, 12, 118, 126
Side casing, attaching, 93
Sliding combination square, 33
Sliding compound miter saw, 39
Softwood, 65
Solvent-based finishes, 192, 195
Spalting, 75
Specialty molding, 102
Speed square, 33, 51
Spirit level, 34, 119, 135, 184
Splitting, 74
Spring angle, 160, 161
  common, 160
Square columns, 182
  building, 184
Squares, 33, 101
Stagger joints, 175–176
Stained finishes, 195
  finishing, 195
  trim prep, 195
Stair stringers, base trim and, 131
Stationary tools, 49
Steel rulers, 32–33
Stickers, 75
Stick style, 26
Stock
  cutting, 50–53
  molding profiles, 63
Stool, 13
Stool and apron, 108–111
  installing, 109–110
Stud finder, 35, 120
Surface planers, 75

T
Table saw, 49, 77
Termination points, 175
Three-piece base trim, 118, 126–127
  cap molding for, 126
  installing, 127
  shoe molding for, 126
Tile floor, installing baseboard for, 122

Timbers, rough, 21
Tongue-and-groove bead-board
      wainscoting, 140–145
  adjoining wall, 142
  baseboard and chair rail for, 143, 144
  corner construction, 142
  cutting, 140
  electrical boxes and, 145
  installing, 140–142
  outside corners, 142–143
Traditional box beam, 174
Traditional-style casing, 98–99
  installing, 98–99
Trends, 19
Trim
  basic techniques, 50–59
  complementary, 72
  integrated, 22
  types of, 12–15
Trimwork finishes, 191–195
  clear or stained, 195
  painted, 192–194
Try square, 33, 138

U
Utility knife, 89, 140

V
Victorian style, 26
  casing in, 104
  cornices in, 158
Vise, 45
Visual balance, 182
Volatile organic compounds (VOCs),
      192

W
Wainscoting, 14, 21, 22, 116
  Arts and Crafts, 134, 136
  baseboard and chair rail for, 143, 144
  designs, 136
  door and window casing and, 146
  finishes for, 146
  flat-panel, 146–151
  Georgian, 136
  materials for, 78–81
  modular construction of panels,
      152–153
  tongue-and-groove bead-board,
      140–145
Wall frames, 14, 15, 22, 116, 137–139,

      154
  attachment, 138
  cutting jig for, 138
  designs, 136
  installing, 139
  layout, 137–138
  nailing base trim to, 120
  orientation of, 137
Wall paneling, 14
Wall registers
  cap and reveal surround, 130
  cap surround, 130
  working around, 130
Walls, trimwork for, 116–155
Wall treatments, 14, 154
Walnut, 173
Warping, 74
Water level, 34
Window(s)
  baseboard cutting sequence for room
      with bay, 121
  with flat-panel wainscoting, 146,
      148–149
Window casings, 87–115
  Arts and Crafts, 105
  assembly, 111
  casing drywall opening, 90–91
  Colonial, 93–95
  Neo-classical, 100–103
  routing a molding profile, 96–97
  scribing backband to wall, 99
  stool and apron, 108–111
  traditional-style, 98–99
  trim, 106–107
  troubleshooting problems, 112–113
  Victorian, 104
  wainscoting and, 146
Wiring, planing, 128
Wood cornices, 159
Wood moldings, selecting, 66–70
Work-holding tools, 45
Worm holes, 74, 75

PHOTO CREDITS

All photography by Neal Barrett/CH, unless otherwise noted.

page 1: davidduncanlivingston.com **page 2:** Mark Lohman, design: Janet Lohman Interior Design **page 6:** Jessie Walker, design: Britt Carter & Company **page 7:** Brian Vanden Brink **page 8:** *top* Tria Giovan; *bottom* davidduncanlivingston.com **page 9:** *top* davidduncanlivingston.com; *bottom* Lisa Masson, design: A.P. Browne **pages 10–11:** davidduncanlivingston.com **page 12:** *both* davidduncanlivingston.com **page 13:** *left & top right* davidduncanlivingston.com; *bottom right* Rob Melnychuk **page 14:** davidduncanlivingston.com **page 15:** *top & bottom right* davidduncanlivingston.com; *bottom left* Tria Giovan **page 16:** Lisa Masson, design: T.L. Knisley **page 17:** *top right* carolynbates.com, design & builder: Pat Pritchett, Vermont Vernacular Design; *bottom right* Tony Giammarino/Giammarino & Dworkin; *left* davidduncanlivingston.com **page 18:** *right* davidduncanlivingston.com; *top left* Tony Giammarino/Giammarino & Dworkin, design: www.willowpondfarminn.com; *bottom left* Tony Giammarino/Giammarino & Dworkin, design: The Hope & Glory Inn **page 19:** Tony Giammarino/Giammarino & Dworkin **page 20:** carolynbates.com, design: Kim Brown, builder: Roy Dunphy & Chris Dolan **page 21:** *top right* Jessie Walker; *bottom right* Jessie Walker, design: David T. Smith; *left* Nancy Hill **page 22:** Jessie Walker, design: Diane Wendall **page 23:** *top left* Phillip H. Ennis Photography; *top right & bottom* Jessie Walker **page 24:** *top* Jessie Walker, architect: Paul Janicki; *bottom* Mark Lohman **page 25:** *top* Jessie Walker, design: Glen Meidbreder Bath Designs; *bottom* Jessie Walker, design: Alan Portnoy **page 26:** *right & top left* Jessie Walker; *bottom left* Tony Giammarino/Giammarino & Dworkin **page 27:** Jessie Walker **page 28:** Jessie Walker, design: Jim & Jean Wagner **page 29:** *top left & top right* davidduncanlivingston.com; *bottom* Jessie Walker, design: Chris Garrett **pages 30–31:** John Parsekian/CH **page 32:** *bottom* Gary David Gold/CH **page 33:** *top group* Gary David Gold/CH **page 34:** *top left group* Gary David Gold/CH **page 35:** *top & center* John Parsekian/CH **page 36:** *coping saw* Gary David Gold/CH **page 37:** *top right & bottom right* Gary David Gold/CH; *left* John Parsekian/CH **pages 38–39:** *left sequence* John Parsekian/CH; *top right & bottom right* Gary David Gold/CH **page 40:** *top right, center right & bottom right* Gary David Gold/CH; *left* John Parsekian/CH **page 41:** *top* Gary David Gold/CH **pages 42–43:** *top* Gary David Gold/CH; *bottom sequence* John Parsekian/CH **page 44:** *right group* Gary David Gold/CH **page 45:** *bottom group* Gary David Gold/CH **page 46:** *top right, center right & bottom right* Gary David Gold/CH; *top left & bottom left* John Parsekian/CH **page 47:** *all* John Parsekian/CH **page 48:** *top* John Parsekian/CH **page 49:** *both* Gary David Gold/CH **pages 52–53:** *all* John Parsekian/CH **page 55:** *top right, bottom right & center* John Parsekian/CH **pages 56–57:** *all* Gary David Gold/CH **page 58:** John Parsekian/CH **pages 60–61:** davidduncanlivingston.com **page 63:** *bottom* Jessie Walker **page 64:** *top* davidduncanlivingston.com **page 65:** *bottom* carolynbates.com, design & builder: Harry, Carolyn & Ken Thurgate, H.R. Thurgate & Sons, LLC **page 70:** Tony Giammarino/Giammarino & Dworkin, architect: Fransis Fleetwood **page 71:** *bottom* Tony Giammarino/Giammarino & Dworkin, architect: William Darwin Prillaman & Assoc. **page 72:** *left* Brian Vanden Brink, architect: John Morris **page 73:** *top right* Tony Giammarino/Giammarino & Dworkin, design: Marge Thomas; *bottom right* Brian Vanden Brink, architect: Jack Silverio **page 76:** *bottom right* courtesy of Fypon **page 78:** *bottom* Tony Giammarino/Giammarino & Dworkin, design: Beth Scherr Designs **page 79:** *bottom* Mark Samu, courtesy of Hearst Specials **page 81:** *bottom* Jessie Walker **page 82:** *top left* Brian C. Nieves/CH; *top right* John Parsekian **page 84:** *bottom left* Brian C. Nieves; *bottom right* courtesy of Solutions Miterless **pages 86–87:** Brian Vanden Brink **page 95:** Rob Melnychuk **page 97:** *top right* Tria Giovan; *bottom right* K. Rice/H. Armstrong Roberts **page 107:** *bottom right* Brian Vanden Brink, design: Martin Moore, Coastal Design **page 108:** Gary David Gold/CH **page 114:** *top right* Gary David Gold/CH; *bottom* courtesy of Fypon; *left* Jessie Walker **pages 116–117:** Mark Lohman, design: Lynn Pries Designs **page 119:** *bottom* Gary David Gold/CH **page 123:** *right* davidduncanlivingston.com **page 132:** *bottom left* Jessie Walker **page 134:** Gary David Gold/CH **page 136:** *both* Gary David Gold/CH **page 138:** *both* Gary David Gold/CH **page 141:** *top* Tria Giovan **page 152:** *top right* davidduncanlivingston.com; *bottom right* Gary David Gold/CH; *left* carolynbates.com, architect: Sandra Vitzthum **page 153:** *top* Gary David Gold/CH; *bottom* davidduncanlivingston.com **page 154:** *top left* Tria Giovan; *top right & bottom* Gary David Gold/CH **page 155:** Mark Lohman, design: Janet Lohman Interior Design **page 156:** davidduncanlivingston.com **page 159:** *top both* Gary David Gold/CH **pages 166–167:** *all* John Parsekian **pages 168–169:** *top sequence* John Parsekian; *bottom left* Jessie Walker, design: Cynthia Muni **page 173:** *bottom* Jessie Walker **page 176:** *bottom* Jessie Walker **pages 178–179:** *top right* courtesy of Fypon; *bottom right* Ivy Moriber, design: Keith Mazzi, DiSalvo Interiors; *left* Tony Giammarino/Giammarino & Dworkin; *center* Jessie Walker, architect: Hugh Plunkett, ASID **pages 180–181:** davidduncanlivingston.com **page 182:** *top* Jessie Walker, architect: Stephen R. Knutson; *bottom* Jessie Walker, design: Meidbreder Building Group **page 188:** *top* Gary David Gold/CH **page 189:** *top* Gary David Gold/CH **page 190:** Mark Lohman **page 192:** Gary David Gold/CH **page 194:** Brian Vanden Brink **page 195:** carolynbates.com, design: Milford Cushman, The Cushman Design Group, Inc. **page 196:** davidduncanlivingston.com **page 197:** *both* davidduncanlivingston.com **page 198:** Tony Giammarino/Giammarino & Dworkin, architect: Fransis Fleetwood **page 199:** Brian Vanden Brink **page 200:** courtesy of Fypon **page 201:** Mark Samu, courtesy of Hearst Specials **back cover:** *top* www.carolynbates.com

If you like **Trim Carpentry**
take a look at these other Best-Selling Books

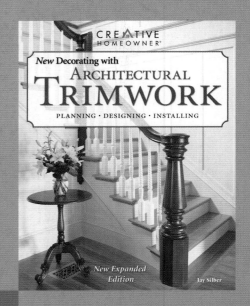
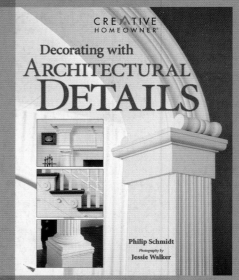
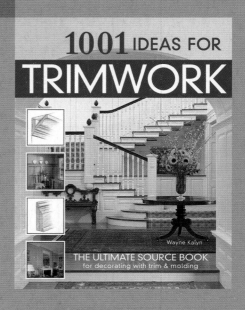